EYEWITNESS

BOOK ONE

"THE TEARS OF THE SAINTS"

The Miracles of Christ

CHARLES DE ANDRADE

Cover art by Dennis Assayag

Published by Scribblers Press   Printed By: Trinity Press
9741 SE 174 Place Rd   3190 Reps Miller Road, Suite 360
Summerfield FL 34491   Norcross, GA 30071

Book Design copyright © 2019 by Bestseller Management. LLC

Library of Congress Control Number:2019947947

Published in the United States of America

ISBN: 978-1-950308-02-6
        1. Fiction / Religion
        2. Fiction / Religious

Follow Charles on Social Media or Join Mailing list.
www.charlesadeandrade.com, www.scribblersweb.com
@scribblersweb

ACKNOWLEDGMENTS

I have found that every book I write, has a similar group of people that both provide encouragement to me and corrections to the work. I owe a great deal to my family, many of whom have said they like this book the best of the books I have written so far. Special mention must once again go to my mother, Pearl de Andrade, who both helped proof the early manuscript, and also echoed her appreciation of this book. My daughters, Jennifer Teter, Stephanie Pardee and Kathryn Marshall also played a real role in encouraging me to get this book out, as well as my first reviewer and most avid critic and supporter, my wife Gloria.

A special thanks to The Scribblers Christian Writers Group (www.scribblersweb.com). This group of authors has been a constant encouragement to me and to my writing efforts. Surprisingly, at least for me, is the host of others who having read the early drafts of this book encouraged me as well. There are too many for me to list here, but to all those friends and family, thank you.

I also must mention the work of my new marketing firm and other individuals involved in this new book. Rodney Bell and Thomas Blackburn of Best Seller Management have worked diligently to ensure that this work is as well-edited and presented as possible. They are masters of this new digital age we write in and are helping me present this book in the different formats now available.

Also, Joe Dye and his team at Trinity Press continue to support me, as I begin to publish through Scribblers Press, the publishing arm of Scribblers Christian Writers Group.

To all these people and companies, I owe a great debt of gratitude. Most of all, I am grateful to the Lord and to his providence that placed me here at this time and gave me both the desire and the ability to write these stories.

Charles A de Andrade August 2019

DEDICATION

For my mother, Pearl de Andrade, who has raised seven children, of whom, I am the oldest. She read many of the recorded stories coming from the oral traditions to me as a child. Her parents read to me from the Bible. The combination of those historical traditions and the all-powerful Word of God bore fruit much later in my life. It is a true statement that our family gets to experience our sinfulness up close and personal. It is a great mystery to me that I ever came to faith. But I know that mom had a role in that outcome as well. It is a great blessing to me to know she follows the Lord and prays for me continuously. She has spent countless hours poring over my words and helping me craft much better stories. All I can say is thank you, and the Lord bless you mom. I love you.

Your son, Charles

FORWARD

About twenty years ago, my wife Gloria gave me the New Testament on audio cassette. Most of my life I have found myself alone in cars driving for hours, and the cassettes helped fill in the time. The version my wife bought for me was a "dramatic" reading of the scripture. Having read much of the various passages before, this dramatic reading brought to my attention several passages that I thought I knew well. It was as I heard the Gospel of John that I suddenly realized that for the first time, I was hearing the voices of the people who had lived the events. It wasn't that I had been unaware that people's words were recorded in the scripture, it was that I had never taken the time to "hear" their voices, and to realize what their words meant. As I pondered this, one witness' voice stood out among the many found in the Gospels.

This one voice attracted me back to the scripture again. As I contemplated and listened to this witness, I was touched by what he had experienced. It was the testimony of a man born blind, whom Christ touched through a miracle, which led me to a new appreciation of this portion of the scriptures. To use this witness's words, "Nobody has ever heard of opening the eyes of a man born blind. If this man were not from God, he could do nothing." (NAS - John 9)

His voice touched something in my soul that had been strangely lacking. There is a display of boldness, courage, and experience in his voice that I long to share in. It was the beginning of my new reading and understanding of the scripture. I now read the scripture, trying to put myself into the life of the people who testify to what they have experienced and point to the Lord God who shaped their lives. This effort has returned many rewards to my soul. My former intellectual staleness of much known and little lived began to change. Also, an idea was born, of which this book is hopefully the first of the fruit of that idea. I hope that the boldness, courage, and faith of the witness revealed within the scriptures might flood through my novel and point the reader to the one, of whom the blind man saw and said, "I believe Lord!" May it be so for many that read this novel.

TO GOD BE THE GLORY

Charles de Andrade   August 2019

CONTENTS

EYEWITNESS - THE TEARS OF THE SAINTS - PROLOGUE

The two men slipped through the night, appearing as mere shadows walking along the path. The older man led the way, bearing the greater weight of the burden that swayed slightly between them. He knew the way having walked this path every day for over two years.

The wall appeared as they broke through the covering. Even in the night, it was an imposing sight. A tall shadow for as far as the eye could see. Its whiteish hue lite by the stars made it appear even more imposing, a line separating the two areas of gray on either side of the wall.

They approached the area where the wall formed a corner. From here the wall made an abrupt right-angle turn. At the turn, the wall was more than double its normal thickness. The corner was their destination. It was here the space for the burden that they now carried waited. Together they stopped and gently laid the burden down next to the wall.

Reaching for the wall, the first shadow felt along its base until he felt the mark. He pulled at the stone and felt it move. Removing this stone began the unveiling of the hiding place. Handing each stone to his partner, together they began the slow process, aware of the soft clicking sound as each stone was laid in order on the ground. Each stone was individually cut and shaped to fit together. If they were careful, they would simply reverse the process, and the stones would all fit back together. No one else knew of the space in the wall. They had been very careful, and they had been protected. Their burden would be safe here.

Together the two men worked the better part of three hours removing the stones as quickly as they dared. Without light, they depended on the moon and the stars to provide what little light they needed. Neither spoke. Each knew the task at hand and what role was required. They knew the consequences of discovery. What would happen to the contents of the box was their greatest concern. Finally, the space was revealed. As quickly and quietly as possible, the two men hefted the burden and found it fit the space perfectly. Both cringed as the slight scraping sound of the box sliding into place, screamed into the night. Nothing stirred, the sound unnoticed except by their own ears.

The older man hesitated briefly, running his hand over the chest one final time. The younger man could not see the tears in the older man's eyes, but he knew they were there. He placed his hand softly on the older man's shoulder and whispered,

"Father, we must hurry, it will be light in just a few hours."

The older man nodded his understanding yet remained stooped, lost in memory.

Time swirled in the old man's mind. He relived his own father's last words, first the offered forgiveness for the great harm he, the son, had done and then the explicit direction and the commissioning of his mission. Directions he followed exactly. The strange tears, which flowed down his father's cheeks to the sand, were ignored by the others, quickly forgotten in the confusion of the moment.

The old man remembered that the tears coalesced and turned the same strange green color of his fathers' eyes. He remembered the sight, the events of that day still swirling around him. He went to that spot and dug in the sand until he found the two gleaming stones hidden under the surface. They seemed to have burrowed their way under the thin layer of soil as if to escape detection. He pondered this only briefly before scooping them up and leaving the area as quickly as he could.

He had accepted his burden and held these emblems close to his body for over thirty-two years. The scrolls of testimony and the other emblem that his father called his emblem of hope and joy were also added to his charge. He had been their steward and guardian ever since that day. He also marked that day as the day he became whole. Thirty-two years were but a short time to bear such a burden.

He waited for further direction. For thirty-two years, none came. Then the voice disturbed his slumber only a few months ago. He heard the words clearly but saw no form. The messenger gave him the task and the warning of what was about to happen to himself and his family. He prayed fervently for two months while preparing everything as directed. He was not afraid for himself. It was his family that he prayed, cried, and mourned over.

After two months of anguish and activity, the messenger again returned, this time in the noonday sun. He was outside working on the wall when the voice returned. Try as he may, he had not been able to focus on the messenger. It was as if the noonday sun had been replaced by an even greater brilliance. The message filled his heart with gratefulness and joy. Falling at the feet of the messenger weeping his thanks, he discovered only the shards of rock carved off the stones he was shaping.

It would take most of the three months to both prepare the resting spot and the chest that would protect the testimonies into the future. The command related to the chest was exacting. It was to be in fact not one chest but five. Each one embedded in the next, forming a single capsule that would ferry the contents to the time waiting for their arrival.

The first chest held the testimonies that his father left him and his own just recently completed. The order that the testimonies were to be placed in the chest had been outlined in detail. In the bottom of the chest lay his own testimony with the warning the messenger had related to the reading of what would be the last testimony reached. On top was his father's testimony on which he was to lay the emblem of hope, still in the pouch his father had made for it so many years before. Between these two testimonies lay three other testimonies, those of individuals he knew and had listened to in awe of their experiences. Each, by themselves, was a precious burden, together they were priceless. Together they provided a glimpse into the history of the events, already disputed by many, and disbelieved by most. These testimonies bore witness that the events recorded were true. They were the audible voice from those people who had lived the events.

On the lid of the first box, he carved two spots where the two stones, the tears of his father, were to be placed. Under the stones he carved in the tongue of his people these words:

"He hears the weeping of his children. He will wipe their tears away, turning their tears to laughter."

He wrapped each testimony individually in the cloth-like substance that came from the tree known as the river widow. The tree's bark once collected and peeled was then soaked in water. It was separated into even thinner sheets. Finally twirled like wool and woven into cloth-like material. The bark after drying became a skin that repelled all moisture.

He placed each item in the first chest as directed. As he prepared to close the lid for the final time, he had rested his hand upon the little pouch with the coin it contained and prayed in faith that what the messenger had said, would come to pass. As he prayed, the voice spoke again. He opened his eyes, once again seeing no form. Obeying the new command, reaching down he took the pouch and opened it. Two identical coins slipped into his hand. He took one and returned the other to its former resting spot as the voice had directed. He had little time to ponder the significance of this latest event. He went to his mat, found the small pouch he had acquired on impulse in the market days before, slipped the twin coin in, and once again slipped the pouch around his neck, as he had borne its mate for so many years.

He closed the lid, wondering what age would need this gift more than his own. Yet, he knew that he did not own the emblem or the testimonies. He willingly passed them on to a people and a time that he did not know.

He had carefully carved the holding spots for each of the tears, and the required statement as well. Although he tried to prepare the openings for the tears, he was unprepared for the first fitting to occur as it had. He expected to need to reshape the openings, but after he laid the tears on the cover to check their fit, they seemed to melt and reshape into place, and no further adjustment was possible or required. He sat back in amazement the tears once again two stones. A small cry escaped from his throat as he realized that they were perfectly spaced and shaped. They looked exactly like his father's eyes.

After sitting in silence, the urgency to complete the task spurred him on. This first chest was laid into a second. This second fit almost like a skin for the first. He hesitated again, as he prepared to close the lid on the chest with the tears. Finally, an internal voice forced him forward.

This chest was then placed in the third. In this chest, he had been instructed to place a layer of coarse salt covered by two inches of river sand in the bottom. Then along the sides of the third chest, after the second was inside, he filled the gap with the same river-sand. The lid to this box fitted into a groove on the sides of the box and when it slid into place it snapped shut. This box was then fit into the fourth box where he had placed a pitch like compound that covered the outside of the third box completely. He filled the final areas around the third box with the pitch, allowing some to flow down the outside of the fourth box.

Once again, the lid was slid into place, and the oozing pitch created a glue-like seal for that box. He slid it finally into the fifth box. The space between this box and the other was once again filled with pitch and sealed shut. As the lid on the final box slipped into place, the old man was still smiling thinking of the pouch that now hung around his neck and the promise that had been given.

Three nights later, this box was the load that he and his son had borne to the wall. The few minutes he had reflected seemed like hours to the younger man. The younger man's whispered urgency spurred him back into activity. With that they began the reconstruction of the wall, carefully replacing each stone in its place.

The brush that grew on the side of the hill would eventually overtake this spot, and only the two men, and the one who had provided the location would ever know of it. The older man knew that the one who had created this plan also had the power to make sure that the plan worked. As he placed the final stone in place, a great load lifted from his soul, and he whispered softly a prayer for those to whom this great gift was being directed.

Turning to his son, he embraced him and then whispered both his thanks and his urgent appeal.

"You must leave at once. Do not think that they will have any mercy for you or your family. Take your wife, your daughter, my grandchild, and leave this place before the sun rises. They will be searching for you in the morning."

"Why can you not come with us? ", the younger man asked.

The old man just shook his head, saying, "Tomorrow I must testify. I have been directed to remain and not to fear what I must say and do. But he has given me a promise of your life, and that of your family. Do as I have asked and leave immediately."

Reaching under his tunic, he retrieved the little pouch and its contents and slid it over his son's head. He said,

"This is yours now to bear."

He had shared with his son the strange occurrence and the duplication of the coin, but he had not shared the command he had been given to pass it on to his son. He did so now.

"Son, this is an emblem of hope and memory. I was told to bear it until I was directed to give it up. I had spent it when I was directed to, and it has always returned to me. It is now yours to carry and to pass on to the one you will be directed to. Your life will be filled with many heartaches, but never forget the past and what we both have heard and seen."

With that, the two embraced again, and this time, the tears were in both of their eyes. After kissing each other on the cheeks, they parted with the familiar words,

"Until we meet again."

Both knew that it would not be in this life.

They came for him in the morning just as the messenger had said they would. He had slept but a few hours having returned from the task just an hour before the day had broken. They had not knocked at the door but had simply plowed it open. They had seized him from his mat, hauling him to his feet with his arms pinned behind his back.

"Where is your son?" the commander had demanded.

"He is not here," the old man replied.

The soldiers made a great effort searching and, in the process, destroying everything in the small room during their search. The one soldier returned to the commander and said,

"There is no one here, and neither are the objects we have been commanded to bring back."

"Where is your son?" the commander asked again, and then quickly tearing the old man's garment he searched for the little pouch he had been told the old man wore around his neck.

"Where is your pouch, old man? And where are the fables you speak about so often."

"I am no longer the guardian of these items," the old man said in response.

"Who did you give them to?" was the immediate question.

The old man said nothing. The blow was not unexpected. The old man felt the blood in his mouth and the broken tooth on his tongue. Once again, the question was asked,

"Who did you give them to?"

He said as best he could with his damaged mouth, "They are now in the hands of the one who gave them to my father and then to me. "

The next blow was not a surprise, but the merciful darkness was.

1

OXFORD, ENGLAND
AUGUST 2023

The voice on the tape was a woman's. The disembodied sound left little trace of the physical individual. In his mind, he saw her face clearly, as if it had been only this morning that he had last seen her. Laura was a beautiful woman. With her pointed nose and her wonderfully thick brown hair that fell just below her shoulders, she had looked more like a model than the professor her father remembered. The rest of her also had turned many heads over the years, but it was her intellect that had brought her father the most joy. She had looked like her mother but had inherited her keen powers of mind from her father. But her gift, he knew, was from someone else, for certainly, she had not received it through him.

Her tone revealed that she was both anxious and excited.

"I have received this evening the first photographs of the box and the first few pictures of the first manuscript removed from the box. I can tell you that the language on the lid of the box is Aramaic. It appears to be of the form used in the period from 200 BC and 200 AD.

It reads, "He hears the crying of his children. He will wipe their tears away, turning their tears to laughter".

"I will need to do further study on a few of the words to know for sure, but this does appear to date your discovery. The words for crying and laughter changed slightly after about 200 AD. So, if what I am seeing is correct, you have found what appears to be an artifact that is almost 2000 years old. "

With that, her voice increased in excitement. She said,

"The first few photographs of the document that you sent me are even more remarkable. They appear to be written in Greek and contain what appears to be a testimony or better an autobiography of an individual. The photographs seem to show that the document is in incredibly good condition. Might I come down to have a first-hand look at this find? If this document is as old as the box itself, these might be the best-preserved written artifacts yet found from this period in England's history and perhaps the most complete from this period of Roman occupation. I will call you tomorrow midday but thought I should record these first impressions for you. This may be a truly historic discovery. I understand from your call that there are other documents as well?" The note of excitement in her voice was palatable.

"I will read to you what I have been able to make out from the first few photograph's, but I will need to spend more time with the writing to be sure of this first translation. Father, what an amazing find! Looking forward to seeing it in person. Here is what the first few pages contain." With that, her voice filled with her trademark melodic tone that had always captivated her father.

He hesitated, wondering if he should continue listening to the tape. He knew what it contained, having listened to it many times over the past twenty years. Yet, as a moth is drawn to light, so too he was

drawn to this reading that had started his life on a path he would never have imagined. His hand rested on the ancient device, long ago replaced by more modern digital forms of recording. He had kept the device only because he had kept the tapes.

His eyes glanced at the table, and the small collection of tapes. He had discovered the tapes years ago…no that was not quite right, he had been led to the tapes, in his daughters' home, hidden from all but prepared for himself.

He was old now. Should he have shared these with others? No, he decided. He had no desire to be a part of the controversy these tapes would bring. Instead, he had decided that he would include in his directions to his lawyer what should be done with the tapes. Her voice returned him to the present and the task at hand. She was reading the opening lines of the first manuscript. The sound of her voice, reading those words still sent shivers through him.

"I wake once again, the light of the morning driving the sleep from my eyes, bringing me from the rest of one at peace with life. Today, I am old. My eyes have seen more in the years I have been allowed than any person could have imagined. Some, not believing in the divine, claim I am cursed by fate. These eyes have witnessed the death of the love of my heart. It was a cruel death, one that should only be reserved for the worst of criminals and yet applied to one innocent of any wrong deserving death. Others, believing in the gods of this world, claim I must have sinned a great sin to witness so much sorrow in my life. I have seen the woman I have loved since I was a young boy, the mother of my children, my wife of almost 50 years, betrayed by our own grandchild and subjected to terrible torture before finally being allowed to escape from this world of sorrow.

I know both views are wrong. I have neither been cursed nor have I been punished for my sins, although they certainly would merit what I have

experienced and more. No, my eyes bear witness to the fact that I have lived a blessed life. My life has been marked by events that only the very privileged could possibly have hoped to see, much less participate in.

To have lived at this time, to have seen and experienced what I have, I would not trade a moment of it, not for all the short-lived joys and pleasures of those who believe such erroneous views of my life. They have neither experienced my sorrows nor shared in my joys. Therefore, their opinions matter little, although their opinions are shared and embraced by many.

Every age is unique to the people who dwell among the years they are given. But this age, my era, will be remembered forever. Long after the great buildings fall, the roads disappear, and my bones have turned to dust, it will still be talked about, remembered, studied, and most of all, longed for. I would not surrender a single day of my past for any of the days of the future. Many who will live after me will long to see what I have seen, to touch what I have touched, and to know the certainty of what I know.

This morning as I washed my face, felt the water bathe my eyes, opening them again as if the first time, I remember. The water drops falling from my fingers, running along my lids, causing tiny ripples in the water…seeing my reflection in the water…I remember another time, and the drops scarcely hide my tears of memory today as they could not so many years ago.

It has been many years since I have heard that voice, but this morning I heard it again as I remembered. It was unmistakable what He asked of me. "GO….

Today the command is different and yet the same, today He said: "Write." So, I am.

I have never been a man of letters. Instead, I am accustomed to speaking of what I have seen. I have spent very little time writing, and without such practice, my words will not ring with the sounds of our poets.

Others have recorded their memories of these events as they were directed. Some of these have much more authority than my memories as they were there from the beginning. I know now that they too were directed to write and guided as they recorded their memories. I pray that I might be given the same guidance. Perhaps, my memories might also shed light upon the events and support the truth of their testimonies. For those events should be remembered for what they are, the truth.

I have little time to write but much to say. Have patience with my scribbling and my rambling. Life's events like strands in a tapestry do not appear orderly individually and yet like those strands once woven contain design and purpose. Only at key points do the individual strands make sense. It is only as the strands are viewed from the perspectives of those who wove them, that the events are truly seen.

I know why He has asked me to write. My story is drawing to another threshold. I have a journey to take, and I must finish my story before I am allowed to depart. I want to touch, to taste, to hear, to smell, to see… that which I know is true. I will know again and in knowing be known. This is my desire.

If these memories touch but a few, that is fine. It is not mine to decide what impact these words might have. I have heard and read the testimonies of many, most much more moving and important than my own. I do know that the Truth used my life to impact many, and I am humbled by that gracious use. I hope that perhaps He intends to use these words as well in His mission. All I know for sure is that He has said write and write, I shall. It is my prayer that should you be reading these memories of an old man, that you will think not more of me but instead know the truth of the events I record. For they are real, and my eyes bear witness to their truth."

He turned off the tape. His eyes filled with tears from the longing in his heart to see his daughter again. He thought back, to the discovery and wondered why he had been chosen to play the role he had. He realized now he knew the answer to that question and many more. It had been there all the time, and he had steadfastly refused to accept it. That knowledge brought some relief, but his loneliness still tore at his mind. Placing his hand on his head, he slowly bowed to the tabletop as his tears and weeping increased. The sorrow swept over and through him.

Why had it taken so long for him to accept the truth?

2

WRAPPING UP – THE PAST

The old man awoke in the small cell barely large enough for him to crouch in. How long he had been here, he did not know, but he knew it had not been too long. The blood on his lip and tongue had not dried. The dull ache of the loss of the tooth had not grown unbearable yet. The darkness of the cell and the odor told him that this cell had been frequented by many poor souls in the past. He prayed silently that he might have the strength to bear all that was about to happen. And then the promise surged through him, and he remembered the words:

"Do not be afraid when you are delivered up, as to what to say, for it will be given to you what you must say. You will be my witnesses to kings and all men."

They found him on his knees in prayer. They dragged him into the light, and he squinted, the light hurting his eyes after the darkness. He knew it was now mid-afternoon on the same day. All that the messenger had said would occur, had. He trembled at what was about to occur but clung desperately to the promise,

"I will be with you."

He was hauled out of prison and down the street that ended at the place of trial and execution. From this vantage, he could see the wall above and the spot that now held the charge he had laid down just hours before. The governor did not take long. The old man looked upon the governor knowing the price that had been paid for this political appointment. He also understood the service this governor performed for the emperor here in this land so far removed from the seat of power. He had indeed paid a great price for his position, but it was one that the governor did not recognize.

The governor had that pompous look that comes from one filled with one's own worth and grandeur. The governor sat in his seat just slightly higher than everyone else present.

But there was no mistaking the resemblance between the prisoner and the judge. It was not often that a son got to sit in judgment over the father. The younger man smirked, relishing the opportunity.

There was a smaller crowd than normal for today's spectacle. But the tar pot was boiling, and the cross upright was already in place. The old man thought it was odd, but two cross uprights were placed looking at each other. The sight filled his soul with foreboding.

"So, you have hidden your son and his family as well as the other items we seek old man?" the governor spoke as fact not looking for an answer.

"Do you really think your son can escape me? Do you forget that I know him, as well as his wife?" I will have everyone in this district paraded before me. And I will find him."

Seeing that the old man was not about to be forthcoming with any response, the governor said to one of the soldiers,

"Bring her out."

The old man had expected this, but none-the-less at the sight of the woman following the soldier, his heart fell, and he groaned an audible cry. The governor grinned at the discomfort of his prisoner. The woman walked to the dais and ascended to a step below the governor. She did so unaidedly and unforced. She looked upon the old man, her father.

Then looking at the governor, she said,

"I am ready lord to do your bidding."

The governor nodded and then said, "You know what is required."

Turning and looking at the small crowd of townsfolk that had been gathered for this occasion she said,

"This day before all of these witnesses, I swear allegiance to the emperor, and I do proclaim that he alone is king on this earth. I also deny loyalty to any other king and proclaim that I do not believe or follow the one my father professes to be God. There is no such God, only the gods that we all acknowledge and the god on earth embodied by the emperor himself."

To this, she added her voice raised as a taunt towards her father, "I have this day brought a sacrifice before these gods and have petitioned that the emperor and his governor live forever."

The sound of the old man's crying was the only response. The governor's laugh and response quickly followed: "Where is this God of yours that you have so much confidence in. Certainly, your daughter does not believe in him, nor do I."

To this, the old man said through his tears, "I pray that she might still believe before it is too late, as I also pray for you. I know for one of the two of you it is too late, although I have not been told which of you will, in the end, be lost. I still hope and pray that even that might be changed."

The governor raged, "It is already too late old man. Now tell me what I seek to know, and I will make your death swift and as painless as possible. If you do not, I promise you it will be long, painful, and without any mercy on my part."

The old man looked up upon this judge and then felt the promise surging through and around him. He understood the warning about the sword that the messenger and his message would bring to families. The words that flowed forth were his but not his. He proclaimed in a loud voice, "There is but one king in heaven or on earth. There is no other that I will worship, I cannot deny what I know to be the truth, and I will not to either prolong this life or shorten this death."

Hearing these words, the governor snarled, "You forget old man, you denied this God of yours before, and that denial brought you long life. Do you forget that you denied your father as your daughter has denied you, and as I have too! How can you speak such foolishness? I will have what I want now or later, but no one will stop me from what I seek."

The old man bowed his head and said, "Yes, you are right."

The hushed crowd murmured at this statement, but then he continued, "I did deny my father and brought witness against him that resulted in his death. I saw him die, as many of you did as well," the old man pointed at the crowd that was once again hushed.

"You know my father's story well, and the story of my own traitorous acts towards him."

The old man's voice took on the qualities of a much younger man and his voice resonated with an inward strength he no longer personally had,

"But, I was a different person then, I believed a lie, and I traded the truth for that lie. I saw my father die, I heard his words, and I saw his witness. He spoke the truth, and I have long ago repented from my denial and can tell you that each of you has the same opportunity as well. Please, I beg of you all, flee the lie, and embrace the truth. For there is only one God, and we are all going to give an account to him. It is only through his Son, my Lord, and the Lord of my father that you can escape the terrible judgment to come."

At this, the governor screamed

"Silence!".

But the old man would hear none of it. He went on with his testimony only to be clubbed by a soldier and fell again to the ground, stunned into silence.

He heard the governor's voice and looked up, hearing the words but only slowly understanding their import. He cried again and reached up towards his daughter. His daughter had heard the words as well but had not believed them. The governor had said,

"If you will not make your own death swifter, perhaps you may do something to ease your daughter's pain?"

He heard his daughter protesting, "But I did all that was required of me, I have denied this God and my father. "

To this, the governor said, "You forget Eunice, that I decide the fate of all traitors. Even those who repent that belong to the family of such a traitor may forfeit their life. Of course, your father can change all of that. All he needs to do is tell me what I want to know, and I will spare your life."

To this, his daughter cried out, "He is your father as well."

Again, his daughter turned, and as the soldiers seized her, she cried out,

"Father!"

The soldiers dragged Eunice from the dais across the small court to where the tar pot lay simmering in the flames. The steam and smell had filled the courtyard with its sickly-sweet aroma. The old man cried out and prayed aloud not to the governor, but to one unseen by those around him.

"Lord, please mercy, have mercy on my daughter."

The governor smiled at those words thinking they had been said to him but looking upon the old man suddenly realized they had not been.

"I am the only one who can have mercy on her now, deny this God again, give me your other son, and what I seek, and I will spare her. If your son recants, I will also spare him and his family," the words spoken by the governor sounded like a low growl.

The old man knew the lie well. He knew the truth better. Standing back up, he looked the governor in the eye and said, "I will not trade my Lord, for myself, my son, my daughter, or for even you. As for this lie you speak, you will not spare either my daughter or my son, even if I did as you asked. Both of us know that to be the truth."

Then from somewhere, he did not know, came words that he had not thought to say,

"And know this as well, before I die, so that all will know the truth of what I have said, my eyes will see your death first."

The governor laughed again.

"You think you can outlive me! We will see about that! Do it!" the governor commanded.

The old man felt the hands of the soldiers as they lifted and dragged him with ferocity. He looked frantically for his daughter knowing all too well the shortness of both of their times. She still had time, and he knew he had to try again. Having been spun around, he sought out her eyes and found her. The soldiers were already smearing

her clothes and body with the hot tar. He could hear her cries and wailing. His heart broke each time he heard her cry, "Father."

He found his voice and again spoke above the clamor of the preparations,

"Daughter, the Lord loves you, remember what you were taught as a youngster, remember the tears of my father. They were real, his testimony is real, God is real. Even now, he will walk with us both." He locked eyes with his daughter again, and in those few seconds, he saw in her eyes the unspoken sorrow of her betrayal. He continued, "You are forgiven daughter, Can I do any less? Remember that I betrayed my father as well, as we all have betrayed our Lord and God as well. If they can forgive me, they can forgive anyone, even you."

The old man was again struck violently. He had no breath to speak. He tried to lock eyes again with his daughter but saw that she was focused behind him. In her eye, the wildness that comes from fear was evident, but as he watched he slowly saw that the look changed to one of puzzlement, then amazement, then sadness, and finally, joy. He turned to look where she had been focused but only saw the shimmering light of the sun reflected off the building side. But he knew, and in knowing, he once again understood that his prayer had been answered and the promise kept. His daughter believed and now knew as well.

The governor gained a morbid satisfaction from executions. These two were bringing him particular pleasure. He raced down the dais and watched as both the old man and his daughter, now covered with tar, had their hands affixed to the horizontal member of the cross. After they had been lifted onto the cross, he took the flame from under the pot and walked before the old man.

"Old man, one last chance for your daughter?", he said.

Seeing both the sorrow and the joy mixed in the old man's face, he crossed quickly to where the daughter's cross had been raised. It was directly opposite the old man's cross. The governor had designed it this way, especially for this occasion. He wanted to be sure that the old man saw it all.

He looked up at Eunice and said, "Well, Eunice, what do you think of your father now?"

And then a voice he did not expect to hear came from her. It was the voice of someone still afraid but with a growing peace that was not the peace of resignation but of knowledge. She said, "I love him."

She continued, "He has been right all along, and I have been a fool. There is but one God, and I do believe in him."

With that, the governor rumbled in disbelief, saying, "He was right. I would have killed you even if he had given me everything I wanted."

With that, the governor touched his brand to her clothes and the tar lit. The fire swept up her body, enveloping her whole body, and she cried out in her agony. Her last words though were not what the governor, or anybody but her father might have expected. "Father, forgive them…"

The governor realized she had not been speaking about his father. With that, the fire whooshed higher, she cried out, in great agony and then went silent. The sweet nauseous smell of burnt flesh filled the courtyard.

Turning around, he walked with the same brand over to the other cross. Upon it, the old man seemed lost in prayer, although the tears flowed freely from his eyes.

"So old man, it is your turn to lose."

He motioned to one of his soldiers and asked for some wine to be brought to him. Once the soldier returned, the governor lifted the cup and said "A toast old man, ...father", added as an afterthought to cause more pain.

"To the wondrous torches your God provides me with. Do not think I will forget your son when you are gone, or the figments of imagination I am sure he bears for you. I will find them and then I will do to them what I am doing to you. Take that thought with you into the darkness!"

He drank a long drink and then touched the flame to the old man's tar-covered feet. The flame licked up the old man's front.

Raising the cup of wine, he toasted the old man again as the flame reached his middle. It was the act of taking a second drink that suddenly filled the governor with wonder. He choked and spewed out the wine. He was having difficulty catching his breath. Falling to the ground, his soldiers surrounded him trying to help, he locked eyes with the old man on the cross.

The fire now was burning brightly, but the old man's eyes were upon his son's. The governor was still jerking and coughing and suddenly realized that the old man's eyes that should have been filled with pain were instead filled with pity. Pity for him.

Rage filled the governor's heart, but as anger covered his being the governor realized that his father had told the truth. It was too late for him. As he looked up, the sky was filled with an inky blackness that mirrored the hate in his heart. The sky was alive, and then its brilliance overwhelmed him in fear. He remembered what he had been taught as a youth and uttered two words: "Hide me!"

He was being swallowed whole, and the last thing he knew in this life was anger and fear. The governor's soldiers looked at one another in

wonder for in that last moment they had seen the fear etched on the governor's face. The commander of the guard spoke the thought that his troops were thinking. He wondered aloud: "Hide you from what?"

The old man died shortly thereafter. He had spoken no other words and had simply bowed his head as he closed his eyes for the last time.

As his eyes closed, he suddenly was aware that he saw with a different sight. He was not alone; he and the cross were surrounded by a multitude, and then he saw at the center of the throng the one he longed for most of all. Yet even as he reached out to this one, he was aware of his daughter's, his mother's and father's presence as well. His father's eyes gleamed with the same excitement and hope that they had in his memory. And then he heard those words he so desired to hear.

"Well done." The words were echoed in the voices of all those who surrounded him, welcoming him home.

3

THE DISCOVERY – PART ONE
NEWCASTLE, ENGLAND 2003

The noise in the room was unbearable. Everyone was talking, arguing over who was to blame. Rubin had allowed the confusion and dissension in the room to go on unchecked for several minutes. He began to pound his hand on the podium, slowly restoring silence to the elite group of scholars that up until this moment had acted more like a bunch of rowdy high school students. Finally, silence was restored. He continued with his statement.

"As you all know two nights ago, we suffered a very grievous loss. The fire destroyed the entire discovery. We still do not understand the cause or nature of this fire, but we know that it appeared to be spontaneous, without any cause currently being identified. "

What Rubin did not tell his audience, was that the fire had been so unusual that there did not appear to be even any evidence left, to indicate that the discovery had ever been made in the first place. That had been a surprise even to him. Rubin continued:

"The fire inspectors are continuing their review, and our staff is also reviewing all potential causes. Professor James had finished

translating the first of the testimonies that had been removed from the box. We still do not know the coincidence of that testimony erupting into flame at the same instant as the others. There appears to be a connection, although the events took place over twenty miles apart. Professor James was conducting the final translation at the university, where she had been allowed to take the first testimony."

This was a lie, she had not been given the approval to remove the testimony, yet he thought it best to cover the error, so as not to raise even more questions about what had happened.

He continued: "She was severely burned in the fire and is still not out of danger. It appears that not only the testimony but also her notes and computer were destroyed in the fire. If she does not survive, we may never know what she learned from the final parts of the scroll. We have searched her flat, and her office at the university and there appears to be no backup or other notes related to her work on the testimony. As for the other documents, they were destroyed before we had an opportunity either to open them or examine their contents. "

The room had once again erupted briefly with discussion but a single slam of his palm on the podium once again restored silence to the room.

"I do have some good news, though. The translations and photos of the portion that she had finished translating are still in safekeeping. I have ordered multiple copies be made and that they are held in different secure locations. Each of your universities will be afforded copies for your own keeping, as well as the ministry's offices. "

Rubin nodded to the two men who through the confusion of the last three hours had kept to themselves in the corner of the room. Rubin thought the academics had acted more boorish than those stuffed shirts from the ministry department. Rubin promised to keep everyone

informed on any new developments and announced another briefing for everyone the next day at the same time.

Rubin James stepped from the platform and ignored the questions and protests that erupted from his colleagues. He simply wanted to return to the hospital and his daughter's side.

Rubin was of medium build, slightly overweight, with a round face and graying hair. As the acknowledged expert on Roman antiquities in England, and as the Chair of Greek and Roman History at Oxford University, it had only been natural that he be called in to examine the discovery over three years ago. He was at that time already approaching retirement age, and yet this discovery had allowed him to delay that retirement that he had no desire to enter anyway. Today he wished that he had retired and with that removed his daughter from harm's way.

Yet he knew that was foolishness as well. Laura was an expert in her own right, being recognized as one of the most brilliant linguists that England had produced in the past fifty years. Her expertise in ancient languages would have made her a logical choice regardless of his involvement. But Rubin still blamed himself for what had occurred.

His car and his driver were at the curb where he had left them in the morning. The driver immediately began the car moving even before the door had completely closed. He knew where Rubin wanted to go and was amazed that they had been able to pry him from his daughters' side. It appeared that Rubin had not slept in the last 48 hours. The driver relaxed slightly as he saw Rubin put his head back on the plush seat and close his eyes. What the driver did not know and could not see was that Rubin had not escaped into the rest of sleep. Instead, Rubin's mind was once again replaying all that had happened in the last three years.

His right hand had also reached into his pocket, where the small pouch resided and hid the precious cargo that had a history that only he and Laura knew. He held it tightly in his hand within his pocket and did something totally foreign to his atheistic beliefs. He pleaded for his daughter's life as a few tears escaped his tightly closed lids.

It had all started only three short years ago when a group of high school students studying the history of Roman occupation in England had decided to take a tour of the Hadrian Wall. The wall, constructed in England under the reign of the Emperor Publius Aelius Hadrianus, had been designed to stall the barbarian Picts from overrunning the Roman territories in Britannia as the Romans called their province. The good Emperor Hadrian had been the third in the line of the so-called "Good Emperors" of Rome. These men had been appointed to the role of emperor based on their skills and not necessarily their lineage or ability to do away with other competitors.

The wall stretched 73 modern miles, 80 Roman miles, from the North Sea to the Irish Sea and it marked the northernmost boundary of the Roman rule. Constructed entirely of stone, the wall varied from 8 – 10 feet wide and stood over 15 feet tall. In a few sections the wall was much thicker, and when it stood on a small hill it appeared much taller than it was.

The wall had never worked for the purpose it had been constructed. Like modern-day screens that could do little to keep pesky mosquitoes out, the wall did little to prevent the attacking barbarians from infiltrating into Roman territory. The wall had survived almost two thousand years and remained one of the most visual testimonies to the Roman presence on the island. The wall had remained for more than 1500 years after the last Roman had abandoned the island, leaving it to the tribes that had continued the quarreling and vying for final control of the island. The ferocity of their own arguments simply meant more blood to spill killing each other rather than killing the Romans.

The high school students had chosen to visit the wall in Newcastle, one of the terminus points of the wall. It was during their hiking along the wall that two of the students had made the discovery that had been the focus of most of Rubin's life for the past three years.

John Adams and James Tuton had never meant to be the focus of so much interest. John was slightly taller than his friend James and had been the first to hoist himself up on the wall. James, however, was by far the more fit and looked something like a Greek god with his bronze skin, and proportionate muscles. Both students enjoyed the daring of doing what was forbidden but especially enjoyed the sight of the rolling countryside as viewed from the top of the wall.

The two students, like so many others before them, had been walking on top of the wall at that point when they had been spotted by local constables who had ordered them off the wall. As everyone knew, walking on the wall was now greatly discouraged since it was now understood to be a historical artifact of significance. Yet as everyone also knew, students and others could not help but want to walk along the top of the wall and see the view.

On a grassy knoll that overlooked what remained of what was believed to be one of the locations of one of the Roman governor's homes and guard stations, the students had stumbled on to the site. The students had chosen a corner where the wall had made a sharp right-hand turn, to attempt to scamper down off the wall. On the way down the side of the wall, a stone about four feet above the ground level had moved and drawn their attention. With the naturally curious nature of teenagers, and the burning desire to cause a little more heartburn for those that had driven them off their desired path, James and John removed several other stones as well.

What had started as an apparent accident had quickly unearthed a much more significant find than anyone had discovered in England in many years. Having removed about a two-foot section of stones, John had suddenly become aware that there was something inside the wall that was not stone. By the time the local constables had reached the two students and had begun to arrest the poor mischievous culprits, they too were also aware of something unusual in the wall. The discovery was made. The students were still charged with mischievous destruction of a historic site, but neither would ever need to give an account for their actions. Instead, Rubin and several other scholars had been summoned to the site, and the careful excavation had begun.

4

WHAT IS IN A NAME?

His hands released his head, and the tears began to recede as all tears in this life eventually do. Wiping his face with his sleeve, he once again punched the machine into life, and his daughter's voice continued. He sat transfixed upon his chair, remembering the words almost verbatim but now understanding their importance. Again, he thought,

"Why had it taken so long for him to understand?"

Her voice brought him back to the tape:

"None of us remember the day of our birth, although our parents, relatives, and older siblings and government officials are fond of recalling the event for us. Of course, for some of us, those who are called upon to witness our arrival remember the event most vividly. I was born to Samuel and Lydia in the tenth month on a day remembered as a dark day, although, the darkness had no impact upon me. I arrived late at night, fortunately after the workday was complete and before the light of the next day required work to begin. I was always told it was appropriate that I be born in the dark of the night instead of the light of the day. I was the fifth of six children. My parents were neither destitute nor rich in worldly means.

My father made his living in clay, creating jars, basins, and other items used by all sorts of people for everything from washing, to water-bearing, to food serving.

I have always been grateful for my father's trade, as I understand much more clearly now the lesson related to the lump of clay. As a friend and teacher have said: some for noble use: a jar to hold fine perfume, and others for ignoble use: a pot to hold and carry out the waste of the night. I know how blessed I am to have been made into a noble jar by the master potter when by all rights, I deserved something entirely different. It is a great peace at my age to know this truth.

My first memories of my youth were those of my mother and of her feel and smell. She would hold me tight to her breast, and as I nursed, she would sing, I thought, to me. I remember holding on to her finger and searching its curve and joint. I remember her hair, its long fineness, its light fragrance of perfume, its ability to tickle my face. Although I was allowed to nurse beyond most of my brothers and sisters when I relayed these memories to her later in my life, she did not believe it was possible to remember such things, but I have often been a surprise for both of my parents.

Of my father, I remember the smell of my fathers' clothes, the roughness of his hands as he would pick me up and hurdle me into the air when he arrived home and then catch me. If I was outside, his launching me into the air brought new sensations, the taste, and sound of the air rushing around me. As I came hurtling back towards my fathers' arms, the warmth of the sun upon my cheeks replacing the coolness of the shade where I was often to be found.

I remember my oldest brother's voice. The voice of Samuel, named after my father, but more importantly, after the prophet that waited upon the Lord in the tabernacle and was blessed with hearing the Lord's voice as a child. My parents named most of us after a relative, and since all our relatives were named after someone in the holy writings, the relationship was established. It was a method to drive home the lessons taught to all of us from early on. Our names bore not only the memory of the generations but of our people's history.

I remember most of all our Sabbath dinners. This one night each week, we would sit around the table, in order of our birth, except I was always allowed to sit next to mother, even after Naomi was born. Every Sabbath evening after the dinner, father would tell us the stories of whom we had been named after. His favorite story was the story of Samuel, and I was envious of my brother and his story, wishing it had been mine instead.

After dinner, my father would ask us all which story he should tell. There were five stories ready to be told by my father. My oldest brother Samuel had his story told the most. Then my sister Rachel, second after Samuel. Then Sarah, then Jason and then Naomi stories were always available. During these meals, I never heard my story, although I know it well now and have pondered the significance of my original name often.

I am known as Celidonius by the Jews, and as Restitutus by the Romans. My given name's story was not spoken at the dinner table. It is just as well, as my new names suit me better than that I was born with. I understand why my father never spoke of my story at the table. I was named such because of my mark and the sorrow my condition brought to my parents.

I was known as the marked one, Cain, son of Samuel the potter of Bethany. "

The tape clicked at the end of this statement. His daughter had been very careful, only recording on one side of the tape. Slowly he removed the tape from the machine, held it in his hand and pondered what to do. From where he was unsure, but he heard a voice clearly answering his question. Startled, he looked for the source of the voice and saw no one. His hand brushed over the pouches that had hung around his neck for so many years, and he understood.

He had heard the voice once before, years ago, just before his daughter had left. He had denied that voice all his life, thinking it but a hallucination or worse. He had refused the task the voice had demanded, and the ensuing silence he had thought was acquiescence to his decision. He thought that had been the end of that delusion. Only now he realized it was not a hallucination or a delusion. The voice had not rescinded the command but had simply waited his being awakened. He was awake now, and what had been demanded so many years ago, remained to be finished. He began the task he had been assigned. As he did, he realized that for the first time in nearly twenty years, he was happy. He knew what his daughter had known, there was a purpose for everything. His tears were now ones of joy. The sorrow was gone.

The promise was true, and he was now proof.

He stood and moved slowly over to the bookcase in the room next to the kitchen. Like so much of his house, the bookcase was hemmed in, surrounded by piles of magazines and newspapers. A thin cover of dust also resided on the surface of the case. Reaching in, he slowly removed a small pamphlet with a cracked leather cover. He returned to the kitchen and his seat. The book had not been his. Carol had given it to him, along with her note as she left.

Once again, he opened it and looked upon the fragments of an ancient paper that had been attached to the various pages within. He read from it one more time coming to the place where the scroll had stopped, torn in the middle of a paragraph as if deliberately shorn in the middle of a thought. Its incomplete thought had not dented his former stony heart. It had taken another event to cause the pieces to begin to fall into place.

He returned to the case and opened the old box he had placed on the top of the case. Inside he removed the other small book. It had been in his mothers' files. For years the box had sat in his attic, hidden from both his scrutiny and memory. The papers had been in his possession for years. His mother had few belongings. He had thrown the few items in the box years ago, without reflecting on the contents. They had resided in his attic for over fifty years. It had been what the voice had said that had returned him to the attic looking for the long-forgotten box. He had opened it and sat on the attic steps realizing what it contained.

He returned to his kitchen table, now strewn with tapes and the other book. Opening the newly rediscovered book, Rubin looked down upon the twin. What had been torn was now complete. The short testimony continued, and with it, the light of understanding tore the final shade from eyes too long blinded by the darkness he had embraced. Understanding opened another door, and before it stood the final door. Rubin read. As he read, he did not feel his soul-lifting an invisible hand, reaching for the knocker on the final door. He did not see his hand lift the knocker, nor did he see the door swing open at his knock. He continued to read, unaware that he had stepped through the newly opened door into the world flooded with light. All Rubin would remember was the slow drip of tears sliding down his cheeks as he read.

5

WITNESS

John looked down at the small scroll before him. He had written his testimony as he had been directed. He knew that far greater testimonies were lying in wait for their time. But that strange urging had pushed him until he had given in and wrote his own story, unsure as to why it was needed.

There was so much more he had wanted to say, but the lack of additional writing materials and the need for secrecy had demanded that his own writing be much shorter than the greater testimonies he had helped his father hide. He read slowly what he had written one more time. Moving the scroll, reading what was inscribed there. His eyes watered as he remembered:

"My name is John, son of Jason, son of Restitutus, also called Celedonius formerly known as Cain. He was a witness of the truth and is known as the Restored One.

I am writing this memorial for those of my family who will come after me so that they might know our family history. I have been led to write this, compelled by urges and dreams that I know were sent to direct me. The one who is the author of so much also at times speaks in mysterious ways and through diverse means. I have sensed that these memories must linger within our family.

I do not understand the purpose, but I am compelled to obey the direction. For he who has directed me, has never led me wrong. I have little time to speak of my youth, other than to say that I was named after my grandfather's brother, his twin, who offered himself up, allowing his brother the time to flee the great persecution that broke out against the truth. My grandfather left the great city accompanying my grandmother and three other witnesses of the truth.

I was not present at the deaths of my grandparents, although I have heard the stories often from both my father and those who were present. Those stories are spoken about elsewhere. Therefore, I will move on to the story that has driven me to this day. I was present with my father, and I helped him complete the trusts that he was assigned before his departure. He pled that I flee from what he knew was about to happen.

I, in fact, did flee, only to find myself prevented from leaving and compelled to return and be a witness to his final work. I watched from the crowd as the flames consumed my father. My heart was broken. In one day, my sister, my brother and now my father were taken.

I had hated my brother. My brother had betrayed first, my grandmother. It had earned him his first rich reward, upon which he built his fortune and his fame. His betrayal earned him the ear of the governor, who longed both to put down the superstition surrounding my grandparents and their friends. The fact that they lived among the Picts also had filled the Romans with suspicion, for there was a growing threat from that tribe.

It was bad enough speaking of the blind seeing, the lepers cured, the mute speaking, and the lame walking. But to speak of the dead living and a king other than Caesar, was beyond their tolerance. It was especially my grandparent's call for generous treatment of the Picts that had infuriated the

Romans. The Romans had long sought to put an end to the "superstitions" they suspected both my grandfather and grandmother of spreading. It was hard to understand that believing in one God could be called atheism. The other accusations were even more ludicrous.

I had watched in horror as my own father had betrayed my grandfather, out of anguish over the death of his mother, my grandmother. His betrayal had pleased my brother as well, who had reaped another handsome treasure for that event.

But my father repented of his betrayal, and in the final hours on earth, my grandfather had entrusted to him the testimonies of his friends and himself. My grandfather's own written testimony he had but completed the morning of his own death. He had passed over to my father, a small pouch holding a mysterious coin. I have been told my grandfather's words by my father:

"I have been told to give this to you. I suspect many trials and tears before you, but this is your emblem of hope, as it has been mine. Hold on to it and remember that all I have told you is true. You will be told when to give it up. You may spend it often, for it will never leave you until it is meant to."

And then my grandfather added, "I long to be started with this journey, my eyes are tired, and I wish to once again see the Lord, who gave me these eyes. I have been told that I will shed tears this day, and I have been directed to tell you that you should collect them, for another generation must benefit from what I have been given. I desire that they have their tears wiped away as mine has been until this day."

I know my father did not understand this cryptic saying until my grandfather died. My father witnessed his father's death. He had seen the strange tears, the luminous liquid flowing down my grandfather's face and dropping to the ground in a great flood.

He had gathered the tears up, for, amid the confusion of my grandfather's death, few had seen the tears that spilled to the ground and solidified into two gleaming green stones, the same color as my grandfather's eyes.

As they had fastened him to his own cross, my grandfather had cried out in a loud voice, "Look, I see one like unto the Son of Man, standing with a great host beckoning me to journey with him."

They lit the tar that had been spread upon him. The wind had blown mightily, and the fire had jumped from his cross to several of the close by rooftops. It was as if the fire being driven by the strange wind had leaped from my grandfather's own being. That fire desired to set the whole world ablaze. The evening that had fallen was suddenly filled with light as the darkness was driven back.

Soon, every building within three hundred feet of the cross was ablaze. The soldiers were running around, madly attempting to douse the fires. My brother also was beside himself, for one of the houses ablaze was his own. Still, my father watched, and heard his father say in a voice filled with joy, with a voice of greeting and longing, my grandmother's name,

"Mary," and then in an even more wondrous voice he was heard to exclaim, "Lord."

And then he fell silent. My grandfather had started the journey he had longed for and finished the one he had begun so many years earlier.

My father broke my hatred of my brother after his own father's death. He often shared with me his own story, reminding me of his own betrayal of his father, and the love that had flowed undeservingly to him anyway. He had told me his story many time and finally had pierced my heart. So, I wept now, among the crowd, as I saw their deaths. Even as I watched my brother light the cross with my sister fastened, my heart prayed for him. When I heard my father's words, I knew he spoke from a force outside of his own spirit. His words were in his voice but guided by the one he now called Lord. I watched as my father's words were proven as true, and watched as my brother slumped to the ground, surrounded by soldiers who could do nothing to protect him. I stopped praying for him when I realized that he had chosen the sin that led to death. I watched from the distance, a witness to all.

I had obeyed my father's original urging. I had gathered my wife, Solam, and my son, James, and started on the path away from the place we called Newcastle after my brother's reconstructed palace and into the hills. It would be a long trek to finally make it back to the area from where Solam had come. Her name had not always been Solam. Her family knew her as Hiedoanoa, and she was from the tribe commonly known as the Picts.

Yet as we approached the path that would take us away from the Romans and the events unfolding this very day, the voice stopped me. I was directed to return to witness what was about to happen and that my family should continue with their journey. Included in the directions was the promise that I would indeed join with my family, but after I witnessed what was going to happen. Neither my wife nor my own child heard the voice, although both sensed the conversation that was occurring in their presence. I bade them to continue and told them I would join them as soon as possible. With that, I had made my way back to the town and my father's final stand. I left my wife as she journeyed back towards her parents' home.

The Picts had always been a querulous group, but even more so since the Romans had come to Britain. Like so many other tribes, they had taken exception to the idea that Rome should rule the world, or at least their piece of it. It had been my grandfather, the one known as "the restored one," that had chosen to settle with his wife in Britain, outside the protection of the Roman garrisons. My grandfather had frequently walked among the Picts, learning their language, and then speaking of the strange things that had happened in his life.

While the Picts had normally killed or made sport of any Roman or other tribe member that had come into their area, my grandfather's sparkling green eyes and his mastery of their language made him an oddity. What was even more unusual, was that neither my grandfather or my grandmother ever showed fear. They walked among the Picts and knew that they were protected. From time to time, another of my grandfather's friends would visit us and would walk with him as well. Whoever was with my grandfather was always protected.

After my grandfather's death, the legend grew among the Picts of the protected one, with the emerald eyes of fire, and the invisible legion that had protected him during his visits with them. They could never explain how it was that the Romans had been able to kill him. They say to this day that on the day of his death, some of their spies had been in the midst of the crowd that witnessed the carnage of that day. They say that the wind that appeared to spread the fire from house to house had borne upon its invisible wings, beings of light with blazing brands. Their story explained better the strange occurrence of the fire that day.

My father had continued my grandfather's walk among the Picts, until his own death. He had spoken openly about his father, his father's friends, and the Lord that they, and now he served. Out of respect, and a little fear, the Picts had accepted his presence among them. My mother had joined my father. It was among the Picts that I was born and grew.

My older brother and sister also were born among the Picts, although both chose to leave at an early age and return to the area controlled by the Romans. The Roman culture and comparative wealth attracted them more than the freedom I experienced among the tribe.

My father had chosen to return as well to the Roman territory after the death of my mother. He was compelled into harsh labor, building with many others the wall that now bore his testimony. It was punishment for his years among the Picts as well as for the truth he spoke that were considered strange beliefs. After his own repentance of the betrayal of my grandfather, he had become a zealous teller of the story of my father and the Lord he served. That had not stopped when he returned to the Roman territory. It was that testimony that finally led to his death. My brother had become the governor of the province and desired to prove both his allegiance to all things Roman as well as his disdain for what my father now taught as truth.

It was not a surprise to anyone that as a young man, I would fall in love with Hiedoanoa. She was and is the most beautiful of all the women of the Picts. She was thin in statue but proportioned with strength and pride. Her bright blue eyes and light flaxen hair set her apart from all the other women. Her mind was quick. She was the only one of her tribe, I knew that not only mastered her own language but the languages of the invader, as well as my father's own language. It was a gift that never stopped amazing me. My father had taken to calling her Solam. It was the name she adopted as it became clear that she and I were to be more than friends.

She often spoke of her strange gift and revealed to me that every generation in her family line where the eldest child was female, that child was blessed with this gift. It had been four generations since the eldest child had been a female. The memory of the gift had almost died out within her family, until after her fifth birthday when it became obvious, she had been given the strange ability. The story was related to her by an ancient aunt, who recalled the last daughter that had displayed the gift. Every time this gift appeared; many other events revealed the purpose of that gift.

Now I know the reason for her gift in my time, and I am recording this so that others in the family might remember the fact of this gift as well as the truth of what will certainly become legends in the future. I witnessed the death of my father and saw his courage as he proclaimed that which he knew to be true. I also was a witness and participant with my father related to the testimonies that we have hidden as he was directed.

I suspect that the author of all gifts has intended events to occur that are foreshadowed by the birth of one daughter, given the same gift. I also suspect that my testimony might be of some aid to those that will certainly be confused by both the discovery of the testimonies that are hidden as well as the revealing of the strange gift my wife bears as well. I am writing this, so you might know, that this gift is both a blessing and a warning of the events that will follow the display of such a gift.

I also have directed that the final gift of my father to me, the emblem of hope and memory as he called it, be passed down through my household, always to the eldest. The voice that directed both my grandfather and father only spoke to me the one time, preventing my immediate departure with my wife and child. The voice has not spoken to me related to the emblem as it had to both my grandfather and my father. Instead, now that I know that my death approaches, I have taken what I feel is the best measure. Of course, if the voice should return, it may overrule my preparations. Otherwise, this emblem waits to be matched with its twin, as evidence of the truth of what all the testimonies reveal."

Rubin finished his reading of the original text and saw on the next page further notes, in another hand. It bore a signature he could barely make out, but the language was old and one he recognized.

He read on: "John left this scroll on his table with a short note of explanation that I found when I returned home. I am sure He wished he could have said more, but neither space nor time permitted it. He must have slid the pouch he had borne for so many years over his head and placed it beside the scroll as well. I can only imagine the scene.

Both his testimony and the emblem he now entrusted to the One who directs the affairs of all men. The noise from outside continued to build, and he realized that it was time for him to depart. He walked to the door and looked back on the life he had known and stepped into the light.

Outside the village was in an uproar. With many of the mighty men of the village gathering together, with war emblems and swords, the men of the village were preparing to depart to once again attempt to repel the advancing Romans. It had always been a debate as to who was advancing or repelling invasion. History will likely record that we, the Picts, were the invaders, although the truth is less clear. The Romans have never been anything but imperial, and their goal is to conquer the world.

He said goodbye to my mother and me the night before. We did not know of his decision to go with the other men from the village, although I believe my mother suspected it. We went to visit my grandparents on the morning of his departure. When we came back, we found this testimony and the emblem.

The twenty years since my grandfather's death have seen many such skirmishes between our village and the advancing Romans. My father returned to the village after his father's death. He completed what the voice required of him that day so long ago.

This day he had finally decided that he too must fight against those who would destroy the only family and peace he had ever known. His internal voice I am sure told him he would not return. It did not matter, for he longed to be with his father and his grandfather. He also desired to continue his conversations with those who were going to the battle as well. There were several who had heard the truth and were close to accepting it as the truth. He would walk with them, hoping that they might embrace the truth before it was too late.

There was much harvesting to do before the chaff was burned with the fire.

I am sure He prayed that he would be given the words to say, and the strength to fight beside those he chose to call brothers. He saw the small group of men he had spent many hours within discussion and walked over to join with them. They did not comment on the short sword he had brought with him. Instead, as they began to walk, they fell into other conversations.

My father died two days later, in a forest surround by the men he had come to love. Two had accepted the truth during their long walk. Both returned to the village to recount all that had occurred. The arrow that had found him also had been accompanied by thousands of others. Most of his small group had taken more than one. As he lay on the ground, his final thoughts would have been of thanksgiving, that he had been permitted to draw two more individuals to the light. He thought of my mother and I, his daughter, and prayed that we might be protected.

I am sure he thought of the testimonies and wondered what their future would be.

I have dreamed of his final moments, as he finally closed his eyes. I know that he suddenly saw better than he had ever seen before. The hand that grasped his was familiar and caused his heart to flame with joy. Beside Him stood his father, his mother, (my grandparents), his sister, and his grandparents. The one whose hand had grasped his spoke and his grandfather's eyes shone with a flame that seemed to burst forth from his green irises. It was a fire that could consume the world. It filled my father's spirit with peace.

I bear now the emblem, passed from my mother to myself. I, in turn, will pass both the emblem and my father's testimony to my oldest after me. I hope that my father's words, and the few I have added, might bring some insight to the gift I also pass on to the next generation."

It was signed in a scrawl that Rubin read easily: Carolinenin, daughter of Hiedoanoa.

6

THE DISCOVERY – PART TWO

The first task at hand had been to photograph the site as they had found it. To everyone's surprise, Rubin and two of his aids had started to reassemble the wall that the students had dismantled. Rubin saw the logic of the stones.

Each stone had a small groove cut in it that fitted it exactly to its mate above and a tongue protrusion that fits into its mate underneath. Only one mate would match exactly. The tongue and the grove stopped four inches behind the face of each rock and therefore were unobservable from the outside. He murmured to his aids: "whoever engineered this, made it in such a way that the stones could be assembled with your eyes closed."

It was as he approached the last two stones that the first curiosity occurred. He was sure that he had reassembled the wall to this point correctly but try as he may he could not get the last two pieces into place. It was one of his assistants that came up with the solution and taking the two stones had joined them together on the outside of the wall and then with an angle where their fronts met, slid the two stones into the remaining hole and pushed them into place. When he did an audible snapping sound was heard, and the wall was once again in place.

After they had photographed the reconstructed wall, the decision was made to reopen the wall. Rubin moved to the final stones and pulled on them. The wall remained intact. Taking a small pry, his staff had brought he wedged it between the stones and began to apply pressure to the stone. Soon he was pushing down and out with all his weight behind the effort. The pry bar began to bend. The stones would not move.

Try as Rubin and his team may, no amount of pushing, shoving or prying would free any of the stones from their places. Frustrated Rubin asked that the boys who discovered the hiding place be brought back. When they returned from the local detention where they were being held, Rubin questioned them closely about what they had done that allowed them to open the hiding place. Rubin even directed that they once again scale the wall to see if perhaps something else would trigger the opening. The boys spent a better part of an hour scampering up and down the wall, all to no avail. The boys lost some of their earlier bluster and now hoped that their cooperation would buy them some forgiveness related to their earlier activities. Rubin took full advantage of their willingness to cooperate.

Rubin finally stopped them after two hours of fruitless activities. He pondered what the next move should be. He was about to order a wedge and a much larger pry bar when one of his assistants' eyes went wide and pointed behind Rubin at the wall. Rubin turned in time to see one stone finish swinging out as if pushed from the inside. It stopped propped on its mate. Nothing further occurred. Rubin searched for the cause but could find no reason for it.

That the stone had moved was even more confusing since it still had the same tongue and groove assembly that each stone had. Yet neither the tongue nor the grove showed any signs of having been forced to part. The stone had simply given up its former properties and seemingly obeyed his desire to find a way to open the hiding place without damaging the stones.

After several long moments, Rubin had the urge to push the stone back into place to see what would happen. The stone would not return to its former spot. He realized that the stone that had moved was also not one of the last two he had snapped into place. For the first time, an emotion best described as fear surged through him, and his mind said: flee! Something was going on that was beyond scholarship and science. He shook that brief feeling off, laughing at his own gullibility. He was a man of science and of history. Everything had a logical explanation. He laughed at his own initial reaction and exclaimed: "This is ridiculous."

Curiosity and logic won the debate, and his earlier emotion faded into the background.

"All right let's see what is behind this strange wall!" were the words that emerged from his re-found sense of purpose.

Directing his assistants to get both the movie camera and the still camera, he prepared to record everything that was to occur moving forward. Any future surprises would be recorded for future review. Easing themselves around the small crowd of local folks that had begun to gather to see what all the commotion was about; the assistants ran to get the required tools. By the time they returned, Rubin knew that they could not complete the opening before dusk. He requested that the local constables provide barriers for the site. Picking his way around the crowd as well, he made for the nearest local phone. He made the call to several more colleagues and other assistants.

Rubin returned and decided not to wait for his additional help to arrive. Slowly he began the tedious job of removing each stone, numbering it and photographing its original position and condition. He had removed and cataloged almost two square feet of stone when his first colleagues arrived with the portable lights and generator. He had stopped briefly to direct the setting up of the site and then had returned to the work at hand.

It took the entire evening and the better part of the next day for the team to remove the remaining stones. What was revealed appeared to be a wooden box that had been entombed within. Rubin had not slept during those two days. Adrenaline, caffeine, and focus kept everyone unaware of the passing of time. The team took numerous pictures again of the area before the first attempt was made to move the box from its resting spot. It would not budge.

Rubin inspected the box again and realized the shape had been deceiving. There appeared to be protrusions still unseen that locked the box into the block wall. The team removed another two feet of stone on each side. When the effort was made to move the box again, it moved freely, swinging out into the light.

The box was laid carefully on the tarp that was brought to protect it. The find measured 1½ meters in length and appeared to be about half that size in both depth and width. The two protrusions that had locked the box in place now were obviously grips that permitted the box to be carried between two individuals. Rubin realized it would have been difficult to carry the box without the added holds. Even with them, he could not imagine carrying the box either up the hill or over the wall. The box was heavy for its size. The two men that bore the weight of the box when they moved it had lowered it to the tarp quickly.

The wooden outside was remarkably smooth. Its condition caused Rubin to doubt the degree of the discovery made. While some aging and spotting appeared on the surface of the box, surely no box of any age would have been in the condition that this one was. With no observable metal parts, Rubin still doubted whether the box would turn out to be more than 100 years old. Nothing older should have looked as good as this box did. It would explain the engineering that had gone into the hiding spot. Surely it was of modern vintage.

Rubin returned to the wall. Examining the opening for other indications of its purpose and age, he was struck by the top and bottom areas that had surrounded the box. They were solid, a single slab cut and shaped so that the outside of each appeared to be many stones, while they were both single stones providing both a shelf and a lid for the area. Both were slightly slanted. Any moisture that would have collected on their surfaces would have run off away from the box. The engineering was truly amazing. Rubin thought again, that whoever built this hiding place must have had access to some very formable tools and engineering skills.

For the second time, he thought that all of this effort was for naught, for surely what had been discovered was much newer than what he had hoped. He was wrong. Logic failed a second test. The box was transported to the university and to Rubin's research area. The area at the wall where the box had been, was roped off.

It would remain open and guarded for almost three months before local pressure would encourage Rubin to permit the rebuilding of the wall. When Rubin and his team had finally tried to put the wall back together, they found that without the box inside the stones kept falling inward. The void created by the missing box would not allow itself to be enclosed. Finally, Rubin permitted a mold of the box and created a duplicate shape to fill the area. Once done and in place, the stones were replaced, and the wall returned to its former condition.

The area had remained a location of discussion and interest. To prevent scavengers and souvenir hunters, the local constable posted a permanent presence at the site.

It took more than another three months of work before any attempt at opening the box occurred. Nuclear Magnetic Resonance Imaging, sonogram, and radiological techniques brought the first images of what lay inside the box. The first clues to the actual age of the box also began to emerge. Rubin's first thoughts about a relatively new age for the box were quickly laid aside. The dating of several slivers taken from the outside of the box came back as over 2000 years old. Rubin's heart pace accelerated when the first reports had returned from the lab. Excitement began to fill the lab, and open discussion of the magnitude of the discovery surged through and around his assistants.

At the same time as those reports stirred expectation, the first images of the interior of the box created frenzy. Robert Fleger, a research scientist that had pioneered the use of un-invasive means for reviewing enclosed objects in mummies had joined Rubin's team. His procedures brought Rubin the first images of what might lay within. Several things riveted Rubin to these pictures.

The twin outlines of stones stared at Rubin on the first image produced by Robert. The strange formation of the outlines bothered Rubin, but it was the unmistakable roundness of a coin and shapes of scrolls that sucked the air out of his lungs. Later that evening, as Rubin lay down on his bed and reflected on the day, a smile crept across his face. He turned his bedside light off and closed his eyes. The images of the stones flashed before his eyes. In that brief moment after he had turned out the light in his room and closed his eyes when his retina still held the brief flash of the light on his own eyes and projected their own glowing orbs back upon themselves, did he understand what he had seen.

Logic departed, fear, cold, and numbing returned. He sat up quickly in his bed and turned the light back on, sweating a cold chill that had run through his entire body. He would not turn the light off again that night. Eyes. Those were eyes …. staring at and through him.

It was then that he heard the voice for the first time, "You are a witness, and you will record all that you learn. You will be told what to do after you have finished. "

Jumping from the bed, he searched in vain for the location of the voice. The voice did not return. Cold sweat and fear accompanied his thoughts. Once again, he wondered if he should have run from the site the first time, he had heard his own internal voice pleading for him to flee. Now he wished he had.

He was trapped, both by the desire to learn what the scrolls contained and by the desire not to be the one to find out. It was the beginning of the torment that would haunt him for the next twenty years.

7

REWINDING AND RELIVING

He heard his daughter's voice on the second tape say, "Well Professor,," she always called him "Professor" when she had something academic to discuss. It was Laura's method of putting the appropriate distance between their familiar feelings and to focus on the task at hand.

"That appears to be all on the first set of photographs you have sent me. If I had not seen the box lid with its carving, I would be telling you that someone was playing an incredible hoax on you or should I say us. Yet the Greek contained on this portion of the find appears to be that of a pedestrian everyday person. It does not contain many of the flourishes of someone educated in the language and fits his description of himself. The word he used for potter is also unusual. Most of today's scholars would not recognize it as coming from this unique time. The document contains some obvious grammatical and spelling errors, but those lend credence to the assumption that this is an original and not anything that has been copied and corrected. Those errors point to either the document being genuine or a real genius at work going to great lengths trying to deceive us. I tend to think it is genuine although

I really need to see the document and the rest of the text before I put my name behind that last statement."

His daughter had grown in the understanding of her father's reluctance to certify anything as genuine. To do so and be wrong, could spell the end of even the most promising and successful career. Academia frowned on errors, especially any of the magnitude they now might be facing. Her voice continued:

"The style of the writing seems to show that the writer was using something akin to the stylus ink method of writing we have always thought was the prominent method of that time. When we get together, I will go through some of the finer points of what I have seen. I would wait for you to call me, but I have decided to come down on Friday for the weekend after my final class is over. I hope you can then introduce me personally to this find! I am sending this tape by carrier and look forward to seeing you on Friday evening. Take care. Love you!
'

The tape clicked at the end, and the old man carefully removed it from the machine. He carefully took another of the labels he had purchased just last week and wrote on its face,

"Laura James, August 2000 – Tape Two – First Thoughts.

He affixed the label to the tape, realizing that the newness of the label would cause many of the reviewer's concern about the age of the tape. Again, he thought that he would be glad to be absent from those discussions. Academics like to argue about trivia. In fact, he thought he had made it an art form, arguing over the little points while ignoring the thrust of the whole.

He reflected on how often he had approved graduate student's thesis selections on obscure and basically unimportant topics while turning down the more obvious direct hitting selections as being "too obvious." He shook his head again at the realization of how much of his life had been spent examining the microbe while missing the elephant, the microbe had been housed in.

With that, he picked up another tape, placed it in the machine, and pressed the play button. His daughter's voice returned as if nothing had occurred since the last tape. There was little introduction, simply

"What follows is the reading of the next section of the find made by Dr. Rubin James. The date today is Friday, August 25, 2000. I am picking up on the next plate although I have read the same on the original document that is housed at Dr. Rubin's facility at Oxford. This is a continuation of the first transcript that I recorded. After I have finished the complete first reading, I will spend more time defining the next steps in the review of these documents and the protocol required to establish their authenticity. "

With that, her voice took up the reading of the manuscript. The old man remembered how he marveled at his daughter's ability to read and translate such a complicated language without fumbling. It was a gift. He remembered having heard his colleagues speak of his daughter as having the gift of "reverse" referring to her amazing ability to translate ancient language without stumbling and hesitation.

When he asked what reverse meant one professor spoke up saying it meant the ability to reverse the curse of multiple languages. Translation was always difficult. Language employs words that described thought or concept. In one language, the word might have action tied to it, in another its closest match might require three words to describe what the other language meant by the word. The problem had always been one of understanding. Laura seemed to have a gift beyond normal for understanding and being able to translate not only the words but their intended inflections and hidden content.

Her melodic voice drew him back from his reflection.

First Words, First Requests

"The event of our first words is an event often recorded and hotly debated by those who claim the knowledge of that event. In my case, there is no debate as the event was well remembered among my siblings. Although Naomi would not remember the event, being only one at the time, my other brothers and sisters, as well as my parents, have faithfully recorded the event. The similarity of their remembrance gives credence to the accuracy of those memories. Of course, my memory of the event has been added to by the constant retelling of the story, especially later, after it was fashionable to speak more clearly of my early days. Once I was considered whole, it was easier for everyone to discuss at length my early days. Even after all of these years, I still have small flashes of the event that I believe was recorded within me, separate from all the stories that were later told.

The event was a Sabbath meal. I was already three, and as everyone already knew, I was much slower than the normal child in speaking. In fact, my parents had come to suspect that I could not speak and would never speak. I was to be a double burden for my family to bear. They tell me I was prone to different high-pitched squeals, something similar to the turning of my father's potters' wheel without the water normally used both to quiet the turning and shape the clay. I did laugh, and often, that was my response too much that bought me joy. But my laughter was unlike normal laughter, something crossed between the cry of a mule and the cackle of the rooster. But it was laughter, although many did not know it to be such.

As was my father's habit, at the end of the meal after the normal prayer of thanksgiving, he asked for whose story he should tell. That night my brothers and sisters were slower than normal in their answer, and I suppose I had been busting with the desire to hear my favorite story. So, before anyone could say anything, I spoke that single word that brought astonished silence to the table, and tears from both my parents. "Samuel,," I said loud enough for everyone to hear. That I had spoken such a difficult word first would only be reflected on later. That I did not ask for my own story, never was a surprise to me. Little did my parents or any of my brothers and sisters understand how much I had come to love Samuel's story.

They did not know that I had often dreamed of myself asleep thinking of young Samuel, serving in the great tabernacle under Eli, the priest. The wonders of being young and hearing the voice of the Lord without seeing the Lord himself overwhelmed me. Samuel had not seen yet he was allowed to hear the voice of the Lord. All he had done was answer, as prodded by Eli, "Speak Lord, your servant is listening." How often I had dreamed of my standing where Samuel had stood and answered as Samuel had answered. I knew for certain that if I only had the chance to talk to this great Lord, that He would explain the burning questions that were already forming in my young heart.

Once again, I said to the hushed room, "Samuel" and then added my second-word "father."

I do not remember more than this in my record of the event. I have heard often that what happened next were whispered prayers of astonishment, mingled with tears of joy from my parents. They say that my father asked me, "Do you want to hear a story? ", and that my response again was simply the repeated word, "Samuel."

They tell me that my father could hardly get the story out. He finally did. On that day, for the first time, and the only time in anyone's memory, he allowed me to sit upon his lap as the story was told. I do not remember, though I have been told that I held on to one of my father's tassels, from the robe that he wore only on Sabbath evenings. After the story began, I know *that I once again escaped into a world that I longed to see and heard the voice I needed so much to hear.*

My childhood memories are like this story, simply flashes of memory in most cases, surrounded by the tales told of the events by those who knew me. As with most memories, I believe that events of great magnitude of emotion are those most remembered. Unfortunately, these are also the ones either embellished or diminished the most by the memories of those around us. After all the years, I find it still amazing how my memory works. From time to time, I wish that I could forget some of the events that were burned in my memory. Of course, as I look back now, I know that those memories I would selectively erase provide the background upon which the rest that I wish to keep is seen and understood.

8

MEETING MARY

*A*ll boys, my age, dream of being taken to the temple. Boys younger than adulthood are required to stay outside the main gathering area where the men are allowed. All get their turn to enter the great area and hear and experience the great periods of worship and sacrifice that occur daily there. My family lived less than two miles from the temple in a small village known as Bethany. It was but a mid-day's walk to the great city and temple from our village along a well-traveled path.

Being so fortunate to live so close to the temple, my father would take his sons there more often than those who could only make the trip on special occasions. These special occasions were usually around the High Holidays and festivals when specific events of our history were recalled and remembered. Of course, the greatest of all the festivals was the Passover festival, and it was this event that always drew the largest crowds and the most pilgrims.

It is the duty of each father, to train sons in all that is required of them, to become a full member of the community. Samuel, as oldest, needed to be especially well trained and prepared for his role in the community. My father began taking Samuel and then later Jason with him on those *occasions he made the trip to the temple. On most Sabbath evenings though we would journey but a block from our house to the building that housed our local assembly where we would join in the community worship that took place and hear the teaching from the writings led by those considered the most learned and pious among the community.*

My father took me along with my brothers to those meetings. My mother and my sisters would come as well but would remain in the back of the building, in an area set aside for them. Most Sabbaths, I would remain with my mother and sisters. With my condition, I was still the object of curiosity and discussion. Often, I would sit alone in a corner and listen to all that was said and taught.

My father delayed taking me to the temple for many years. Finally, when I was nine, he brought me as far as the entrance to the city. I was left among some kindly folks who had agreed to watch over me, for a fee, while my father and brothers went on.

It was not a Sabbath, but Samuel was approaching the age when he would become an adult. He and father were required to prepare for that event. People, such as I, were considered blemished and therefore could only enter the city but were not allowed into the temple courts. How I envied Samuel. How I wished that I could enter and stand like the Samuel of old. How I longed to hear the Lord speak to me.

It was on this first trip that I learned about beggars. The group I was left with made their living by asking those who were passing by for mercy. I did not understand it then, but begging was expected of these folks, and the fee paid by my father, was but another form of mercy. Those who were begging neither seemed to regret or shy away from asking.

As I sat among these beggars, I realized that there was much to be learned both from the words and melodies employed by these people. I learned quickly the sound of the various coins being dropped into the bowl used as a vehicle to transport the money from giver to receiver. As you grew accustomed to the sound and weight, you would not even need to look or feel to know the value. They mostly received copper coins, but from time to time, a generous soul might give a silver coin. Those truly redeeming themselves or seeking to earn favor might on occasion give a gold coin.

I had known for many years the use of money and the great value placed on it. I was amazed at the ability of these people to glean the harvest of coins. I learned that the goal was to sound both pitiful and broken, which was not difficult after many years, as that is what we became. But when one is young and still unaware of the full scope of one's circumstance, you are not yet either weighed down with care or broken with sorrow. This was my case the day I first met Mary.

I had been among the beggars from about midday and the afternoon was fast drawing into the evening when the ruffians came. There were four of them. I knew there was a problem as I heard one of the beggars' melodic chants for mercy change. His shout of surprise was coupled with the sound of his bowl knocked from his hands. I heard the scattering of the few pitiful coins on the stone path. His day's efforts were lost. The ruffians sounded to be little more than unruly boys. I heard the voice of one call out,

"Barabbas, you should have taken the money!"

Then the laughter of the other boys continued as another of the beggars' bowls followed the earlier launching. I remember standing and saying: "stop, leave them alone," only to find myself doubled over from a punch and feeling myself being thrust towards the ground from a fast kick to my back.

I remember the boys' laughter and my feeling of helplessness. And then a voice filled the air around me.

"God sees what you are doing, and He will not leave unpunished the acts of the wicked. We stand in the light of His temple, and you would injure those who cannot defend themselves?" The words seemed to come *from an adult, and yet the voice was that of a child. The ruffians stopped, and I realized they had turned to look upon her. I heard Barabbas breathe and expected a retort from him, but all I heard him say is "Let's go and leave these losers."*

And then they quickly disappeared, still laughing down the path.

A hand clasped my arm and slowly helped me up. Her touch was not magical, but there was a firmness there, that stunned me. I would learn later that despite her family's wealth, and the many servants she could afford, she had taken it upon herself to draw the water for many years. She had strength beyond her years.

She was only ten, one year my senior and yet she spoke with a dignity and assuredness that I would not have for many years. Her first words were those of concern,

"Are you alright?"

"Yes," I muttered and then bent down still sore from the blow to my middle. She placed her arm around me and led me over to the ledge that ran along the path where I could sit.

"Sit here and let me get you some water," she said.

That ledge would become my perch for many years. I would never sit there without recalling this day, and the events that continued to unfold around me.

She returned sooner than I imagined possible. I thought the nearest public water was far away. However, she had darted into the nearest shop, that of the olive oil seller, and had returned with a bowl of water that was cool beyond anything I expected to find here. The water had a slight chalky taste that marked it as water drawn from one of the wells outside the city walls. Later I would discover that the shop belonged to her father and that there was a deep crevasse inside. He was able to store his water and keep it cool in the earth below until it was drawn up for use. She had been at the shop looking in on her father when she had witnessed what was happening. As was her nature, she had jumped right into the fray unaware of any potential danger to herself.

Her father had returned with her. I listened as she quickly recounted the abbreviated event and my meager role in it. Listening to her, I was the hero of the event, instead of the helpless, inept, bungler who managed but a few words before being soundly trounced. Her father put his hand on my shoulder and said,

"You are a very brave young man to have said anything. Most would have just let these ruffians have their way."

I was at a loss of for words, but turning to where she was could only think to ask,

"Who are you?"

Her quiet laugh was followed with a quick response

"My name is Mary, and this is my father, Joseph."

At just that time I heard two other sets of feet arriving and heard their exclamation,

"Father, what's Mary getting into now?"

I remember her father saying, "Martha, Lazarus, as normal she is only getting into good!"

With that he laughed and said to me, would you like for me to go to the temple and get your father and brothers?"

I quickly dropped my head and said, "No."

And then the rest just sort of tumbled out in a flood:

"I do not want them to know that I have gotten into trouble already. You see this is my first time this close to the temple and I want to come back. Please do not tell them anything."

After a brief silence, he said, "Alright, young man. But you should sit on the side and in the shade until they return. I must return to my shop, but I will check in on you from time to time to be sure you are okay."

And then to his children, he said, "Children, please return to the shop." As Mary started to leave, I said, "Thank you," knowing that I said it to her back.

I heard her stop and turn, and then she asked, "What is your name?"

She was the first person to ever ask. "I am Cain, son of Samuel, the potter."

"You are most welcome Cain," she said and then she left.

Before my father came back, Mary's father Joseph returned to check on me and handed me a coin, wrapped in a small piece of cloth.

"This is for you, to help you when you need it when sorrow is ready to wash over you. I suspect that life will have many sorrows for you but never lose hope. There is a time coming when I believe that our sorrows and tears will be wiped away. Until then never forget how to smile! May God bless you!".

The coin Mary's father gave me was a gold one. I did not know how often I would spend that coin only to find that it never would allow itself to leave me. Now, after all these years, I understand it was an emblem of hope given to me. I had nothing to do with its coming to me, and once given, I was its steward, and although I would use it many times, it always returned to me.

I sat in the shade by the ledge for the rest of the day. My father and Samuel came back about two hours after the event. By then there was no sign of the skirmish although my middle would be sore for many days. I did not tell my father what had happened or about the coin. Yet, I think my father knew something had happened as he said, "You look happy."

I did not realize that my condition had started taking its toll on me. My face already showed the sadness of my condition. But this day, my physical condition was overwhelmed with a new experience. Her name was Mary. She had asked my name. She had touched me with tenderness, not pity. I was already helplessly in love. I was smiling.

The tape clicked once again. He punched the button, removed the tape, labeled it, and inserted the next tape.

9

GAINING AND LOSING

Rubin's driver pulled the car to a halt just outside the entry door to the hospital. Like so many hospitals, it was a large brick building standing in stark contrast to the neighborhood that contained it. Rubin had sensed the turn into the drive and had reopened his eyes to focus on the task at hand. Even before the car had fully stopped, Rubin was already opening the door.

The John Radcliffe Hospital was equidistant between Rubin's Oxford facilities and Laura's university. Laura had been brought here on Rubin's insistence. Rubin knew and trusted the hospital administrator as well as the chief of surgery. They had all been classmates until their chosen fields had separated them for their university experiences. He could trust them to provide excellent care and ask a minimum of questions, although he knew he would need to answer some, and probably too many. No matter, he thought, it would be worth it if they can help Laura.

What had happened he had never intended. It was as if events were under the control of someone else and that he was but an actor on the stage. Shaking these thoughts from his mind, he entered. Rubin pushed through the doors and was greeted with the familiar gleaming terrazzo floor, medicinal odors, and sterile atmosphere. He crossed immediately to the lift that took him up towards the intensive care unit where Laura waited. As the lift doors opened, Dr. Louis Belton was just exiting Laura's room and crossed immediately over to Rubin. Dr. Benton stood slightly over six feet tall and was distinctly thin.

During their school years together, Louis had been called "the stork" by his friends and detractors alike. The large black eyeglasses with the heavy lenses gave him a fishbowl specter. His bright brown eyes and crooked teeth completed an appearance hiding the intelligence and expertise that Rubin had seen displayed often by his friend. The only thing about Louis that had ever bothered Rubin was Louis' steadfast belief in the supernatural and his religious convictions. These had always stood in stark contrast to Rubin's own indifference and outright disbelief in such things. Despite these differences, the two had remained friends, although both had schedules that had made their social contact limited over the years.

The two men embraced, and Louis said quickly, "her condition has not changed."

"Can I see her?" Rubin asked.

"Of course. We are keeping her heavily sedated. The pain has started, so she may not respond to your presence," his friend replied.

They entered the room together. Besides the normal beeping sound of the monitors, there was a quiet blowing sound coming from the special bed that was filled with floating silicon pebbles. Rubin knew that the bed was designed to put as little surface pressure on any part of the body as possible. It was specially designed for burn cases.

Coming to the head of the bed, Rubin looked down on Laura's hidden face. She was completely covered with gauze with even her eyes hidden. A narrow slit exposed where her mouth was, and her nose was also recognized through the small area opened for her breathing. Tubes still entered and exited both if the areas.

Her hands lay still beside her uncovered and normal. They represented one of the few areas apparently untouched by the flames. Rubin looked and simply could not understand how it was possible that Laura was lying here. It was not supposed to have happened. He also found it impossible that she had suffered such terrible burns, and yet her hands were untouched. If anything, he had expected that they would have experienced some of the most extreme burning, yet there they were, looking healthy and not scared by the recent events.

He gently picked up one of her hands and squeezed lightly and bending down, whispered in her ear.

"Laura, I am here, and I am so sorry. "

And then silently kneeling to the floor, he bowed his head and began to weep.

Later, after he had gained control of himself, he wiped his eyes with his sleeve, stood and looked over at Louis. Louis had been watching from the door and had not tried to intervene in Rubin's sorrow. They left the room together, and Louis brought Rubin current with what had been going on.

"We continue to treat the burns but still cannot determine their cause. As you know, they still appear consistent with some form of flash burn, but we still have no idea what Laura has come in contact with. There appears to be no toxicology present, so we have ruled out any type of chemical reaction causing the burns. Whatever it is that she encountered, the burns are severe. As with all burns, the real danger is still the infection that can set in as well as the dehydration that results from the exposure of underlying tissue to the air. We are particularly concerned about her eyes. We do not know to what extent her vision has been affected. She may well be blind, although there is no apparent physical damage to her eyes. She will need cosmetic surgery to repair the damage to her face. "

The "if she survives" was unspoken but the concern hung heavily in the words.

"We have kept her heavily sedated to allow her as much comfort as possible. Laura was in great shape, and she has a real fighting spirit, but in the end, it will depend on her body's ability to heal itself. We are doing everything we know to do, now we must just wait."

Rubin took his friend aside, knowing that he needed to reveal part of the secret that had haunted his conscience for the past three days. Sitting his friend down in a corner, Rubin continued to stand as he spoke quickly and urgently to his friend. As he spoke, Rubin realized that instead of limiting what he was saying, he was instead pouring out a confession that was bubbling up from his soul. He needed to share this horrible burden, and he hoped in some way to gain some absolution from the guilt that weighed him down. He did not care any longer about the consequences. Instead, he longed for release.

Louis' face remained impassive through the entire discourse. Towards the end, Rubin's face fell, tears leaking from his eyes. Finally, he stopped and waited for Louis to respond. Louis rose slowly.

"I am not the one that will need to judge your actions, Rubin. While I would like to speak further about your actions, I have to tell you that your explanation does not fit the facts, " he said.

A surprised Rubin sank slowly to the chair, replacing Louis' position. Louis slowly explained the tests that had been run and their results.

"Despite what you might think, the compound you mentioned is, in fact, well known by both myself and my staff. Two years ago, we were called in related to the explosion at the McHenry Industrial Plant in Newford. There were five badly burned survivors of that explosion that we worked with extensively. You probably read about that in the newspapers at the time. That explosion and fire leveled a three-block area and killed over thirty people.

What you do not know, and what was withheld from the public is that McHenry held the rights to manufacture this compound and was, in fact, producing their first samples when everything went terribly awry. Those facts were kept out of the newspapers. Not only was the propellant considered a secret, the last thing anyone wanted was to reveal the presence of such an unstable, highly combustible compound being manufactured near any neighborhood. Since the accident, the manufacturing of this compound has been limited to the most remote areas and under security and safety standards hundreds of times more stringent than before. All those injured and any others with knowledge of the compound's presence were paid handsomely to keep that secret.

I had the opportunity to see firsthand the effect of this compounds burning capabilities on human flesh. I treated the five survivors, who came in contact with the compound as it was released through the explosion. I know what it can do and what it looks like. I also know that despite what you might think, Laura's burns are not consistent with that compound or any other I have experience with."

Louis continued,

"The compound is indeed difficult to trace, and it is highly specialized. Very few facilities would have been able to detect the residue or know what the residue was even if they had detected it. But it was not present on Laura, and as far as we can tell, it was not the cause of the fire."

Rubin stared at his friend and replied,

"I do not understand," and then fell silent.

In his mind's eye, he relived his role in the events of three days ago. He knew the compound was there. He had arranged for it to be applied to the chest and the documents. He expected the compound to combust at about the time the fire occurred.

He desired to destroy the chest and the contents.

Rubin did not know that Laura would stop by and remove the scroll to take it back to her lab that evening. She normally would have asked him. Little had been normal since the discovery. Security should have also prevented its removal, and it was a serious breach in security that allowed it to occur at all.

He once again rationalized his actions arguing with himself again that he had not intended this current evil. He believed that Laura's interest in the manuscripts was consuming her. The testimonies were leading her to believe that which he could not accept.

He forgot to include his own fear in the list of reasons for his actions. His actions had resulted in the destruction he had desired and the injury that was unintended. It was the only explanation possible for what has happened.

"Are you sure that you know what to look for? ", Rubin asked.

Again, Louis nodded and said,

"The compound was not present on Laura, or anything brought to us."

"Of course, I have not tested anything from your lab. Do you still have something with whatever you applied to the chest and documents?"

Rubin slowly shook his head.

"No, I left everything in the lab. I wanted nothing to remain that would point any fingers at me. "

Rubin told him that portion of the story as well. Louis knew that Rubin had been a double major at the university. Brilliant in both chemistry and history, Rubin's scholarly bend towards history had drawn him professionally that way. What he had not realized was that Rubin had continued to stay abreast of developments within the chemical industry. He continued to maintain a small but well-equipped laboratory at Oxford. His credentials and contacts, not to mention his chair at Oxford, opened many doors thought to be closed to all but a few.

After Rubin related the story, he added,

"I think you should look at the samples from the lab in Oxford where the other books were housed. I believe that you will find that I am telling the truth and that the only explanation for what has occurred is the one I have provided you with. I will get some samples sent over for you to look at right away."

With that, he got up and strolled over to the phone in the waiting area. After speaking on the phone, he returned to Louis.

"The inspector is sending some samples over immediately, I told him that you needed these to try to verify whether any chemical there can explain the burns on Laura. "

Rubin returned to Laura's room while Louis waited for the samples. They arrived in less than an hour. Louis left to take them to his lab. The inspector had taken upon himself to deliver the samples personally. The inspector's name was Kirby Watson and had the reputation of being very thorough in his investigations.

"No change with Professor James?" the inspector asked.

"No," said Louis.

"Can you tell me what you hope to find in these samples?", asked Kirby.

"I am not sure that we will find anything, but Rubin insisted that I check these out to see if they can tell us what happened to Laura. "

"I have had every battery of tests known run on these. There is nothing there to give us a clue as to what happened. You will let me know if you find something we missed?", the inspector added.

"Of course," Louis's answered.

Silently Louis prayed that there would not be anything to report. Two hours later, he knew the answer.

Rubin listened in unbelieving silence as Louis shared the results of the latest tests. For the first time, Rubin dared to hope that perhaps he had not been the cause of Laura's injury. But what had happened?

"If this is not the cause, how is it possible that absolutely no trace remains of what I applied. I am not dreaming, I know what I did," Rubin said.

Louis only shook his head.

"I believe that you believe you applied the compound. All I can tell you is there is absolutely no evidence to prove that. In the end, you can convict yourself of this tragedy, and certainly, you had an intent that would allow you to plead guilty to the event. But I could not prove that as fact," Louis said.

Rubin retreated in time. Reliving the days and events leading up to his decision to destroy the discovery.

The opening of the chest occurred almost six months after the discovery. After using every means available to produce an opening without damaging the box, it was determined that the boxes had been fused together. What had been five different boxes were now three. The outside three were now a single unit. The decision was made to drill a small hole into the base of the box, entering into the area where a granular substance seemed to separate the outside boxes from the inside ones.

The drilling occurred without difficulty, and the small sample of the interior contents revealed sand and surprisingly salt. A larger pilot hole was drilled and then a small saw inserted, and the process of removing the covering boxes began. It was a four-hour process as the saw was carefully and skillfully moved around the base of the box. Finally, the saw met its starting point.

The box had been enclosed in a vacuum hood, and all work was done using the gloved entry areas. All the dust and debris were captured within the hood, and any floating particles were removed to another chamber by the vacuum induced in the hood.

After six hours, the team was able to lift the first three boxes over the top. The sand that had capsulated the remaining boxes slid harmlessly to the bottom of the hood area. The sand was remarkably dry.

A day was spent cleaning the first removed boxes. Numerous tests revealed that no harmful properties appeared to be present. Another week of X-rays, consultations and other tests preceded the decision to move ahead.

The next chest appeared to have a lid that had a tongue that had slipped into grooves carved for it on the sides. Rubin's team began to apply pressure to the lid and found that it slid easily out. As the cover moved, the carving and the eyes were revealed. A hushed silence filled the room as the hidden box top came into view.

Slowly that box was removed. Rubin had allowed his staff to handle this step. His decision had brought a surprise. Rubin had never allowed his staff before to take the lead on a major step in any discovery. Rubin had never shared his night experience with his staff. Nor did he reveal the near panic he felt as he came face to face with the eyes in reality.

Rubin stood in the corner of the room. Present but removed from the sphere of activity. As the box was revealed, there was an audible sucking in, as all the assistants and Rubin as well, reacted to the scene. The assistants spoke excitedly about the box cover, the carved words, and the strange green stones that stood out on the box cover. Rubin forced himself closer, curiosity replacing fear. Finally looking down on the box lid he saw the carved words and the two stones. Stones that is all they were after all. The nights of cold sweat and fear faded quickly from his consciousness. Now that they were exposed, he felt instant relief. He also felt glad to be only one among many in the room. Nothing ever happened with many witnesses' present, was his thought. He became the analyst and director his assistants remembered. Once again, he took control of the theatre of operations.

Pictures had been taken and then the decision about the final opening was made. Careful examination of the top showed that the final step was similar to the last step. Rubin and an assistant both used their gloved hands and reached to the final cover. It was then that the next curiosity had occurred.

Just before their hands touched the surface of the lid, the lid had slid open. Rubin had simply looked up at his assistant, Carol Anders.

"Did you touch the box?"

Rubin knew from the look on her face that she had not. She confirmed it with a quick shake of her head. The old concern crept back into Rubin's mind.

Anger surged through Rubin. He was tired of fear. He said aloud,

"Enough of this foolishness. I am a scientist, and do not believe in cheap tricks, or activities that have their sole purpose of scaring me."

Looking around the room, he suddenly realized that no one else seemed to share his conviction. Rubin took hold of the cover and slid it the rest of the way back until it was removed from the box. He laid it aside still on a small stainless-steel table inside the containment area. He willed himself not to look at the top again. He wanted, no needed to see the contents of this box.

Peering inside, he saw what they had seen in the x-rays and other pictures. A pouch with a thin string-like wrap, small scrolls, and a slightly larger scroll lay exposed to his sight. Excitement once again built, replacing both the fear and anger. After the required pictures were complete, he reached in and removed the little pouch. Even though the fiber and with his gloved hands, he could tell that the object inside was round and distinctly coin like in feeling. He did not open the pouch. Instead, he passed it out of the containment area through the door provided and placed it on the steel tray provided quickly by another assistant.

Rubin decided he would look in the pouch later. What he wanted was to get to the first parchment. Reaching again inside, he lifted the first parchment gently with its strange woven cloth-like covering. The first parchment he laid gently on a tray still within the containment area. More pictures and then Rubin examined how the parchment was covered. It was a small scroll. He had seen a few fragments of this type of document before.

Most fragments from this time were from former scrolls. The scroll fragments remained since the rolling process produced layers of protection for the interior areas. This was the general practice of that age. As the document was written, the written portion was rolled under to allow for more writing on the adjacent area.

Unlike the fragments and pieces, he had seen before, this scroll was whole. It appeared neither brittle nor dried out. The realization that he was looking at a complete scroll slowly took hold. The feeling that he was being duped once again raised its specter.

He slowly unwrapped the scroll from its wrapper. He sensed through his delicate grasping of the scroll that it was still pliable. "How was that possible given the expected age?" was Rubin's thought.

With that, he broke normal protocol and slowly attempted to unroll the scroll. It unwrapped easily, much to his surprise and the astonishment of his staff. Carol had started to say "Professor…" wanting to warn him about opening the scroll without the normal protection being taken but had stopped when she realized both that it was too late and that the scroll had opened easily.

Rubin recognized the writing immediately. It was Greek. The quality of the scroll, the clearness of the writing, everything was speaking against the age that had been assumed. No written document had ever stood the test of two thousand years and appeared in the condition this scroll did. Once again, Rubin was certain that someone was pulling an elaborate hoax on him.

Despite the reading of the age of the wood boxes, despite so much evidence that was indicating that this find was indeed ancient, Rubin once again believed that the scrolls were of modern invention. But he needed to be sure.

Simultaneously he directed both that pictures be taken of the revealed writing and the box lid and sent to the best ancient language linguist in England. That linguist also just happened to be his daughter. Then taking a small sample of the covering of the scroll he gave it to

Carol for more tests. He was sure that one and probably both directions would result in readings that would date the discovery and expose an elaborate modern-day hoax.

He was wrong on both accounts.

The note from his daughter and her first tape, arrived at his office only a few hours after the lab tests had placed the age of the wrapper as close to two thousand years old. He did not share his daughter's excitement, that was evident both in her note and on the tape.

Once again, dread began to squeeze his heart. What exactly was he dealing with here?

10

REMEMBERING

Rubin never grew tired of listening to his daughter's voice. Her voice brought his memories into sharp focus. As he prepared to play the next tape, he hesitated, remembering the only two women who had meant more to him than his daughter had. It had been years since he had spent any time remembering either of them. The death of Laura's mother had driven a cold spike into his heart, separating him from belief in anything. The death of Laura had driven the other woman away. Rubin had sworn never again to trust or be exposed to anyone.

His first wife's death cemented his belief that led him to accept only naturalistic explanations for events. We are born, we live, and we die. It was a cycle that was natural and not directed or planned. Any other explanation was too difficult to understand and too painful to accept. His daughter's death shrouded his life with pessimism. Now not only was the cycle of life natural it was slanted towards grief and misery.

But now he knew the truth. For the first time in years, he thought back to both and began to unravel the mystery and each woman's influence upon him.

Laura's mother, Anita, had touched Rubin like no other person before her. Rubin met Anita in graduate school. She was completing her doctorate in the Romance languages and literature, as he completed his doctorate in ancient British history. Anita Brown was not brilliant, but she was gorgeous and persistent. He had seen her in the library where so many students gathered to study and research their various assignments.

Anita was 5' 6" tall. She was decidedly skinny but in a way that did not make her appear undernourished. Instead, she had a frame that accented her face that was beautifully shaped. With her slightly pointy nose, her bright brown eyes and her pixy haircut, she looked like a model from one of the magazines instead of a student. Rubin had already begun to take on the slightly pudgy shape that would be with him all the rest of his life. With his round face, thinning hair, and demanding nature, he had decided early on that he was not likely to be of interest to a woman like Anita.

Doctoral candidates were required to explain their thesis in a public forum. Most of these forums occurred in the students' final year. Supporters of the candidate, normally family and friends, attended hoping to lend visible support to the student. Other aspiring candidates attended seeking insight into what might occur when it was their turn.

Then there were the critics. Normally comprised of critical professors and other detractors, whose delight it was to ask probing and sometimes absurd questions in hopes of embarrassing the candidate. Of course, the candidates own moderator and sponsor, who had the most to gain should their student excel in their future career, also came to both guide and lend support to their prodigies. Often the attack on the candidates was a thinly veiled attack on a rival professor who might be in line for a chair or some other honor the attacker desired. Sometimes, it was just the desire to show the attackers own superiority.

In reality, these forums served as the preparation for the oral presentation and exam that would be required of each candidate. This was the great "final" or "passing through the fire" as it was known. Here the panel of professors and experts that held the student's hopes and future in their hands would do their best to humiliate the candidate while probing for the candidates' understanding of the subject matter being presented. The forums were but a foretaste of the greater roasting still to be experienced.

Rubin had sat through a number of these presentations and had watched as detractors had asked questions both insightful as well as meaningless. He had seen the announcement of Anita Brown's forum and decided to attend.

Her doctoral thesis focused on the understanding of the supernatural in British writing from 1300 AD to 1700 AD with a focus on the view of that time related to evil. Her focus was on the various views shown about evil especially as revealed in the personage of Mephistopheles in various writings of the times. He had not gone to the forum to listen to her topic but instead to see how she handled herself among the many critics that her topic would certainly raise.

As a modern man, Rubin found it amusing that anyone might still believe in the supernatural. He found it even more puzzling that someone with the looks of Anita, and the aptitude to reach for a doctorate might hold to these views. He had heard through his friends that Anita not only held to a belief in the supernatural but was more than willing to discuss this belief when the opportunity presented itself. This alone, Rubin thought, would make the evening interesting. He admitted to himself another fact, he liked looking at Anita. Despite all of his protests to himself, he found that at times he went out of his way to be where he would have the opportunity to see her. He had never worked up the courage to speak to her.

The evening of her presentation, Rubin was suitably early enough to garner as close of a seat as he might desire. He chose to sit several rows back so as not to be too conspicuous. Her presentation was to begin at 7:00 PM. By 6:50 PM, Rubin began to get the feeling that he might end up being the only spectator present. For whatever reason, her forum appeared to be shaping up as one of the poorest attended forums he had seen.

When Anita had taken the podium to begin her presentation, only 15 people were in the auditorium. At least 13 appeared to be professors assigned the role of probing and questioning. The only supporter appeared to be an elderly man that Rubin had never seen before. With his obviously old suit and ruffled condition, it was obvious that this individual was neither an academic nor a casual spectator. Therefore, Rubin reasoned this must be a relative. "Where were all of her friends and other supporters?" Rubin wondered.

Anita had taken the podium exactly at 7:00 PM and started her presentation. As with most presenters, she focused on a friendly face or two among the spectators as she began her thesis and explanation. She had little to choose from that evening. Her focus was on the elderly man that Rubin had guessed was a relative and upon himself.

He began to realize that while her focus would shift between the two of them, by the end of the first fifteen minutes, her focus was almost entirely upon Rubin. Rubin had never been so scared or happy in his entire life.

It was not until almost an hour later at 8:00 PM that noise interrupted the presentation. Much to the disliking of the professors present, about 25 more people poured into the room. The cavalry had arrived, and Anita's friends, while late were there in force. He would learn later that Anita's friends had been given the wrong time for the presentation.

The mistake that would be traced to a particular individual who had never liked Anita or her "superstitions." That individual had carefully doctored the announcement of the time and had made sure that Anita's closest school friends had received the "corrected" invitations. While much would be said later about the event and the meanness of the action, Rubin could not have been happier for the outcome.

Rubin had expected that with so many other real supporters now there that Anita would shift her focus to the new arrivals. He was wrong. Despite the arrival of so many obvious supporters, Anita had first flashed a smile at her friends and then refitted her sight once again upon Rubin as she completed her presentation. Rubin's anxiety level increased exponentially. Near panic took control of his heart as he tried to make sense of her focus. Finally, she came to the end of her prepared remarks, and her focus shifted to the scholars and her mentor as she asked: "Do you have any questions or comments for me?"

The real torture began. Her mentor and guide asked the first question, one that was designed to boost Anita's confidence and gird her for the grilling that would come at the hands of others not as disposed to her wellbeing. Anita had flashed a grateful smile and answered the question smoothly, displaying both her command of the subject matter and her ability to play the role that the setting demanded. The trouble started with the second question.

The professor that asked the next question was none other than Rubin's own mentor and counselor. Professor John Howard was a particularly brilliant scholar whose disdain for any belief in the supernatural was known throughout the academic world. His works had included several scathing attacks on many of the beliefs displayed in the so-called "Religious Era Writings" of the Middle Ages. Rubin noted, however that his mentors' writings were peculiarly silent about many of the belief systems outside the one that seemed to be the focus of his hostility.

The Professor had also gained a reputation as leading the charge against many of the Christian writers that had been emerging from the English academia over the past 20 years. Writers like CS Lewis, JR Tolkien, and others were regular targets of Professor Howard's disdain and criticism.

Anita's entire thesis neither attempted to support the view of the supernatural world as displayed through the writings she reviewed or to deny their view. She instead based her focus simply on what the writers had believed, how it had influenced their writing, and how their writing shed light on the belief pattern in the society at that time. She also focused on how the writers own influence had either supported or begun to change the views of the society that were their immediate audience.

Rubin knew immediately where Professor Howard would be going and what might lie ahead for Anita. He had started simply, asking a question seemingly innocent but that Rubin realized was the proverbial bear trap.

"Ms. Brown, what do you think of the views these writers held?" Rubin held his breath, expecting Anita to step on the trap and be caught in the jaws. But Anita surprised him, she said,

"What I believe really has nothing to do with the topic at hand professor, what matters is what did they believe, and how did that belief affect both themselves and their society. They understood good and evil in different ways, and we see a progression in the changes in their society as that view begins to change as well." She had danced around the trap. She had sniffed the cheese and chosen not to partake.

The professor moved the trap and put new bait on the spring.

"I understand that, but I am curious as to what you believe anyway. Any truly scholarly work must admit the scholar's own prejudice to give the reader the ability to judge for themselves the effect of the scholar's own views on the supposed facts spelled out by that scholar."

There would be no dancing around this trap.

It was then that Rubin did something almost unthinkable. He laughed. Not a chuckle but a full-blown laugh had erupted from Rubin. The irony of the question had taken hold of Rubin.

The entire audience turned to look at Rubin. Professor Howard also turned surprised to see Rubin and recognize his laugh.

"You find the question humorous, Mr. James? "Professor Howard asked.

Rubin swallowed hard; his whole future flashed before his eyes. He realized he had jumped on the trap in Anita's place.

But anger and pride also welled up within Rubin. He heard his voice, although he could not believe he was saying what he did.

"Professor, you never reveal your own prejudices in any of your writings that have received such acclaim. Why should she or anyone else be held to a different standard than the one you live? Or is it your position that others be held to a higher standard?"

The professor's mouth dropped open to quickly be replaced with a steel gaze that Rubin understood immediately spelled trouble.

To his surprise, Anita came to his rescue.

"I will be glad to answer your question, professor, as I too agree that it is important," she said.

Professor Howard turned back to Anita. Rubin felt the Professor's eyes glaring at him through the back of his head. His offense would not be forgotten.

Anita answered his question.

She also endured a barrage of other questions, but she never flinched. Nor did she seem concerned at the scoffing that accompanied many of her answers. Rubin listened, amazed. Not only was Anita beautiful, but she was also a woman of intellectual substance. She stood her ground never yielding anything but the respect that her audience had a right to expect. In the end, Rubin would describe the exchange as a draw, which was as good as a win in Rubin's eyes. Professor Howard was no longer unbeatable. Try as he had, all Professor Howard was able to show was that Anita believed what he disdained. There was no verdict reached as to who had more evidence for the truth of the matter. In the end, Anita had successfully returned the discussion to the matter at hand. Her dissertation and her thesis were what mattered in this forum. Her beliefs were not on trial. In the end, Professor Howard's colleagues understood this and helped stir the questioning to a more positive and understandable conclusion.

Rubin changed counselors the next day. The change caused him to lose a year of his work. In the end, it had been worth it, although he had to endure Professor Howard's additional attention at his own forum at the end of his final year of work and study.

It had been with difficulty that Rubin had found another professor to serve as his sponsor. He finally found one professor who was at the end of his career and would not benefit in the future from any relationship with Professor Howard. Professor Howard had never forgiven Rubin's outburst. What made it doubly infuriating was that Rubin had never disagreed with the conclusions reached by Professor Howard.

Rubin's own intellectual capabilities and his growing reputation, as a scholar would soon exceed Professor Howard's. To add to Professor Howard's angst, when he retired as the head of Oxford's English History Department in 1963, the chair would be given to Rubin who had already surpassed his former mentor and adversary both in statue and in publication. By then Rubin had replaced Professor Howard as a champion of intellectual detachment and disdain for all supposed "superstitions." Despite this fact, Rubin and Professor Howard would never be friends, and the slight was never forgiven or forgotten.

Anita and Rubin were married three years after the forum and within a year of Rubin accepting an assistant professorship of history at Oxford University. The old man at the forum was indeed Anita's closest relative. His name was Harry Brown, and he was Anita's father. He also was an Anglican priest with a deep faith but a small congregation and church that was both his ministry and his support. His wife had died years before the victim of an outbreak of polio that had claimed many in his small parish. He had raised Anita by himself from the time she was four. Anita and Rubin were married, by her father in his church, on August 25, 1954. Laura was born less than a year later.

Rubin had never been much of a religious person. His parents were nominal Jews. Like so many of their generation, they had lost faith in their God. Their leanings towards social concern led them first to socialism and then finally communism as the great remedy to the ills of society. After the war, when the Holocaust was revealed for what it was, the final blow to any belief in any power other than the human spirit was cemented in his parents' minds.

Neither understood nor accepted a God that would allow such extermination to take place. Rubin's father had fought in the war and had been critically wounded at the Battle of Dunkirk as the English fled in one of greatest defeats and most miraculous retreats of the war.

Rubin's mother died shortly after the war. A cancer discovered shortly after his father's departure for Dunkirk and before that news could rescue him from his own destiny, finally took her life. Rubin had grown up taking care of his father, who never really recovered from his wounds and whose bitterness over his wife's death had hardened his own heart towards any mention of God. His father died in 1946 when Rubin was eighteen.

Rubin's own brilliance was recognized earlier. His real home had become the schools he attended. It was the only place Rubin ever felt free to be himself. A perpetual student, Rubin had decided that academia was where he wanted to be.

Despite Rubin's lack of belief and Anita's father's warnings to Anita of the perils involved in such a relationship, Anita had finally broken down her father's resolve. He agreed to the wedding.

Theirs had been a passionate romance. Anita's father wrestled with the wisdom of marriage despite the problems that were sure to lie ahead for his daughter. It was better to be unevenly yoked than to be unfaithful to the demands of purity he reasoned. He argued with Anita passionately trying to change her thinking. He told Rubin to his face of his concern. Rubin assured the old man that his love for Anita was genuine and that he respected her faith despite his own doubts.

Anita died before the demands of her faith had an opportunity to come into real conflict with Rubin's lack of faith. On a Sunday, as she walked to her father's church that was but a few blocks from the flat that she and Rubin had acquired, a car struck her. The driver of the car, a victim of a heart attack, had also died. Rubin was at home with Laura, who was only nine months at the time. Anita's death traumatized Rubin into a paralysis state. Once again, Rubin's certainty of fate, uncontrolled by any reasonable force, took hold.

Only Rubin's position at Oxford, his daughter's wellbeing, and Laura's father held him together for the first year. Anita's father took over raising Laura for much of her first ten years. He continued his ministry right up to the end, never complaining about having raised first Anita and then Laura.

Rubin thought back to Harry. Harry had cried. Rubin saw his own sorrow and brokenness mirrored within Harry. Yet Harry had officiated Anita's funeral with quiet dignity. Rubin remembered he had never seen Harry defeated. There was something internal that had knitted Harry together and held him through everything.

Rubin understood now. Harry's faith, while often challenged, also showed itself true. It was the glue that cemented Harry's peace. Even amid great sorrow and tears, Harry's faith showed itself with its quiet acceptance of what Rubin had not been able to accept.

It was Harry who first discovered Laura's natural abilities in language. Laura would spend most of her day at Harry's home while Rubin taught his classes. Harry went about the daily process of preparing for his Wednesday and Sunday sermons. Unlike so many other Anglican ministers, Harry still believed the truthfulness of the scripture. He was intent on bringing those truths to his ever-dwindling congregation.

Harry's beliefs were considered outmoded in this modern age. He did not seem to care, continuing to prepare wholly committed sermons to the truth he found in the scripture. His particular disdain for the so-called "modern views" caused many young people attracted by the intellectualism of the new ideas to look instead for a church where they could hear what they wanted to hear. Harry referred to this as the "tickling ears" phenomena. He continued to attempt to find a way to speak the truth to the younger generation, praying that they would hear it and stay. He longed for the truth to be an anchor for the youth being blown about by the storms of their own generation.

It was his normal procedure to spend hours pouring over the material he would be teaching. This included reviewing the original languages to see what nuances or other meaning had been left out in the translation to the English language. As with so many translations, even those attempting to be faithful to the intent of the original writing, there were always areas where decisions were made. Those choices might leave out some additional emphasis or meaning understood in the original language.

Laura had started to sit with him, first on his lap, then on a chair that he had placed in his study for her when she was four. Harry had tried to spend time with her playing as much as possible. He had found different opportunities to expose her to other children. Rubin had agreed to allow Laura to attend a toddler group that met every morning close to both of their homes. Harry would pick Laura up from the group and walk the few blocks home every day. He would make Laura her lunch and then set up some toys in the room where he would be doing his studying. She had kept coming over to his desk. He had picked her up and soon added the chair when he realized that she had little interest in the toys. She seemed content to sit close to her grandfather.

As a youngster, Laura was unusually subdued and focused. She would sit with Harry for hours. Harry would talk to her about what he was seeing and doing. Harry did not believe that she could understand but was surprised at her willingness to sit for so long and listen. It was when she was five that Harry realized that Laura had been more than just satisfied with being close to her grandfather. She had been learning.

Wrestling with a passage, Harry was often prone to ask himself questions out loud as he prepared his lessons. He quoted himself a definition and then was trying to say the Hebrew word that the definition fit when Laura answered the question for him. She spoke in flawless Hebrew the word he had sought. Harry was stunned.

Taking Laura on his lap, he had pointed to the text he had been reading and then listened in amazement as Laura read the entire passage speaking in English what was written in Hebrew. Harry had looked again to be sure that it was not his lexicon that he had been reading from, it wasn't. Laura had just read an entire paragraph of one of the most complicated languages known to man and had translated it into English without error. Harry had spent most of his life trying to master this language, to do justice to his calling. Laura, it seemed already had a command of the language beyond his own. Harry looked in wonder at Laura and said aloud,

"Dear Lord, what have you given this child?"

He hugged Laura tightly realizing she had been given a gift that he had heard about but never personally experienced. Later that evening he brought Laura home to Rubin. He shared with Rubin what had happened. Rubin, at first did not believe his father-in-law. Laura demonstrated her ability for her father. Rubin sat down in amazement. Rubin took Laura to be tested by some of his colleagues at the university the next day. They returned the report that Laura had an amazing gift. They recommended that Laura be started in a special school focusing on language immediately.

Laura had blossomed from that day forward. By her thirteenth birthday, Laura was already recognized as one of the most gifted linguists of her generation. Rubin realized now how those years played such an important role in both his and Laura's lives. Rubin realized now the impact of Harry Brown's life on Laura and himself.

Harry died in his sleep of a massive stroke when Laura was ten. He had known that his time was close. He had made preparations for both Rubin and Laura's care with the few remaining members of his congregation. Laura's gift and Harry's death snapped Rubin back into reality. Anita's death was finally released, and Rubin once again took control of his circumstances. He determined to raise his daughter quickly ending the preparations Harry had made.

After Harry's funeral, Laura's focus was on language. God was never mentioned in his home. Laura was given many other works to study from. Rubin's unbelief had been challenged by Anita's love and Harry's faith. His unbelief was rekindled by Anita's death, and sealed by Harry's death and Laura's gift.

The old man turned the tape on again and heard Laura's voice returning him to a time not as distant as that he had been visiting.

Her voice said:

"The first time I spent my coin."

"As I have told you, my father was a potter by trade. His workshop, like so many of the other artisans of our city, was directly attached to our home. By the time I was five, I had mastered the home and shop. Although still clumsy, I now made the rounds of the area unaided and with some speed. I also spoke clearly, and it was obvious to my family that I was not the dotard they had first assumed.

From the time I was very young, I sat much of the day in my father's shop observing the various comings and goings as displayed through the various sounds, smells, and textures. The day my father had placed my hands upon the clay in the wheel, it turned in my mind. His hands guiding my hands around the clay lump, fashioning my first crude bowl, is a memory cherished. However, I would not be long for the shop, or blessed family memories, as events would overtake me.

My father created mostly common wares for sale. A small shop attached to the house and a spot in the local market served as the distribution network for his wares. The market was located along the path that led through our village towards the great city. My father often set Samuel, as the oldest, at the market booth to oversee the display of the wares and to handle the selling there. It was a meager living but one that housed, clothed and fed the family. From time to time a special commission would provide a much-anticipated surplus in the family coffers.

I remember Samuel, hurriedly returning to the shop well before the market closed, with the news of such an event. Breathlessly he reported to my father the good news. A wealthy neighbor, a merchant in the olive oil and perfume business, desired to place a large order for jars.

I knew from Samuel's description that it was Mary's father, Joseph. Unlike my family, Mary's family conducted their business in the great city. They also had one of their homes in the same village as ours with a small shop attached.

I had not returned to the great city since that first trip. I had not been anywhere where Mary or her family had been. It had been a year since my first encounter with Mary. I had thought of her every day.

My father left quickly with Samuel and was gone for much of the remainder of the day. As the evening meal was being eaten, my father announced that indeed a very large order had been placed. The delivery was *needed in a very short time. He would be working late and early every day for the next two weeks except, of course, for the Sabbath.*

If all went as planned, my father would make enough off this one order to support the family for most of the year. The order had conditions, as all such orders did. Substantial penalties for underperformance could quickly reverse good fortune to a disaster.

For much of the next week, I remember that my father was already in the shop when I awoke, and still there long after I had returned to my mat that served as my bed.

As was my custom every day, I would find my spot in the workshop where I was not in the way, and yet could be a part of all that was going on around me. On the last day before the order was due, I came to the shop early. Sitting in my normal spot, I listened attentively to my fathers' activities.

My father took a brief break from his work. Standing up, he walked outside to stretch. What happened next is a blur in my memory, although the consequences of what happened are pressed upon my soul.

I stood to follow my father. Somehow, I missed the detail that my father had moved several of the finished and dried pots to an area beside the doorway. As I rushed to follow my father, I missed the normal markings that guided my path. I ran headfirst into the stored pots. I felt more than heard the shattering of the pots. I remember the stunning awareness that I had started a canopy of events. Pots crashing against one another ended shattering as they tumbled into one another and then onto the floor.

The loud crashes halted my father. He quickly returned only to witness the final foray of pots coming to their final resting spot. I never heard my father curse before that day. I do not believe I ever heard him curse since. The anguish, in his voice, as he spoke my name, communicated more than the words. Although I never heard the words before I fully understood their meaning. He picked me up from among the damaged pots. These were not the loving arms of the man who had thrown me into the air, but those of someone I had never known. Their roughness created a black wall of fear that rose inside me. His words were a branding iron, searing, and marking both memory and soul.

I remember saying "Sorry father" but as I was hurled out of the door of the shop. His words stung more than all of the damage done by the fall or by his rough handling. His words were simply, "You worthless piece of camel's dung, look what you have done."

I remember thinking I should retreat to my mat, but instead, my fear caused me to run from the yard onto the path beyond our wall. I had never adventured alone outside these walls. It would be the first of many lonely journeys.

I stumbled and ran as best I could from our house up the short path to the main thoroughfare through our village. At the corner stood a small tree that halted my progress as I ran face-first into it. I collapsed by its trunk, wrapping my arms around it and burying my face in its side. My mourning was quiet, although my sides heaved with the pain inside. It was mourning lacking the tears that would have come from most normal people.

It was the week before the great feast, and many people were passing through our village on the way to the temple and the festivities. While I had heard the noise of the people passing by, my broken soul did not care if others saw me. I continued to mourn, replaying the words recently spoken in my mind, cursing both my condition and my inability to fix what I had just done. My hurt and anguish turned against my father and the God I had heard about but never experienced. "Why!" I yelled silently in protest.

I did not hear his approach. Instead through my anguish almost as if answering my last protest and question, I heard his words,

"Cain, why are you here?"

It was a young voice. A voice I had never heard before. A voice filled with the tone of recognition that I could not understand. I sensed that he had sat beside me. A gentle hand rested on my head. I turned my face to him, a stranger I did not know. The story erupted from me unintended but relentless. I left out my real sorrow. One does not share the scaring of one's soul by those you love. He listened and then softly said, "Come with me."

My face still stung from the collision with the tree, and my sides were still weak from the trembling of my sorrow. I stood and took up his hand and slowly joined his pace as we walked on.

I would realize much later that he had known my name. When I would ponder this, I became convinced that someone else must have told him my name. I was certain that I had not met him before. Much later, when I understood the truth, I would remember the event in wonder.

I learned quickly that he was journeying towards the great city with a group of pilgrims that included his family. Those around us spoke of going to the temple for the upcoming feast. He was the age of my brother Samuel. He was traveling with his parents and family to the temple as they did every year for this holiday. His father was a carpenter, a trade's person like my father, but their shop was not as fortunately placed as my father's. They were much poorer than my family. There was a joy among this family that money had not bought. I listened to the banter among them and realized that he was the oldest of the children. Like Samuel, he was close to the age of becoming a full member of the community.

Walking, his hand in mine, guiding my steps, I realized that we were going to the temple. I did not think about what my parents would say. I was unprepared for what happened.

The closer we came to the city, the greater the press of people. The noise of the gathering of a large crowd filled me with awe and anticipation. In but a short time we had passed through one of the gates of the great city. We continued to walk past the area where I had sat the year before. I stopped when I heard the chant of the beggars, instinctively expecting that this was where we would part. His voice was soft, and his hand persuasive. His words few, simple, and yet a command: "Come with me, you belong inside."

I was filled with frantic joy. The traumatic morning was forgotten. I was aware of the odors and noises surrounding me. I was going where I had only dreamed of being.

The sounds of the people and the odor in the air told me what was occurring here. Finally, we came to the great door. Just as we passed through the door, I felt a much rougher hand thrust upon my shoulder. An older voice accustomed to immediate obedience said to my guide,

"He is not allowed in here."

My heart fell. I understood that I was not allowed. Then I heard my guides voice and the single word question I had asked in such a different context only recently: "Why?"

The commotion around us continued, the throng of people continuing to pass us by. All disappeared into the background. All I heard was two voices, that of my guide and that of my detainer.

"Look at him, I do not need to tell you why he cannot go in," said the detainer.

To this, my guide said simply, "Which does the Lord command? A whole body or a humble spirit?"

When the detainer made no response, my guide continued:

"Which does the Lord inspect first, the condition of the body or that of the soul?"

Still, there was no response. The silence was more painful than the tight grip upon my shoulder. Then I heard my guide's answer to his own questions:

'The requirement is not that our body be whole but that we be humble in spirit and realize that we need to be made whole. He is concerned about our soul first. That is what our God teaches. That is why we offer sacrifice. Surely, you must know that?"

Then with a much softer voice, one filled with longing and love, I heard my guide say:

"Let him enter."

I felt the hand on my shoulder go slack. My guide's voice drew me again,

"Come."

I walked. released, I entered. His voice was young, yet his words bore authority. My soul and body trembled at his touch, yet I gripped his hand tighter. Not understanding the reason until much later, his touch suddenly filled me with a longing I had never known before.

Once inside, my guide led me over to a small porch, where there was room for me to sit.

He said, "I must tell my parents that I am here, and then I will return.
"

With that, he left me, and my thoughts traveled back to my dream. I am in the temple! And in my heart, I spoke those words that Samuel spoke so many years before,

"Lord, your servant is here, speak?"

I waited, but there was no answer, just the continuing bustle of the people passing by moving into the main area.

How long I sat there, I do not know. My longing to hear the Lord's voice did not fade, but I began to realize my surroundings and the activity that was taking place. Suddenly my guide was back, and he had someone with him. I recognized this voice, and he said,

"Hi, Cain. I have come to take you home with us. We are finished for the day."

And then Lazarus had turned to my guide and said simply, "It was good of you to bring him, I will be certain he gets home before night falls. Will your family stop in Bethany on your way home?"

"No, it is a long journey, and they will want to be on their way, "my guide said.

Lazarus took my hand and slowly helped me from my seat. But before I turned with him, I said to my guide,

"Thank you. I have dreamed of sitting here and speaking with the Lord like Samuel."

To that my guide's voice changed, and I knew he was smiling when he asked,

"Did you ask Him your question? "Did the Lord give you your answer?"

I remember my head falling to my chest and my answer: "No, but `I am grateful all the same."

His final words I understand now although I did not then.

"He heard your question and did speak with you. Perhaps you do not realize that you have heard his voice and have your answer. One day you will."

With that, he was gone. Lazarus guided me efficiently through the throng and back to the path back towards Bethany. It was not until I was well away from the temple and through the gates of the city that I realized that I had not known who my guide had been. I asked Lazarus about this mysterious guide. Lazarus said simply that he had never met the guide before today. He had simply followed when the guide had said:

"Cain is here, and I need you to take him home. "

I pondered this while we walked.

97

After a couple of hours of walking, the events of the early morning returned to me, crushing the joy that had welled up within me from going to the temple. Lazarus sensed the sudden change in me, and asked,

"Cain, what is the matter?"

With that question, the memory and sorrow of the morning's events tumbled out of me. Lazarus listened quietly to all that had occurred.

After I had poured out all that I could share, Lazarus said:

"Cain, I am sure that it will all work out. Do not be afraid."

With that, we continued our walk, although the darkness that hung over me grew with every step closer to my home.

We arrived back at our village about an hour before dark. Lazarus brought me to my home. "It was good to see you again, Cain." Lazarus departed saying: "I am sure that everything will be fine."

In my haste to creep back into the house, I forgot to even thank him for his kindness in bringing me home. As I sat on my mat, I wondered how any day could compare to this one. This day had been both the greatest sadness and the greatest joy of my short existence. I thought no day would compare. Later I would realize how wrong that belief was.

Wrapping my arms around my knees, I pondered the day's events. What could I say? I had destroyed my fathers' work, and now he would both lose this valuable commission and face the ridicule of his neighbors. Of course, I was to blame, but in the end, it would be my father and family that would pay. Despair, creeping like a fog, slowly wrapped around my mind and heart.

It was then I remembered the coin given to me by Joseph. The despair withdrew as the sunshine of hope rose. I knew what I must do. Finding the wrapped coin, I moved slowly towards the workshop door. I sensed my fathers' activity within, and I stood in the doorway until my father took notice. His words were only slightly less branding than earlier.

"What do you want, Cain?"

The words were fairly spat out although I realized that some of the earlier harshnesses had tempered.

"Father, I have this for you. It is not much, but perhaps it will help a little?"

I felt the coin lifted from my palm and knew it was being examined.

"How did you come by this?" my father questioned.

I did not tell him the whole story.

"I was given it when you took me to the great city, while you and Samuel were in the temple."

It would not be until later that I would understand that this action on my part sparked an idea within my father that would direct a good deal of the next twenty years of my life. My father said nothing else.

No absolution or pardon was offered. I had hoped at least for an acknowledgment that the calamity had not been deliberately planned by me, but my father said nothing. I returned quickly to my mat and my thoughts.

It was late at night when I woke. How I had fallen asleep or for how long I had slept, I did not know. Nor did I understand what woke me, but I heard my father and mother in conversation.

I heard my father say, "I do not know why this has happened, but Joseph stopped at the shop to let me know that he did not need the order for another month. He said something about going away after the holiday and not wanting to have to move the pots to his shop until he came back. Then he added another order to the original order and paid me an advance for the materials. It is amazing. He even increased the price we had agreed upon saying the original price was too low. I never mentioned to him that the original order had been damaged and that it would have never been done."

My mother's tears and my father's laugh-filled me with gratefulness, and I remember saying,

"Thank you, Lord, for Lazarus, and thank you for Joseph's mercy upon my family and me."

Then I heard my father say in an all-together different tone,

"I do not want Cain in my shop anymore. I think he is old enough to begin to learn his only occupation will be with the beggars. We cannot afford to have him sit around here and do nothing. He will need to learn how to support himself. After all, it is not fair to the rest of the family that he is a burden upon them."

I waited for my mothers' protest but heard none. Suddenly I realized that the two people that meant the most to me had agreed. I was a burden to my family. I was to learn to beg. I turned my face from the room, clenched my fists, and rolled back into the corner where I could be alone with my thoughts. I did not dream of Samuel, or of Mary, or of my strange guide that night. Instead, I nursed the hurt until I barely could contain the raging question within: Why?"

Rubin turned off the tape. The question asked on the tape had been his for many years. He reached into his pocket and felt the familiar roundness of the coin still within the same pouch that he had removed years ago from the box.

As he held the little pouch, the question that had bothered him for close to twenty years again emerged. He looked at the next tape in the series and knew what it contained. There was a gap in time between the tapes. While the next one would pick up where this one had left off, there was a gap as if part of the story had been untold.

He had pondered this mystery often, and finally, he knew what he needed to do. He had started this step twenty years ago, but his anger had prevented him from completing the step. Getting up, he walked across his cluttered room to the bookcase in the corner and withdrew a book that had been given to him by Anita's father so many years ago. The book had seldom been opened over the ensuing years. Like so many others in so many other houses, the book had been available, accessible, and ignored.

With trembling hands, Rubin returned to his seat by the table, and slowly opened it to the point that he had marked but chosen not to read almost twenty years ago when he had first made the connection of the gap in the timing of the tapes.

This time he read. After he finished reading the passage the first time, he went to the beginning and read the entire passage with its context and the outworking of the events. History unfolded before Rubin. For the first time, he not only knew the history, he believed the history.

Suddenly, the box, his father-in-law's faith, his wife and daughter's death, fell into place. He now knew. More than that, he believed. Tears streaming down his face, he laid his head upon the book on the table and wept. Why had he taken so long to come to grips with it?

Finally looking at the time, he retreated from the study area to a little bed he had placed close to his study. He lay down, closing his eyes, and slipped into a peaceful sleep. The first he had experienced in many years. His final thought that evening was about Anita, then Harry and finally Laura and the truth she had discovered so many years ago. His soul was no longer filled with sadness but with peace. He slept the entire night soundly.

11
ANTICIPATION

Laura arrived at Rubin's office at the university earlier on Friday than Rubin expected. He learned that Laura's excitement was so great that she had given her Friday afternoon students a rare gift, an afternoon off. She drove the 90-minute drive from her office to Rubin's without the normal stop at her flat near her own university.

Laura embraced her father as he rose to greet her. Rubin's queasiness was not eased by the anticipation he saw in Laura's face and heard in her voice.

"Can I see the box and scrolls?" was her first statement.

Not her typical, "Hello Professor" or her rare but sometimes playful "Hi Prof."

No, today her anxiousness to see the find overrode everything normal. Rubin thought to himself that everything was far from normal.

Laura did not seem to detect the hesitancy in her fathers' response. She beamed in happiness as Rubin answered: "Of course." Rubin's reasoning was once again at odds with his gut. But he was not willing to give over to the churning in his stomach that told him more was to come.

CHARLES A. DE ANDRADE

Taking his hat and overcoat, he guided Laura towards the door and then out of this building and towards the building that housed his lab and research area. Laura strode purposely beside her father, without speaking. It was as if Laura had no questions to ask of Rubin, only a driven need to see the discovery firsthand.

The research building looked like so many other buildings on college campuses of the time. While many of the campus buildings were built with the endowment from wealthy benefactors, others were built as "afterthoughts." Functional but not particularly architecturally pleasing, the lab building lacked the finished sophistication that came from having a donor whose happiness with the final product dictated the presentation. Rubin's lab was housed in this simple three-story brick building that was dwarfed by the endowed granite and marble buildings that were its neighbors. Rubin had often thought how odd it was to see this building on the campus of such an ancient learning arena.

Reaching for the door, Rubin took out his key and opened the door to allow Laura to glide through. Entering the first story, they proceeded down the steps. Rubin's lab area and research facility were on the first level below ground level. They reached his lab after passing down a short hallway. The sign on the door read simply "Historical Antiquities Lab – Entry Prohibited Without Permission." Rubin was greeted at the door by Carol, his assistant who greeted Laura with enthusiasm and Rubin with the professional distance Rubin demanded.

Laura greeted Carol with her trademark whimsical smile, which spoke of a knowledge possessed by few others. Laura knew that despite the seeming formality between her father and his assistant that their relationship was much more. Carol was just slightly older than Laura. Like Laura's mother, Carol was also a thin woman with a proud face. Slightly shorter than her father, Carol's golden-reddish hair was tucked up in a bun that exposed her chiseled features. Her face had the sharp angles of the French heritage she bore. Her nose was sharp and perfect and offset by two perfect blue eyes that gleamed with intelligence. Laura was not at all surprised that her father had been drawn to this woman. After so many years, Laura knew that this was the first serious relationship her father had entertained.

Laura also knew that Carol had been offered several different lucrative positions both at Oxford as well as other universities, but she had instead chosen to continue on as Rubin's assistant. It was obvious to Laura, and she suspected too many others, that there was more than loyalty working here.

Few people knew of how the relationship between Carol and Rubin had begun. It had started innocently enough. Carol had been a post-doctorate student looking for an intern position as her next step into the academic world she had chosen. She had remembered her two classes under Rubin with fondness, drawn to both his command of the historical arena that was his specialty as well as his dry humor that flowed through many of his classes. She remembered that Rubin had seemed to respect her thoughts, and she had earned two high marks from Rubin's classes. Rubin was a professor who was notorious for sparingly few good grades.

Carol had been wrestling with which approach would be best. She had not chosen Rubin as her mentor or sponsor during her doctorate period. The position she desired would have been much easier for her to obtain if she had been Rubin's protégé. Many post-doctorate internships were rewarded by professors to their own group of students who had been under their tutelage. However, Rubin had attended her public forum related to her thesis and had given her support when one other professor had seemingly taken it upon himself to skewer both her thesis and her presentation. She still remembered with gratefulness Rubin's piercing sarcastic remarks about Carol's detractor's own work related to her subject area.

Even her own mentor had smiled after Rubin had demolished Carol's detractor. She had sought out Rubin after the forum to thank him for his support. Rubin had eyed Carol with those eyes that seemed to penetrate through the surface and had said that he could not stand bombastic portentous academics whose own work was little better than those they chose to review. This had not exactly been the response Carol had been expecting, but none-the-less she had been grateful for his support.

It would only be later that she would discover during her review for her final oral and written exams the paper written by Anita Brown. Anita had written a strikingly similar thesis and reached conclusions like her own. Carol had searched out who this Anita Brown might be and had stumbled onto a potential connection to Rubin's support. His former wife had written a very similar thesis more than twenty-five years ago, and Rubin's support must have been a reaction to the attack of the professor on a thesis that she had also reached and supported. She had learned of Anita's death, and then made the connection to the other person in Rubin's life, Laura.

Laura had by this time, already distinguished herself within the academic circles and was already approaching the status of being the best of the best linguists in the country if not in the world. Carol made an appointment to see Laura, hoping to understand better what made Rubin tick and to see if there was any hope in enlisting Laura in swaying a position for herself within Rubin's team.

Carol dressed nicely, choosing carefully the professional appearance she wished to display. She arrived early at Laura's office and was surprised when Laura greeted her immediately upon her arrival. Laura's eyes did not reveal the internal surprise Laura felt seeing within Carol a distinct reminder of the photographs she had of her own mother. While their faces were distinctly different, there was something in Carol's poise and demeanor that was strikingly familiar. Laura eyed Carol suspiciously saying, "I am curious as to what brings you to me?"

Carol had brought with her both her final written thesis and a copy of Laura's mother's thesis and handing them to Laura had sat and waited for Laura to make the connection. She had almost immediately and sat down as well. After briefly skimming both documents, Laura had looked up and asked, "What is this about?"

Carol had then told Laura her story, and of her desire to work with Rubin. She admitted her nervousness at approaching Rubin directly and admitted her own apprehension of Rubin reading too much into the similarities between the two thesis papers. But Rubin was working in the area and historical arena that intrigued Carol the most. She asked Laura directly what approach she should take with Rubin. Carol remembered Laura's piercing gaze that had slowly softened and the sad, whimsical smile that had crossed her face. Laura had asked simply, "You want to go get a cup of coffee, and we can talk?" To this, Carol had agreed, and the two women had left Laura's office.

Carol and Laura had become friends that first meeting and Laura had arranged for Carol to meet her father. It would only be several years later that Laura would confide in Carol, that she had known exactly what she was doing and what the potential consequence would be. She knew of the emptiness in her father's life, and she had seen instantly the potential attraction her father might have for Carol. It had not surprised Laura at all when two years later she had arrived at her father's flat unannounced and had discovered Carol there. Rubin had been flustered, and Carol had tried to perform a disappearing act, but Laura had simply announced that she had known all along and that neither should attempt to deny what she knew she had arranged.

Carol had been Rubin's constant companion since.

Laura smiled at Carol again as they entered Rubin's lab. Looking around, Laura had focused in on the large hood area and the stainless-steel tables that ran the perimeter of the lab. Each table now had on it what appeared to be smaller hoods, and she walked over to the first. There on the table beneath the glass cover lay the object of her curiosity. Seeing the partially unrolled scroll, Laura had turned quickly to her father, her expression bearing both the surprise and the reproach of one professional to another. Rubin had raised his hands in defense and said: "I know, I know. But the scrolls were very flexible and unrolled easily. I suspected at the time that they were of recent origin and that it explained both the condition of the box and the scrolls. Of course, your comments and the review of our other tests seem to indicate quite a different possibility."

Laura had stepped over to another table and peered down through the cover. Laura was frozen in position. The eyes staring back at her had transfixed her. The eyes had seemingly seized her that first time. They expressed a longing that was at the same time, both inviting and consuming. She had looked down on the writing below the eyes and had spoken the words, "He hears the weeping of his children. He will wipe their tears away, turning their tears into laughter." She stood transfixed, unable to move.

Rubin had continued to stand back, watching Laura carefully. Rubin's heart was beating a strange rhythm, and he knew he was bordering once again upon a near panic. It had been Carol who had broken the spell by reaching out to Laura and gently taking her arm.

Laura had finally broken contact with the case and looked at Carol with eyes full of amazement and at the same time, a seriously puzzled look. Laura shook her head and said, "Wow!"

Coming out of the trance, she had looked at Carol and said, "I have never seen anything like this." She shook her head again and returned to the first case. Looking down, she realized that the portion of the scroll that was revealed contained a portion she had not seen before.

Her gift kicked in, and her words started without thought:

The life of a beggar – Meeting Mary Again

Six mornings later, my father woke me. It was the third day after the great feast, and though I remember that we celebrated it that year, I do not remember it as being a joyful time. He told me to get dressed, that he, Samuel, and Jason were going into the great city again to continue Samuel's learning. I knew why I had been invited to go. Whether my father knew that I understood what was happening, I do not know. He and my brothers spoke little during the journey to the temple area. We arrived in the mid-morning and as I expected, I was left with the beggars. Except for this time, my father placed a small bowl in my hands and said simply, "learn from those around you and see whether you can make some money as well. We will be back late this afternoon." I felt my face flush red with the anger and emotion that was welling up in me, but before I could say anything, my father and my brothers were off. I was ten, and I was a beggar.

I sat carefully on the ground and listened to those gathering around me. This was the earliest I had ever been here. As new arrivals came to join our band, I began to realize that everyone here had a story and a name. Each took turns welcoming one another back, and even some bantering took place as each prepared for the day.

I felt one of the gathering residents being laid down beside me. It was more like a collapse as his bulk was lowered to the ground beside me. I heard him grunt and then his self-diminishing laugh as he said: "Gracefully done as normal!" Thanking his friends that had brought him, his friends, in turn, told him that they would be back later in the evening.

As his friends left, he said to me, "Such friends! We used to work together until the mast of the boat cracked and took my back and my legs with it." I felt him surveying me, and I felt him reach out his hand to grasp mine. "My name is Jacob," he said. "I lost the use of my legs about a year ago, and now I come here to support my family. I almost died, probably would have been better if I had, but here I am anyway!" His voice had a merry ring to it, and as I took his hand, I realized that he was a young man. I said quietly, "My name is Cain, I am the son of Samuel the potter from Bethany. I was born this way, and this is only the second time I have come here. And the first time I have come to beg."

He heard the bitterness in the last statement and reached over and slapped me on my back. "Do not worry, normally it is only as bad as you might think" he said laughing. "There are times it is even worse! But we all manage to get through the day. At least we are not alone."

I discovered Jacob loved to talk. He had opinions on everything, but he shared them only when the crowds passing by had thinned out. This morning most of the people passing were leaving the city after attending the festival. As such, they were in a hurry and spent little time listening to the chorus of chants and pleas for mercy that arose from our small band. During the slow times, I learned that Jacob was married and had been for only a short time before his accident. He had married one of his friend's sisters. Now his brother-in-law came with other friends to bring him here when they were visiting the great city and the temple.

It was so very odd listening to him. At no time during the morning did I hear of any bitterness in him from the accident. It seemed that he had adapted to his situation, and although I knew that at times, he remembered his former life longingly, it was without bitterness. Around midday, we were interrupted as a man, and his wife stopped and asked of Jacob if he had perhaps seen their son. It appeared that they had come to the festival together with their family and had left in one of the caravans heading back in the direction of their town. It was always better to travel this way, as there were still robbers and other "bad people" in the hills. There was safety in numbers according to what Jacob told me later.

It appeared that both mother and father had supposed their son was with each other, and since the caravan was large, it had been three days before they realized that their son was not in their midst. They described their son, and Jacob said that he had not seen him. They were obviously worried, and I envied this youngster who had parents that would care so much for him, to have returned from such a great distance to search for him. After the events I had experienced, I was no longer sure that if I became lost that my parents would search for me.

My thoughts were interrupted as I heard a familiar voice say, "I saw him walking with the teachers going to the temple. "My heart had skipped a beat at that voice, and I quickly tried to turn away from the voice with the hope that she would not recognize me or see the bowl that was clenched in my hands. I heard the parents thank her, and quickly leave making their way back up the path towards the temple. I had hoped that she had gone away too.

Then I realized that she was sitting down between Jacob and me. "Hello Cain," she said to me. With my face downcast, I turned to her and said softly, "Hello Mary." I had forgotten that her father's shop was so close by. Suddenly I trembled to realize with sadness that she might often see me here when she came to visit her father. See me here, begging. Yet something inside rejoiced at the thought of that as well.

"So, your father has brought you here for more than a visit?" Her question was a statement of fact, and I realized that the bowl had not gone undetected. "Did you tell him about your conversation with my brother?" she asked. Again, I looked down and said softly, "No." Then quickly I added, "Please do not tell him that I spoke with Lazarus. I do not want him to know that I had anything to do with your father's mercy upon us." Mary thought about that for a while and then said softly, "I understand."

Mary stood slowly, and I knew she was looking at me. She said softly, "Lazarus, Martha and I stayed with my father this week, but now we will be returning to our home in Galilee." Mary's family was rich, and as such, they owned several homes. While Bethany was the family's base of operations, being so close to the great city, apparently her mother had decided that the hill country was more suitable for the family residence. "I will not get to see you again for a while, as I must continue to learn from my mother those things necessary for me to know. My father has gone away to the hill country to my relatives there, and I suspect that when he returns, I will be betrothed to someone there.

My heart dropped within me. So, it was not just Joseph's mercy upon our family. He had actually needed to go out of town and had not needed the order from my father with the same urgency as originally thought. Mary was to be betrothed, promised to another.

Of course, my dream had not been real. She was older than I. She was whole and vibrant. I was young, blemished, and broken. Yet I had hoped, and now this hope was gone as well. Her hushed voice continued: "Cain, Jacob is a good man, he will help you. And remember that God does see all things, and He sees and knows and loves all His children, even you." With those words, she was gone. I felt her rise and walk away. Jacob turned to me and said softly, "Such a wonderful girl. She brought water to us here often. She will be a fine wife and mother for some fortunate man." Little did Jacob know that I agreed with his words but that those words broke my heart.

If I had been able to shed tears, they would have flowed freely that day. But at times the greatest afflictions have great blessings, or so I thought since I believed that tears would have only added to my misery.

It would be years before I would hear her voice again. Sorrow and grief would pass through and around me before the joy would come again. Yet I would think about her almost every day and pray that she might be happy.

My father returned with my brothers to collect me. I had but a few copper coins to show for the day, and I suspected that a couple had come from Jacob's hand when he thought I was unaware. Nonetheless, my father seemed content with what had occurred that day.

Once home, at dinner, he had announced that he would be taking me back to the city early in the morning. My life as a beggar had begun. I only remember getting up and leaving the table for my mat. Later that night, my mother had stolen into my room and woke me. She had slid something into my hand and said simply, "This is yours, you may need it later," and with that, she had left. No words of comfort or regret. Yet as I look back on it today, I realize that this simple act was the beginning of mercy in my life beyond my understanding. I did not need to open my hand. I knew from the feel; it was Joseph's coin.

Laura looked up from the glass, her eyes locking with her father's. The unspoken question had leaped between the two, and Carol had watched and listened in amazement. Carol had heard of Laura's gift, but this was the first time she had seen it in action. Carol also realized that Laura's earlier criticism of her father for the opening of the scroll had now been replaced by an almost pleading appearance. She realized that Laura was more the captive of this amazing gift, for once started, it seemed to possess her with a strength that cried out "More." Carol understood Laura's look at Rubin, she was asking for permission to have the scroll unrolled more, so she could continue.

Carol had glanced at Rubin. The few other assistants in the room had gone still and silent during the last few minutes of revelation. Rubin seemed frozen in space. It was Carol who moved to the hood, placed her hands into the gloved area, reached in, and gently rolled and unrolled more of the scroll. She had looked up into Laura's eyes, and saw a respect and a love that she now knew she cherished.

Carol was Rubin's lover and his assistant. She was Laura's friend and the sister she had never had. Carol had smiled at her friend with respect as well and then stood back as Laura had returned to the glass. The spell returned, her gift kicked in, as did her voice.

12

UNDERSTANDING

For the first time in years, the old man awoke from his sleep feeling truly rested. Sliding his feet from the bed and sitting up, he looked over at his table and the tapes that still waited for his listening. He looked around his room, felt its dinginess and its dustiness, and decided that something needed to be done about that first before he continued his task.

He went to his front window and drew back the drapes. The sunlight flowed into the room marred only by the dust and dirt still to be removed on the windows. The sudden light replaced the glumness that had been his companion for many years. He forced a window open, its mighty protest the stillness it had endured for such a long time echoing around Rubin. The fresh breeze began to fill the room. It was time for a change.

In Rubin's mind, he realized the truthfulness of the statement, "All things are made new." The last 24 hours had changed Rubin. Now, that change began to be reflected in everything that touched Rubin as well. Rubin's heart told him that there was little left for him to impact. He would learn again how wrong his heart could be at times.

He spent the best part of the morning cleaning. By lunchtime he had created many large piles of refuse that he now placed in bags and hauled out back to the trash containers that had been seldom used in the recent past. It took many trips, but finally, he entered his room and understood the blessing of orderliness that he had surrendered in his former state.

He prepared his lunch, mindful that while the rubbish was gone that there was still a great deal of dusting and other cleaning to be done. He told himself that he would work on the dusting during his next break. He placed his sandwich on the plate and sat it on the table. Returning to the sink, he seized a freshly washed glass and filled it with water from the container in the refrigerator. He looked at the food in the refrigerator and made a note that he would also need to take care of that situation as well.

He was just preparing to sit down when he heard the knocking of his door knocker. He had not had a visitor for a long time. He wondered who it could possibly be. Looking at his tapes, he wondered if he should move those out of sight first but decided against it. Moving to the door, he opened it slowly and stood stunned at the apparition that stood on the other side of the screen.

It had been over twenty years since she had left. She had aged but had not changed. Her sparkling blue eyes still seized on his as they had done so many years ago. Behind her stood a younger woman, who by her appearance was obviously her child. The two together reminded him of another family he had once had and lost. "Rubin," the apparition said, "May we come in?" The old man stood aside in surprise as this visage of the past slid past him and into his house.

Carol still wore her hair in the tight bun except now its reddish hue was woven with the fine yellows of age. Her bright blue eyes danced around the newly cleaned rooms, and he could tell that she knew of the recent cleaning activity. Turning to him, she said, "It is as I remember it." Then smiling, she turned to the young woman behind her and said simply, "Laura, this is your father, Rubin. "And then to Rubin, she had said, "Rubin, this is your daughter, Laura." Rubin sat down slowly, not knowing what to say but suddenly realizing that another part of the puzzle was about to slide into place. His acceptance of the truth was now allowing him to understand the past even better than before.

Carol had taken off her coat that had protected her from the coolness of the day and had taken her daughter's coat as well. She had hung them from the familiar rack that hid behind the door.

As Carol and Laura sat opposite Rubin, Rubin realized that a simple gold cross-hung around each of their necks. His memory flooded back to another who had also had such a necklace. His other daughter also called Laura had taken up that symbol only weeks before she had left. And he remembered when he had last seen that symbol. Rubin once again walked in the past.

After his discussion with his friend Lewis at the hospital, he had taken up his vigil close to Laura's room. He had fallen asleep when the first crisis started. He woke with a start as one of the nurses had rushed past him and into Laura's room. It was then he heard the warning beep, beep, beep, that caused his blood to freeze.

Lewis had also not gone home and had insisted on staying close by. It was as if he knew that the toughest times for Laura were about to begin. Lewis flew past his friend and from his perch Rubin heard the rapid-fire directions that Lewis was giving to the gathering troops. After a frantic fifteen minutes, Rubin realized that the tension was leaving. With a happy realization, Rubin understood that Laura had overcome whatever this first crisis had been.

Lewis returned to his friend, placed a hand on his shoulder, and explained that Laura's lungs had apparently filled with fluid, which was a common problem with patients that were being treated for significant burns. The buildup at times can occur quickly, and the need for constant intravenous fluids made this form of pneumonia almost inevitable. The fluid had placed enormous pressure on both her lungs and her heart mandating a rapid draining of those fluids. This had been done, and this crisis appeared to be past.

It was as Lewis explained the recent crisis to his friend that the second and final crisis began. Lewis had just finished his explanation when the bleep, bleep, bleep of another warning echoed in the silent halls. Lewis once again turned, moving quickly back to the room so recently left. Lewis's staff also quickly returned. This time there was no recall or second chance.

It would only be after the battle that Rubin would be told that a blood vessel had burst under the intense pressure of the fluid buildup. When the fluid had been removed, the vessel became a fire hose squirting Laura's life into the empty cavity as fast as her heart could pump it. Lewis's team never had a chance, although they had fought bravely for his friend's daughter for hours. When it was over, Lewis had come out of the room, placed his arms around his friend and wept. Rubin had collapsed in his friend's arms, slumping to the floor also in agony. If it had not been for his friend's embrace, Rubin would have pounded his head on the floor in the anguish. Instead, the best he could do was beat his fist on the floor as he repeated over and over, "My fault."

After their weeping had passed, Lewis had helped Rubin up as well. Rubin unsteadily took the steps back to Laura's room and entered. Lewis's team had tried to straighten up while Lewis and Rubin had mourned, but there was little anyone could do to hide the immense effort and work that had been done in attempting to save Laura.

Still swathed in the bandages, she was the same and yet remarkably different. Rubin realized for the fourth time in his life, the powerful absence of life. Without the presence of life, his daughter had shrunk much more than he thought possible. He once again picked up her hand, which no longer had the warmth of life, and holding it sunk to his knees and wept again.

After he had finally been able to leave the room, he had told Lewis he was going home. He said that he would be back in a few hours for Laura and wondered where her body would be then. Lewis had replied, "You do not need to come back so soon, there is nothing you can do. She will be taken care of, and she will be ready for you whenever you are ready." Rubin had simply nodded and walked to the lift and gone home.

The next day started early. Rubin had canceled the conference he had scheduled to update the team on what was happening. His thought was, "they will understand, and if they don't well…"

He had returned to the hospital and found that Laura had not been moved to the morgue. Instead, his friend had moved her to a private room. Rubin was touched by the unexpected sensitivity. He entered the room and found his daughter lying gently on a freshly made bed. Most of the damage and soiling from the activities of the evening had been removed, as had the bandages that had covered her face and head. One side of her face had been terribly burned, but remarkably, her hair was for the most part intact. Her eyes were closed, and Rubin believed that he would never see those eyes again.

Someone had dressed her in a flannel pj's that Rubin remembered seeing her in before. It was against this background that the gold cross stood out. Someone had placed around his daughter's neck; this simple sign of a faith Rubin did not have. He reached over and felt the cross and was about to rip it off when Carol's voice filled the room. "Don't you dare remove that!" Her words surprised Rubin, both that she was there witnessing what he was about to do, and that she dared to speak against his action.

Carol stood in the doorway of the room. Rubin realized that Carol's face was etched with both alarm and sadness. Recent tears had cut their grooves in Carol's otherwise perfect face. He understood that his daughter and Carol had in the past year become sisters in more than just name. They had shared over the past few months not only a deepening intimacy but also a belief that Rubin could not share.

Carol slid over the bed and put her arm gently around Rubin's shoulders. Realizing her first tone of voice, her new tone stood as an apology. "She told me that if anything happened to her, this is what she wanted." Carol slowly sat on the corner of the bed, turned to her friend, and stroked her hand again. "I just cannot believe that she is gone."

It was this day that had spelled the beginning of the separation between Carol and Rubin that finally ended in her departure shortly after the funeral. Rubin's anger at Laura's death had kept re-emerging. Anger at himself for what he felt was his fault, and especially anger at Carol who tried mightily to persuade Rubin that other forces were at work that was outside both of their controls.

Carol had become convinced, as Laura had been before her death, that there was more to this life than what was seen with their eyes.

Rubin's steadfast inability to accept that belief caused his anger to become focused on Carol as well. Finally, Rubin's anger had boiled over. Shortly after the funeral, he had exploded, telling Carol that if what Carol and Laura believed was true, then this God was responsible for both his daughter's and his wife's deaths. It was Laura who had been the catalyst that had brought them together, the glue that had cemented their relationship, and now the pry bar that tore them apart.

While it was Carol who physically left the home, it was Rubin who had insisted that Carol leave. Carol had argued that she needed to stay, but Rubin would have none of it. He remembered the distress in Carol's eyes as she had argued that final evening, attempting to change Rubin's mind. Nothing she had said had moved him.

Before Carol had left, she had written Rubin a long note. In it, she had shared that she now believed, as Laura had come to see shortly before her death, that the scrolls had been but a vehicle that pointed to another greater document that held the keys to the truth that these scrolls had also confirmed.

Both Laura and Carol had spent hours discussing their discovery and had together come to the faith that Laura remembered her grandfather had spoken about.

She had prayed that her father would understand and join them on their journey. She would not live to see her prayer answered.

With her note, Carol had also included a small, leather-bound book. Inside Rubin found pages upon which fragments of a much more ancient nature were attached. Those pages had obviously come from a scroll, whose roll was much narrower than the recently destroyed scrolls. Carol's note told Rubin that this book had been passed down through Carol's family for generations. He set it aside.

Staring at Carol now Rubin remembered his daughter's voice on the tape that he had just finished the night before. He remembered the portion that he had listened to, and he remembered that it had been this portion that had started his first Laura on her journey towards faith. He looked at Carol, and the young lady that he had just learned was

121

also his daughter and began to weep. This time, the tears were ones of sorrow but also of hope. Carol got up and sliding next to Rubin placed her arms around him and drew his head to her shoulder, as the tears continued to fall.

The tears stopped when he heard the tape recorder begin to speak and he saw that his new Laura had gone to the table, slid a new tape in place and pushed play. Rubin did not object but watched and listened as the scene unfolded before him.

New Friends, Family Changes, Old Challenges

I had been a beggar for over five years. I was now fifteen, older than most boys who are recognized as men, and yet I was known only as one of the beggars although I had heard the other names that I was given after people first looked upon me. Jacob had been with me for almost a month that first time before his friends had come and taken him home with them. He had returned on the stretcher between his friends every year since, about one week before the Passover. He would stay anywhere from one week to four weeks, depending on what his friends had planned.

Jacob was from a town far north of Bethany in the region known as Galilee near the Sea of Galilee. It was upon the sea that Jacob and his friends had encountered the sudden storm that had almost claimed their boat and had claimed Jacob's legs. He spent most of his time in the village where his family lived.

During my first short time with Jacob, I learned quickly that the band of unfortunate folks I was among had a great blessing as well. Everyone here knew all the latest news. When you are a beggar, you learn two things quickly, when to listen and when to speak.

With our strategic position along the road, it was easy to hear much of what was being discussed by the travelers of this path. Of course, from time to time, some individual or group would take exception to us being where we were. At the worst of times there would be branches or stones, but most of the time just verbal abuse such as "Away from me, you animal." As if we were somehow less a person than they were. It was easy to believe that we were less than they, for we were certainly different than they were. The worst of times was when I believed I was something less than they were or when I longed without hope to be like them.

I had been a quick study. Jacob had explained the proper words to say to beg for mercy from those passing by. I guess the sight of me must have stirred something in people's hearts for my second day had yielded several copper coins and one silver one in my bowl. I know that my father again seemed impressed by my success when he had returned late in the afternoon from the city.

After the first week, I had learned that there was a stable close by where many of those too weak to make the journey home, or simply too far away to make the journey could stay for a very modest fee. At the age of ten, I had joined this little group.

I simply told my father that this way, I could be here to beg every day without him needing to take me. My heart had hoped for an objection, but I was not surprised at his agreement. He simply stated that he would return with my mat and would bring some food when he could. I remember that my brother was there as well but said nothing to me until my father had started back to Bethany. As my father departed, Jason had come over and done something completely foreign in my experience. He had hugged me. It was only then that I realized he was crying, and for the first time, I realized that he had more feeling for me than I had realized. He said simply, "God will protect you, and I will come as often as I can."

Jason kept his promise. Over the years he had made the trip to where I was many more times than either my father or mother did. I still remember the day, about six months after I had started my role as a beggar, that he stopped by to tell me that Samuel my oldest brother had been allowed to read from the scrolls on the prior Sabbath. He said that Samuel had given his short explanation of the portion he had read. Samuel was now an adult.

I already knew more of the world than Samuel might ever know. Six months as a beggar had exposed me to a world and people that I had never understood existed. I thought to myself that I would never be accepted as Samuel had been, but I was already older than he was. But I kept my thoughts to myself, just grateful that at least one brother had not forgotten about me.

Shortly thereafter, I learned that father had made arrangements for Samuel with another local merchant, a man who specialized in making tents for those patrons who needed portable housing. Samuel was now betrothed to a young lady named Gaila. They were to be married when Samuel turned seventeen, and by then, Samuel would be a full partner in my father's profession. I would not meet Gaila for many years.

It was not Samuel's fault I would tell myself. Once betrothed Samuel's workload increased. Soon only Jason would come to me with news about the family. I was simply grateful to hear his voice on the rare occasion that he stole away to visit me. It was during these brief visits that I would hear the news about the rest of my family and the few other people I knew.

It is strange, but not until I became whole, did I really come to know the rest of my family. Looking back on it now, I suddenly realized that even among my family, I was avoided, by all except my brother Jason, and my mother during my early days. The rest of my brothers and sisters had looked upon me as an oddity. I did not realize it until I understood that my brother Jason was the only one who had taken more than a passing interest in me.

I learned a short time later that my sister Rachel was betrothed as well, to another merchants' son. This merchant imported timber and some food items from faraway places and sold the materials to the wealthiest people in the area. Only the truly wealthy could afford real wood timbers for their homes. Rachel would never lack for money, but as she would learn, money would not bring her happiness. Her husband David was not a good man. Even though my sister was beautiful, David would often wander from his marital bed and would never seem satisfied with anything he had.

David was accepted in the community as someone of importance. He was rich. His family's gifts to the temple were always very large. Everyone was impressed by their generosity. Only later did I realize that everyone knew the scope of the gifts, and that was a reward in itself. I also would learn that the size of the gift did not reflect the true condition of the heart. Some of the smallest mercies to me cost the givers more than all the money that David placed in the coffers of the great temple.

The years passed by quickly, although the days seemed individually long. By the time I was twenty, my brother Samuel already had two children, another Samuel and John. You might wonder how I kept all the Samuels in order? Frankly, I still have difficulty, but my brother was pleased to be able to continue the tradition, and I am sure my father was pleased as well.

Rachel still had no children. David's wandering eyes had already become a report among our small community. We, beggars, learn everything. People tend to ignore the fact that we have ears and hear everything that is said in gossip. It always amazed me how people could act like we were not present even when we were.

Sarah was still at home with my mother and father. Now twenty-one she was already considered to be almost past her prime years and rumor had it that she might never be married. My brother Jason continued to visit me as often as possible. He was married now as well and working with my father and my brother Samuel in the shop. They had prospered, and even now, my brother Samuel was considering moving to another village to expand the reach of the family business.

Now twenty, Jason, had been married for over a year and was about to become a father himself. He had argued that I should be allowed to attend the wedding, but despite his pleas, both my father and his bride's father had determined that it be best that I be excluded.

There are some things in our society that we normally have little control over. Who we marry and what conditions are placed upon the wedding are among those things? Jason brought the news that I was not to be allowed to attend, and although I was angry, Jason's tears quickly overcame me and filled me with guilt. He was truly in anguish over the decision, and I quickly played down the implications of the exclusion.

"It's alright," I said, "and besides this way, I will not be either an object of discussion or stumbling and causing a commotion," I concluded. He married Ruth in a large gathering of family and friends. I later heard that many had commented that he had looked strangely subdued for such a happy event. Jason's wife, Ruth, I was to learn later, had not agreed with the decision either. She understood Jason's attachment to me, and she would bring great happiness to both my brother and myself.

The death of friends

It was the day Jason brought me the news about his approaching status of fatherhood that I also heard the news about Mary's father and mother. For ten years, Mary's father, Joseph, had stopped often by my perch and had brought food, water, and at times other necessities for me. While I never thought of him as a father figure, it was not lost upon me that he had provided more for my needs over these years than my own father had. Every time he had approached me, I felt the burning need to know what was happening with Mary, but I could never squeeze up the courage to ask. Why should I ask, when I was sure that all was fine, and knowledge would only bring me greater sadness?

Joseph had gone with his wife, Ester, on one of the several trips they took each year to look for materials and other markets for their oils and perfumes. It was unusual for a merchant to take his wife with him on such trips, but Ester had an eye for unusual materials and a good nose for fragrances, that other women would find alluring. Joseph also was far from being a traditional merchant, for he valued his wife's opinions. They had journeyed with a small caravan that made its way towards the coast of our country.

Our country is under the laws and protection of the nation that had conquered us, but that still does not prevent bands of robbers from frequenting those spots where unsuspecting travelers might fall prey. This is why almost everyone travels in groups, especially when leaving the vicinity of larger towns and needing to transverse sparse areas.

Many of these bandits also were zealots fighting the occupiers of our nation. Patriots, ruffians, and murders often wear the same face. Often, the current role they fulfilled, depended on their own need, current company, and the appropriate opportunity. Events that often start as a robbery sometimes would turn into something more sinister dictated by circumstance. Such was what befell Joseph and his wife.

There are several passes on the journey to our coast that are particularly noted for trouble. Even though there were garrisons near many of these passes, it still did not prevent those truly intent upon this form of livelihood from its practice. The passes made for excellent locations for both insurrection and thievery. At one pass Joseph's caravan had been stopped, and thievery was the object of the day.

In robbery, anonymity is preferred. Joseph had recognized Barabbas. The shroud of secrecy had a tear. The silence was the bandage. Joseph would not be silent.

The first of the caravan returned to Bethany a day after the event and two hours after Jason had departed. The news did not arrive at my location until several hours later. As with most news, we heard it from those hurrying to the great city with the report. At first, through all of the commotion, it was clear that bandits had struck again. It was only later when Jason came hurrying back to my location, that he breathlessly told me of what had happened, that the full implications became known.

I remember that my heart seemed to stop beating, and beneath my ragged tunic, a small pouch with a hidden coin suddenly became immensely heavy.

Jason spoke of those returning to Bethany with the bodies of Joseph and his wife and the tale of Joseph's loss.

It was Joseph's rebuke, so similar to Mary's so many years ago, that had brought Barabbas's sword upon Joseph. Jason relayed the witnesses' testimony:

"Joseph had looked at the bandits, and apparently recognizing one had spoken saying, "The Lord sees all that is done, even here where His presence is hidden. He will not leave unpunished the acts of the wicked, even you Bar.... before he could finish his name, the sword had been moving and his life was taken. The witnesses reported that Ester had leaped upon Joseph's attacker only to be pulled aside and struck down by another in the band. The deaths were quick. Two ruffians and thieves had graduated into murderers.

Joseph's and Ester's deaths shocked me into silence. How could God allow these peaceful, holy people, to die so suddenly? The question rang out in my soul, and then I thought about Mary, Lazarus, and Martha. What was to become of them? Then I thought of the attackers, and my heart grew colder.

Death in our community of beggars was not a big deal among the rest of the world. The deaths of Joseph and his wife were. Grief gripped the community, shrouding the normal peaceful village with its sad cloak, but anger seized and squeezed my heart.

Those who knew their family began gathering in Bethany to mourn the loss. Joseph and Ester were to be buried immediately in a small cave outside the village-owned by Joseph and designated for this purpose. As with many families, generations of Joseph's family rested within that cave. Normally Joseph and his wife would have already rested in the cave, but the trip back had delayed that burial. Haste was of the essence.

Lazarus was in the shop at the great city when the news arrived. He sent a servant to the North to bring his sisters to him, though he knew that they would arrive many days after the burial had taken place. He was alone and would endure this sadness by himself. He gathered the spices and ointments used for such occasions from the shop and turned to begin the journey back to Bethany. It was not until he turned around did, he realizes that I was standing in the doorway of his shop. He said nothing and coming to me placed his arms around my shoulders and embraced me as dry heaves welled up and shook my body. In his moment of sorrow, he instead comforted me, the beggar.

He led me toward Bethany with him. Arriving in Bethany, I sat outside the door of his house. He went into his home, now inhabited by the remains of death. Already a crowd of neighbors and wailers had gathered. Lazarus went about preparing his parents bodies for their burial. It was still two hours before dusk when the sad procession left Lazarus' house, carrying the twin stretchers with their burdens. We arrived at the tomb in a short time. After placing Joseph and Ester in their resting place, Lazarus with the *help of some of his neighbors rolled the stone back in front of the cave. In the stillness, I heard Lazarus voice as he said softly, "The Lord is my Shepherd…." After he had finished, the wailing started again, but Lazarus was quiet. He took my arm and gently began to lead me away from that place. He said to me simply, "The Lord gives, and the Lord takes away, blessed be the name of the Lord." His tears dripped on my arm, and they fed the anger that grew within my soul.*

Mary and Martha arrived in Bethany three days later. They had left the same day they heard the news and reached the village late on the third day. I heard of their arrival through Jason. I had returned to my perch outside the great city with my surrogate family. Jason said Lazarus was intent on continuing his father's business. He was 24, and he was now the man of the household, and it fell to him to keep the family together.

Mary and Martha had decided to stay in Bethany to be with their brother. Neither had family with them. Try as I may I could learn nothing about Mary's supposed betrothal. I wondered what had happened and now regretted my reluctance in not asking Joseph about her earlier. I would learn the truth from Mary, but only many months later.

In our country, the friends of the deceased often would lay a stone upon the tomb seal as a witness of their friendship. Something akin to the stones Joshua had removed from the Jordan after the nation had crossed the river on dry ground. The stones bore witness to the events of our lives. Several weeks after the burial, I had begged and paid different travelers to return me to the gravesite. Once there and alone, I had stole to the stone that covered the cave, and feeling the many stones piled in memory before the door, I carefully dislodged a large number, took the small pouch from around my neck that that been hidden under my tunic, placed it under the rocks and then recovered the spot. The emblem of hope was buried near the man who had given it to me. Sitting once more by the stone door, I remembered the past. Within my anger exploded against those who had taken Joseph's life, and against God who had not stood in the way of the murders.

Meeting Mary Again – The End of Anger

My rage lasted over a year. During that time, I was given to many bouts of depression and anger. If you have been a beggar, you would understand that anger and asking for mercy, do not mix. I was a surly beggar. Where I had stayed silent before at the comments of those passing by, or at their failure to consider mercy to us, now I spouted off. I no longer cared if they heard my stinging retorts. My already meager daily collection began to dry up to nothing. I did not care.

The beggars around me began to insist that I be quiet. My anger was affecting even their collection.

I had grown accustomed to knowing how many people were passing by based on the footsteps. I also could identify the footsteps of frequent visitors such as Lazarus and Jason. Both Lazarus and Jason had been by to talk with me. But their presence and arguments had not changed my attitude.

I was especially angry with Lazarus who did not seem to hold the same grudge against circumstance and God that I did.

Lazarus caught me in the act of belittling a passing stranger who had failed to give me any money and said, "Cain, What are you doing?" In foolishness, I charged ahead. I exploded in anger. I wondered out loud to him whether he really loved his father and mother. "Why I asked, are you not angry? You have more reason than I to be angry and yet you do not seem to care!" His answer made no sense to me. He said, "Cain, I care. Every day, I long for my father's and mother's presence and wish they were here, *but anger is not the other side of the coin of love. Love impels me to know that there is a reason for what has happened outside my understanding. Not a single day of my life or a single event occurs, without there being an ordained purpose to that day and to those events. God..."*

At the mention of God, I cut Lazarus off. "Don't talk to me about God," I erupted. "If He were real, if He was present, if He cared, He would have done something to prevent this from happening." Although I knew my words were foolish, I could not help myself. I continued on "If God is real, how could He allow this to happen? If He is so caring, how come He allowed me to be born the way I am? What did I do to deserve this life? What did my parents do that I should be cursed this way," I raged.

We had suddenly reached the real reason for my anger. Yes, I had been angry about Joseph's and Ester's deaths, but their deaths had just picked at the unhealed scab on my life. Their deaths had brought the flow of the infection and puss that had been under that scab. I was angry with everyone but especially God about me.

Try as he may Lazarus could not get me to consider other alternatives to my tirade. I was convinced that God, at best, did not care, and at worst, was not there. Lazarus left me with the words that he would pray for me. A lot of good that would do I thought to myself.

The days of anger brought evenings filled with despair and loneliness. While on the one hand, I longed for the old dreams of Samuel and God, and the peace and escape they had brought, I could not bring myself to live the contradiction. If I was going to be angry, it had to be morning, noon and night. It was on one of my restless evenings that my belief in my own righteous anger at my condition was challenged. It was the evening I met Simon.

Simon was not a beggar. He had lived a prosperous life. Simon's family lived in Bethany like my own. He had passed by our small band of beggars many times on his way to the great city. He was one of the few regulars who could always be counted on for taking notice of our plight and dispensing mercy to us. His sudden absence was noticed by our small band. We heard rumors of tragedy, although no one spoke of the nature of that tragedy.

It was his wealth that had insulated him from the spread of the bad news. Late that evening as I sat against the stone ledge that had been perch for so many years and attempted to gain the sleep that eluded me, I became aware of movement nearby. The moon's light had not penetrated the clouds that night, and as such, I was pretty much invisible to anyone walking on the path this late at night. As I heard the noise, I spoke up startling the person passing by. He nearly fell over me but quickly sort of danced around me, never touching me and spoke swiftly under his breathe. "Sorry, Sorry, I did not know you were here." The sound of his voice betrayed both who he was but also that something was terribly wrong.

I said simply, It is okay, Simon. It is just me, Cain." From the hoarseness of his voice and his labored breathing, I could tell that something was very wrong. I heard him sit down slowly about ten feet away from me, and I wondered why he had chosen to sit so far away. After a few moments he said simply, "No Cain, it is not okay. I should not have come out this evening, but I was tired of being cooped up at home and had hoped that no one would be out this late." It was then that he told me what had happened to him.

Simon's tragedy was of the worse sort. In my area, there are few things worse than being the way I am. Simon, though rich, was struck with a malady that forced him to stay indoors and if he ventured out, required him repeating words that everyone in my society dreaded. I dreaded those words when they were misapplied to me. Although I was not whole, the words would have been inaccurate if directed towards me. Those words had a real purpose in our society. Simon was required to cry out these words whenever

133

he was outside and within 30 feet of any other individual. Those words were both mandated by our law and our custom. When he cried out "unclean, unclean," it was because he truly was unclean. He was a leper.

As he told me his story, I was both fascinated and yet like so many others desired to put even more distance between myself and him. As I listened to his story, I suddenly realized that this man had every reason to be as angry as I was. He explained that the numbness had started in his hands and feet and though concerned he had ignored it until the rash on his skin had developed. He had gone quickly to the temple to pray, and as required had shown himself both to the priests and to the local authorities. The judgment had been swift and without comfort or mercy. Judged a leper, he was quickly driven out from their midst and told the requirement.

Simon had spent a great deal of money on both ointments and other treatments hoping that something would reverse or at least stall the progress of this ailment. His parents, on learning of the problem, had quickly left him the house to himself. They had moved to another home that they owned. So, like myself, Simon had been abandoned and was alone.

After he explained his tragedy, I expected that he would join me in renouncing both those around him whose true face he had now seen, as well as the one whose face could not be seen, and yet who seemed to take a perverse pleasure in the suffering of his creatures. But Simon was like Lazarus. He wept freely but laid no accountability for the circumstance on anyone.

Simon stayed with me for about one hour. After his tears had dried and he had emptied himself of his sorrow, he stood again, wished me well, and asked that I keep him in prayer. What foolishness, I thought. Once again, another person had refused to join me in my anger. So be it, I thought. I would be angry for Lazarus, for Simon and for myself. I could handle that with no problem.

That evening as I finally slipped into sleep, I vowed that I would stay angry because of the unfairness of life. I must have been asleep, but suddenly I was aware of a presence. I was suddenly fully aware, and then I heard his voice. He said simply: "Cain, what are you doing? Why are you angry?" I was struck dumb. "Come." I felt his hand on my shoulder and realized that I was standing. I had never heard this voice before yet like the guide of many years ago, this voice also would accept no disobedience.

We walked for what seemed but a brief time in silence. I suddenly knew where he was taking me. How we had made the trip so quickly I did not know. It was late, the doors should be closed. We passed into the city and then into the temple unhindered and unchallenged. The door to the temple simply opened as we approached and closed after we had entered. He sat me on the seat I had sat on so many years ago. And then I heard the second voice, an older voice, but one I recognized. It was the guide. I heard him say with the words that Mary had echoed so long ago, "God is here, and he sees all things, Cain." And then he told me my names' story. I had never heard it this way before. He spoke as if He was present at the event. He spoke as God did. First warning of the danger of Cain's anger and the requirement that if he did what was good; he would experience the joy he longed for. Then came the asking Cain about his brother Abel. I heard an unimaginable sorrow in his voice as he cried out, "What have you done? The voice of your brother's blood is crying to Me from the ground."

After he had told me the whole story, he said simply. "The father makes no mistakes, Cain. All things are under his control. The father loves his own. Joseph and Ester are with the father. They were murdered, but He called them home. He appointed the time, the place, and the method. But woe to those who were used as the instrument of that purpose. Those who were responsible are known. Pray that they may find mercy from the father and not his anger. For only the father has the right to such anger. Not even *you, Cain, have the right to that anger. Cain, as for you, as with Jacob, as with Simon, there are no mistakes...."*

I awoke the next day on my mat in the stable and wondered how I had come to be in the stable. I thought I had fallen asleep by my perch on the path. I remembered the dream. It was then I realized that in my hand was a familiar pouch. I remembered that the guide had pressed it into my hand. He had said, *"Joseph gave this to you. It is not yet time for you to give it up. You will know when it is time, for I will tell you."* I opened my hand and felt through the thin material. It had not been a dream, but what had it been?

I sat pondering the events of the night when I heard her footsteps entering the stable. While I did not recognize the steps, I knew who it was. The mild fragrance of her perfume preceded her presence. I had only smelled that perfume twice before. No one else I knew wore it. She stopped there looking at my back as I continued to feel the small package in my hand. She said simply, *"Cain, I need to talk with you."*

I turned slowly to her, closing my fingers around the coin. Feeling my heart increase in speed, I was afraid of what I would say. I had longed to hear her voice for so long, and now that I had, I was unprepared to respond. *"Not now,"* I thought to myself. *"I have too much to ponder and think about."* Yet, I heard my voice come alive, but it came from a great distance. *"Hello Mary,"* my voice said.

All of the anger of the past year had been drained away in a single evening. How could I explain my behavior to Mary? I did not even understand it. Even worse, I could not explain to her what had happened last night, because I still did not understand it.

She sat down beside me and began. *"Cain, my brother, and your brother are very worried about you. They say that since my parent's deaths that you are no longer the same person. I have come to see if I can help."*

I responded simply, "There is no longer any need, Mary." How could I explain to her that someone else had already touched my heart of stone and my anger was gone.

I continued trying to reach a conclusion I could not grasp. "Mary, I was angry about their deaths," I said. Shaking my head, I continued, "and I was angrier about my own condition. But something happened that, that I cannot explain. It is as if I had a dream, and today, I awoke without the anger I once had. I am perplexed but no longer angry." She started to ask what had happened, but I shook my head and said simply, "I do not know." I started to try to explain what had happened but found the words would not come out. I just bowed my head and stayed silent again.

I finally gathered up my courage and asked, "Mary, what does your husband think of everything that has happened." Mary responded with a surprise question. "Husband?" she said. "Yes," I said. She responded, "I am not married Cain, what made you think" …and then she remembered her last conversation with me so many years ago. She said bemusedly, "Cain, my father never found someone for me…well that is not exactly right, he discovered that I already loved another and he chose not to complicate my life. So, I am not married." I was stunned.

In my country, for a woman to speak of love and have her father pay attention, it was unheard of. Truly, Joseph had been remarkable. But she had said she loved another. I murmured my question and asked, "Is the one you love, unaware of your love?" "I do not know," she answered. "Is he married?" I asked. "No, but he is tied to a task that I wait him completing. When he is done, then I can tell him."

I sat silent again and then turned in her direction. "Can you take me to your brother, I must apologize to him for my anger. And then I must find my family, especially Jason, and ask their forgiveness as well." Having said that I struggled to my feet and realized that I had also not taken care of myself. To put it mildly, I stank. I think she understood my sudden hesitancy, but she had put her arm around my shoulder and had helped stabilize my body. As I felt her warmth and her fragrance, I started to draw away, but she said, "Cain, it does not matter." Together, we walked to find her brother.

The tape clicked off, and Laura turned to Rubin. She had punched the release button on the tape and returned it to its case. It was only then that Rubin realized the tape had not been one of his. She slid it into her pocket and took something from her pocket. Rubin turned to Carol with questions in his eyes, and then he understood: "She made a copy for you as well?" he said more as a statement than a question. Carol nodded and then said, "She had told me that she feared that you would destroy the tapes in your anger. She gave me a set for safekeeping. Once Laura was born, and she was old enough, we started listening to the tapes frequently. You see, I wanted Laura to know who she was named after and why. I also wanted her to have something I did not have as a youth." Looking at Rubin, she said, "Our Laura knows the truth, and she has her namesakes gift." With that, Rubin turned again, looked at his newest daughter and stared, and then whispered, "Tell me everything."

13

THE CRISIS BEGINS

The lab was silent. Except for the whirl of the exhaust fans and the occasional sound from one of the other assistants, the lab was as quiet as Rubin could ever remember. Carol stepped back from the hood to allow Laura once again unfettered access to the document she was reading. Rubin, Carol, and his team watched as Laura once again stooped over the hood, peered down at the document and the words came again.

Rubin thought that this gift of Laura's seemed unnatural. Then he realized that her gift fit the circumstance he was faced with. Once again, a cold shiver passed through his body as he thought of the implications of the connection between Laura's gift and the discovery. It was also the first time he heard his own voice in his head say, "I have to destroy this before it destroys me. "

He shook his head in amazement, wondering where that thought had come from. Nervously Rubin looked around to see if anyone else might have sensed what he had thought. To his relief, his first impression was that no one had seen his shaking of his head, but then he saw Carol's eyes fastened on him. Her eyes communicated everything. She knew or at least understood what had just occurred. Rubin tried mightily not to confirm her understanding, but he could not help but glance away from her eyes and down at his shoes. He heard himself think again, "You fool, you just all but told her what you had been thinking. " Glancing up immediately, he was comforted by the fact that Carol's eyes had turned back to Laura and that she, as well as the rest of the staff, were listening intently to her words.

Rubin heard Laura's words but from a faraway misty place. His mind raced elsewhere, planning, devising, scheming, "What to do?"

Carol had seen Rubin's head shake. Her first thought was, *"He is afraid!"* But then an internal voice told her that while her first analysis was right, it was incomplete. Then she understood, *"He is so afraid he is thinking about getting rid of it!"* The shock of her thoughts caused her to seek Rubin's eyes for confirmation. When their eyes had briefly locked, she saw what her inner voice had suspected. A wildness in his eyes communicated more than just fear, it was a fear backed with a developing plan. She attempted to communicate with her eyes, but he had looked away quickly, as if ashamed of the thoughts that had occurred to him. She looked at him for but a few more seconds. Laura's voice was drawing her back, demanding attention. Laura's gift was hypnotic, as was the story that was unfolding. She turned again to her friend and found herself swept back to the story.

She would hear clearly what Rubin would only recognize later as having vaguely heard. It would be the difference between her and Laura's immediate drawing to truth and Rubin's much later awareness and acceptance of the truth. Laura and Carol suddenly found themselves hearing as if for the first time, Rubin was still miles away, deaf and scheming.

For the next twenty minutes, Laura's voice unfolded a story that would forever change many who heard it that day. Certainly, for Laura and Carol, it was the turning point and the beginning of a journey that would last the rest of their lives.

The start of truly amazing times

Jacob was sick. For eighteen years he had shared this roadside spot with me whenever his friends brought him to the temple area. He had been with me eighteen times in eighteen years.

This year Jacob's four friends had brought Jacob back again from the North. They were going again to the temple to worship. For nineteen years they had made this trip with Jacob in tow, on a stretcher between them. To have such friends was something beyond my understanding. This year Simon seemed frailer than he had in the past. While his words were still the same, the tone in his voice told me the years were taking their toll.

Our band of beggars had both grown and contracted over the years. Many had died or moved away only to be replaced eventually with some other unfortunate soul. I had become a fixture of the area. Everyone knew me.

This year as I listened to Jacob, it was hard to believe that life can go by so quickly. Yet, I think back over those years and realize a few things are as certain as to how fast the days rush by.

Close to the end of this first day back, Jacob confided in me that he did not believe he would be back again. He said simply, "Cain, I am tired. I have been a burden on my friends and my family for too long. I do not regret my life, but I am ready to rest." It was the first time I heard anything close to despair from his lips. But it was not said in despair, simply as a fact.

I remember thinking to myself how unfair it was that Jacob should have had to suffer so much for so long. And as I had done so often before I thought to myself the question "Lord, why?" What had Jacob done to deserve such a fate? To be whole and then suddenly to have been broken was in my mind a far worse fate than never to have been whole at all. How he had not been overcome with bitterness and anger was beyond my understanding.

How does a person accept giving up what was once had? And then I remembered the rebuke of my guide, and I wondered what the purpose of Jacob's circumstance was. I still had not figured out my own.

Jacob must have guessed my thoughts as he said simply, "Cain, it is easier to accept reality than to fight against it." And then he added with the familiar twinkle, "Besides, look at all of the friends I have made!" I laughed but did not bother to say to him that he would have made many more friends if he had been whole.

Just before the dinner hour, I stood up from my normal location and told Jacob I would be back shortly. When one is a beggar, it does not remove the need to take care of the bodily functions that are normal to all people. Fortunately, there was a short distance away an area where such things were taken care of.

While there I overheard the voice of one of Jacob's friends speaking of a traveling teacher who was causing quite a commotion in Galilee. While I had heard about a preacher named John, that was baptizing many by the Jordan River, this was a new piece of news for me. I continued to listen and heard Jacob's friends confide that without something being done for Jacob soon, that he would surely die. Then they started talking about some very mysterious claims that were being made about this newest teacher. Jacob's friends spoke of what appeared to be miraculous healings. It was said that he had already healed many, even lepers and those suffering from demon possession were said to have been healed.

Then they returned again to the discussion about Jacob. It was obvious to me that a plan was forming in Jacob's friends. However, as with most plans of good intention, there was a problem. Jacob's friends needed money.

It was then that I remembered my gold coin and the small stash of money that I had made over the years from my begging. Getting up quickly, I returned to my mat in the stable and found my small set of coins. Over the eight years since my anger had left me, I had managed to save the equivalent of a month's wages for the normal man. It was not much, but I returned as quickly as I could to the toilet and bath area, hoping that Jacob's friends would still be there. They were not.

I started on my way back to my perch when I heard one of his friend's voices just slightly ahead of me. I fairly ran into him in my haste to catch up before we were in earshot of Jacob. "Well," he said as he nearly tumbled from my onslaught…Where are you going Cain in such a hurry?" I was grateful that he had been strong enough to stop my launch and to stabilize me. I quickly explained that I had heard his comments in the bath, and I handed over to him the money I had saved. I wrapped my fingers around his hand and closed his fingers over the money. I remembered the gold coin, and though I had not been told to give that up as well, I did. Sliding the pouch from around my neck, I also added that to Jacob's friend's hand.

"Please," I said. "Take this," Take Jacob to this teacher, for I love Jacob and cannot bear to think that I did nothing to help him." His friend, I knew had looked at the small stash in his hand and then said simply, "Surely you need some of this for yourself?" "I have plenty," was my reply. Where that had come from, I do not know. I had given all that I had, and yet what I had said was the truth. I had all I needed for the day. "All right," said Jacob's friend and he was off looking for his other friends.

I returned to my perch beside Jacob. Jacob said quietly, "You were gone for a while. Is everything all right?" "Yes," I said. "Just took a little longer to *do what I needed to do." And then I picked up my bowl and eagerly awaited what would happen. Within an hour Jacob's friends were back. They told Jacob simply that they were leaving, to which Jacob nearly exclaimed that they had just arrived. One of the friends said, "We have decided to go hear this teacher that everyone is talking about before we go home." And with that, they were gone, bearing Jacob between them as was their burden and joy.*

Jacob cried out to me as he left "Cain if I do not see you again, God's mercy be with you" To which I replied softly, "And with you as well my friend."

It would be nearly two months before I would hear what had happened. It was shortly before one of our feasts when among great crowds of visitors, a person approached whose footsteps I had never heard before. Before I realized it, he was sitting down beside me. "Hello Cain," he said softly. It was Jacob.

Jacob told me his story.

His friends had hurried on the long journey. It had taken nearly one week just to make it to a village known as Capernaum where they had learned that this mysterious teacher was. Once there, they had learned that he was staying in the house of a local religious person. Try as they may, they had been unable to find a way into the house. The area was mobbed with people. All sorts of sick people were there. Everyone wanted a chance at being healed. And all the whole people were there as well, wanting either to see a healing or to listen to the teaching of this man.

The crowd was so great that the closest they could get to the house was more than 100 yards away from the front door. No one would let them by.

Finally, one of his friends had come up with an idea, and had carried Jacob, still on the stretcher about two streets away and then had slowly made their way back towards the back of the house. There as they had hoped a small stairway led to a small balcony just below the roofline of the house. Once there, they had tied Jacob to the stretcher even tighter than normal, and the one friend had lifted himself on to the roof. Then with the other friend's help, they had lifted Jacob on to the roof. What happened next almost did not seem possible. But knowing Jacobs' friends and their devotion to him, I knew that it was possible.

They were on the roof, which was made of a combination of clay and branches. These roofs are often thick, as thick as a man's arm length. Jacobs' friends had started to make a hole. After more than an hour of digging, Jacob began to hear the protests of those in the house as some of the debris fell on them below. Nothing deterred Jacob's friends. Even when some people came around the back of the house and demanded that they stop, they continued.

Finally, a large hole had been opened. Now in one of the most unlikely acts of balance that could only have been completed by men seasoned by fishing and rigging many nets, Jacob was lowered down, through the hole towards the center of the house.

Jacob said that for the few minutes, he was lowered the entire inside of the house went silent. All eyes were on Jacob's prone figure as he was lowered from the heights. And then all eyes were upon the teacher.

Jacob said, "I looked upon this man, he looked like a normal man, nothing special about him. I had expected a kingly looking figure or a wise old man, but instead found myself looking at a sturdy, man in his thirties, with dark skin from constant exposure to the sun."

This teacher had a smile on his face and a twinkle in his eye. He looked up at my friends' expectant faces looking down from the ceiling and then back at me. Then he looked around at so many of the local religious and social leaders that were gathered before him. I also saw him look at those who were his disciples. What he said next shocked everyone. He looked at me again and said: "Son, your sins are forgiven."

Jacob breathed softly now, a slow exhale and then he said, "I was not sure what to expect, but the last things I expected was to have the teacher tell me that my sins were forgiven. But I knew even as he said these words that they were truth. Cain, the thing I was most afraid of about dying was not knowing about where I would go." Jacob almost stuttered but then continued, "You see, I believed in God, but I was so angry about having lost my legs I did not think that God would ever forgive some of the things I thought and said when it first happened." I bit my tongue. I had never realized that Jacob had ever done anything but accept what had occurred to him

Jacob continued, "Suddenly I knew it would be okay to die and the fear I had lived with for so many years left me. I remember thinking to myself, 'It was all worth it.' The trip I mean. But it was not over. Suddenly I realized that there was a murmuring passing through the crowd in the house and then it dawned on me what had happened. Who but God could forgive sins? I knew what they were thinking. This man had claimed authority to do something only God could do.

Then, I saw the teacher looking around at the murmurs, and he said, 'Why are you reasoning about these things in your hearts? Which is easier to say to the paralytic, your sins are forgiven; or to say, Get up and pick up your pallet and walk? But so that you may know that the Son of Man has authority on earth to forgive sins' – and then he said to me, 'I say to you, get up, pick up your pallet and go home.'

"Cain, the next thing I knew I was standing. I picked up my stretcher, bending my legs for the first time in nearly twenty years and with my own arms held it. I walked through the crowd and out the door. I really had not thought about what I was doing, as I was still thinking through his earlier

146

words. It was not until my friends rushed me on the other side of the door, that I realized I was walking." I heard the tears in his voice. Tears of joy, of surprise and of wonder mixed all over again and mirrored in his voice.

I learned from Jacob that he had returned home to his wife first. At first, he said she stood speechless and then had collapsed into his arms, having fainted. Then Jacob said, it was as if twenty years fell off his wife, and the worry and turmoil in her life evaporated. She immediately began to pack her things, and when Jacob asked what she was doing, she had answered simply, "to go with you when you go to follow the teacher." Jacob found himself sharing the event with his family and former neighbors.

His testimony had sent many in the village scurrying on their way to find this teacher. For the past four weeks, he had been following this teacher everywhere he had gone. He reported that two of his four friends had also abandoned their work and followed the teacher. The other two friends had returned home to close their fishing business and planned to join them within a very short period.

Then Jacob said to me, "Cain, this is Mariam, my wife." I suddenly realized that I had been unaware that another person had been present through this entire dialogue. I felt her hand as it grasped my arm, and she said, "Cain, Jacob has told me so much about you. I want to thank you for being his friend all of these years." I sensed happiness within her voice that I suspected had been missing for many years. Then Jacob almost exploded with joy and said, "Not only did I get my legs back, but I am going to be a father!" And so, it was, that I understood the joy in Mariam's voice was doubled by what had happened. After more than twenty years of marriage, she now not only had a whole husband but was going to be a mother as well.

I was speechless again. Finally, I came to my senses and asked, 'Who is this teacher? Is he really claiming to be "The Son of Man?"' I knew that this claim was reserved for the Messiah, the one that was to come into the world, sent by God to return his people to a right relationship with God. Many expected this Christ to throw off the rule of our conquers and suppressors, Yet as I inquired about this teacher, it was obvious that he had no army but a small band of fishermen and other common folks following him. The more I questioned Jacob, the more confused I became.

Jacob relayed that many of the leaders of the people were having serious problems with this teachers' methods and teaching. Jacob said, "He speaks as one with authority to explain things that are only discussed as opinions by the other teachers. He does not quote the older, more famous teachers. Instead, he speaks as one who needs no other defense or support of his position. Cain, he cures more people on the Sabbath than on any other day of the week. The teachers are furious that he is doing this, but they do not know what to say. No one ever, and I mean no one has cured as many people as this man has. Some are saying that he is a good man, while others claim that he cannot be good. There is so much confusion right now it is hard to know what is right. But I know this, I walk, and I am to be a father. I will follow this teacher anywhere, for no one can do the things he has and not be from God."

There was no denying, this was Jacob, he was walking, and he was not the same man that had been ready to depart this life less than three months ago. He had everything to live for. I envied him. It turned out that this teacher was less than a day's journey away, and Jacob had decided to come to visit me with his wife. As he spoke, my mind wandered to the unspoken "What ifs." But then I knew that it could never be. After all, Jacob had walked before, all that had been done was to restore that which had been. I caught myself in doubt and thought, 'Cain, you fool, there you go again, thinking about yourself instead of rejoicing in what has happened for

Jacob." I laughed and clasped my friend in a hug with all the joy that was welling up in my soul.

Jacob and Mariam spent the rest of the day with me and relayed the story many times over to any who would listen. The few of the band of beggars that knew him asked him to repeat the story many times over. By the end of the day, all those that could had packed up and were off to find this teacher. I stayed behind.

As the night drew close, Jacob told me he needed to go and find lodging for his wife. While he had stayed with me before when needed, he was now whole and would be accepted into a more normal resting place. He told me he would be back in the morning, but before he left, he bent down, clasped my hand and placed a small package in it.

"My friends told me what you did after I was healed. They gave me back what they had not spent during our trip. I will repay the rest as soon as I can, but I wanted to give this back to you as soon as I could. I felt the small package and realized that it had come back to me. For some reason I was not surprised and yet I was happy to take it back and slide it beneath my tunic. My emblem of hope had returned, and now I thought it was more than that. It was an emblem of joy, as well. It had been carried by Jacob, who had seen a mysterious teacher, who had made him whole. It was the happiest day I had in many years.

The next morning Jacob and Mariam were at my perch early. The sun had not yet breached the sky, and its warming rays were not yet felt. I had not gone inside that night. It had been cool, and I had slept peacefully near my perch. Their arrival did not awake me, although I had been awake for only a very short period when they came.

I heard their footsteps and recognized Mariam's quiet voice. "Should we disturb him, perhaps we should wait until later?" "No," I heard Jacob say, *"We must be off to be with the teacher as soon as possible." "I am awake," I said.*

Stooping down, Jacob took my outstretched hand and raised me up to my feet. In his bear hug, I found a strength that I knew was new even to Jacob. He said, "I must return to the teacher, but I will come back as often as I can. And Cain, I hope that the teacher will be passing this way soon. If nothing else, you need to hear him teach. While I am glad, he healed my legs, I would give up my legs again, just to be able to hear him teach." At that, I knew that Mariam had given Jacob a guilty nudge indicating that she was not as certain about that last statement. Jacob laughed and then said, "Somehow, I think that he will not ask for them back anytime soon." Then they were gone.

I sat again on my perch and dreamed of what ifs and prayed softly my thanksgiving for the restoration of my friend. I knew the name of the teacher now and yet; I did not know him. I had heard part of the story of his life from Jacob, yet I knew there was much more to that story that neither Jacob nor I knew at this point. I would have to wait but not for long.

There is a sign of God among us is, it is simply hope for the hopeless

Simon's condition had grown worse over the years as well. Leprosy had continued to spread and had begun to erode the tips of his fingers and his other digits. His face also now bore the marks of the spread of the infection.

After that first night's visit, Simon had returned many times always late after the rest of the world had gone to sleep. He updated me during these visits on the progress of his condition. He shared the many different treatments he had tried and their varying degrees of failure. It was obvious that he was spending great sums of money seeking out a remedy to his condition, and all had been a failure so far.

I understood well the loneliness spawned by his condition and his desire for a cure. I also knew the desire that drove him out to find someone to talk with. Although I still was afraid of his condition, I no longer minded his visits. After that evening with the stranger and the guide, I was now convinced that I was meant to be Simon's friend. His visits also filled a need within me. Now I had someone to share my daily struggles with, and I now knew that there were others with conditions as grievous if not more so than my own.

It had been several evenings since Jacob's visit when Simon returned. I told Simon of what had happened to Jacob. He listened with the rapt attention of someone who needed the hope that Jacob's story provided. He plied me with many questions that I answered the best that I could. He also had heard of the mysterious teacher but was much more secluded than I and therefore lacked many of the rumors and stories I had heard.

After hearing the end of my story, he asked me, "What do you think Cain? Who is this teacher?" Simon did not wait for my answer but leaped ahead saying "What an unusual time, first the Baptist comes, raises the anticipation of the people, causes no small commotion by his message and yet uses his speech only to draw people without any miracles or other signs. He challenges the king, is arrested, and then killed. Now a teacher comes not only with words but also with power not seen since the days of the prophets and wielding the power with a frequency that dwarfs any time previously. "Has there ever been a time like this?" His question hung in the air, but I knew the answer. There is another question that hangs in the air, as well. It is palatable. It is a question that lingers in both our minds, but Simon asks it first. "Do you think he could cure me?"

It is the same question that has occurred to me. There is a great longing within my soul that embraces this question and desires the answer. I answered, "What harm is there in asking?" And then I realize what I have just asked of Simon. And I realize how silly it would be for me to ask for what I had never had.

For most of the past eight years, Simon has only forayed out to visit me late in the evening. He has used his wealth to have others purchase his food and much of the other items that were needed for his life's sustenance. He has not been seen over the past eight years. While most, with his condition, would have been driven from the village, his voluntary seclusion and separateness had allowed him to remain. To ask the teacher, Simon would need to venture out into a world hostile to his condition and, therefore, to himself as well. He would be exposing the extent of his condition to the world and risk the life that he had built for himself.

We sat in silence as the great debate raged in both our hearts. As before, Simon is the first to answer the question. "I will go to find this teacher tomorrow. I can no longer live the way I am." With that, he stood with the pain evident in the slowness of that ascent. Once again, a friend said, "God's mercy be with you, Cain." To which I could only answer as I had before.

I would not need to wait long for the answer to Simon's question. Less than a week later, in the middle of the day, Simon was back. I knew what had happened even before he sat down and embraced me. His tears, his presence in the middle of the day, told me everything. Like Jacob, Simon too had been cured. His story also left me speechless.

He had left the next day immediately to find the teacher. He had robed himself in the garments that allowed him to hide as much of his condition as possible, yet he also carried the knowledge of his responsibility. He spoke of his crying out as he walked the dreaded "Unclean, unclean" that sent people scattering from his presence. He spoke of the stones and sticks that had been hurled at him any number of times as he made his way to where he had heard the teacher was staying. And then he told me simply of the meeting.

Simon had found the small village the teacher was staying at. Because of his condition he had stayed just outside the village at a distance off the path leading from the village. It was about midday on the second day outside the village. Simon had exhausted what little food he had brought with him and try as he may he had been unable to find anyone willing to accept his money to go and buy him food. As he had sat on the side of the road wondering what to do, he watched as a great crowd of people began to emerge from the village. The moment had arrived.

Simon shared that when the teacher had come within shouting distance, he had cried out, "Son of David, have mercy upon me." He said that he had repeated that phrase several times each time louder. The crowd preceding the teacher had tried to quiet him, but when they became aware of his affliction, they had fled from his presence. Some had even picked up stones and begun to fling them at him. The teacher had both heard the cry and seen the commotion and had stopped. Then something truly remarkable had happened. The teacher had made his way over to Simon while his disciples and the crowd had hung back, aware of Simon's condition. "The teacher looked at me and asked, 'What would you have me do?' Simon's answer was unusual "Lord if you are willing, you can make me clean." The teacher's answer and action were even more so. "The teacher said, 'I am willing' and had reached out and touched Simon and then had taken his hand and lifted him from where he had been seated.

Simon took my hand, and though I had never felt his hand before, he had described in detail the erosion of his fingers. The fingers were whole, solid, and I could tell I had feeling in them long lacking. He took my hands and allowed me to feel his face, his nose, his ears, and his tears. It was not simply that the condition had been stopped, it had been reversed completely. Simon was whole, again.

He embraced me in a hug that nearly split my sides. Through his tears and his laughter, he whispered what his soul shouted. "I am healed, I am healed." He shared with me the amazement of the crowd at what had occurred. Those who had been ready to hurl stones now surrounded him in wonder. Simon had thrown off his cloak and stared at what had occurred to him. Simon indicated that many were heard to be praising God for this great event. Simon shared that he had fallen at the feet of the teacher as well and had thanked him and God for his healing. I understood his reaction, for I too was amazed and once again hope stirred within my heart.

The question soared within again, "What about me?" And then the doubt came hurling down the same path, "I have never had what I need, how can anyone give what was never had?" But the longing was real, and my answer was but a short time away.

Laura's voice stopped. The spell was broken again. She looked up at Carol who no longer looked to Rubin for approval. She moved to the case and showed Laura how to move the scroll. There would be no stopping until the tale was done. Rubin had looked up when Laura had stopped. Realizing that everyone else's attention was focused on Laura, he moved quietly for the door. As he left the room, only Carol saw. But even she could not hear the voice in Rubin's head that drove him. The voice said, "What I must do, I must do quickly."

14

THE CRISIS REACHED

Rubin tried not to stare at Carol. He remembered their parting and now wondered in dismay over the choice he had made. Accepting emptiness and anger was the ultimate non-fatal self-inflicted wound. After all of the years, her presence revealed the staleness of what had been his chosen life. Rubin had tried not to think about her much since those events that had changed his life. But from time to time, usually, late in the evening, he had felt the emptiness. He filled the vacuum with work and anger. Both were now gone.

He wondered if there would be either the room or time for him to heal the wounds he had created. It was as if he had lived in a mansion all his life but had only discovered today, that there was more than the one room in the mansion. He was sure that as he explored, he would discover that he had chosen to dwell for many years in the cellar. He knew that he could not claim back the time lost.

He understood that there had always been a hole in his life that neither Anita nor Carol had been able to fill. Now that the hole was filled, suddenly he realized how much more room his life had for people. He only hoped that perhaps he could finally truly be the man he was supposed to be. His thoughts turned darker, but the truth pushed back on the self-incrimination that had started to build. The truth echoed in his mind, and it said simply, "No more." The darkness receded, and light and peace flooded in. He heard himself say, "Thank you, Lord."

Carol had looked over to Rubin when she heard his words. She understood that a battle in Rubin's private war had been waged and won. She knew that each person had similar battles. Both her friend Laura, and she had fought their own battles. She had watched as her own daughter also encountered similar battles. But unlike herself, Carol's daughter was blessed with knowing the truth all her life.

She smiled now knowing that the battles continued to be fought, but now a power greater than herself came to her aid whenever she felt that she was in danger of losing the struggle. Joy rushed into Carol and produced a silent tear sliding down her cheek.

Rubin glanced over to Laura and realized how much he did not know, and more how little he understood. With anticipation, he looked again at Carol and said again, "tell me everything."

Carol wiped the single tear from her cheek and then sought for the words to say. Rubin realized that Carol was struggling with a spot to start the story from. Laura came to their rescue, opening the new tape case that was in her hand and slipping it quickly into the player. She looked now upon the man she knew was her father and said:

"Of all of the tapes, this is my favorite." Laura punched the on button and then slowly sat by the table as her name sake's voice once again began to speak.

Rubin heard the first few words and knew instantly that this was the missing segment in his set of tapes. For whatever reason, Laura had not left him this tape. He had been right, there had been a gap. This time his logic had been faultless. He had listened to his set of tapes many times over the past 20 years and knew there was something missing. He wished as well that he had waited until Laura had translated all the scrolls before, he had done what he had. But he was grateful that at least he now had the complete translation of this first scroll. Perhaps, this was as it should be, since this had been all he had needed.

Rubin leaned forward in anticipation. He suspected what this tape would contain. He had read an account of this period only the evening before. It had been this account that had finally let him see the truth. It had burst upon him as an unexpected wave. It had covered him until he felt like he was drowning. Then for the first time, he realized that he was breathing. He had held his breath for so long, and now freshness filled his lungs. Tears had sped down his cheeks, and truth had driven him to his knees.

Now he would hear it from the perspective of the man himself.

Carol looked at Rubin as he leaned forward, and she understood now what Laura had told her so many years ago. Laura had said that she had withheld a little from her father to spur his curiosity. She had known that the gap would cause her father to search for the missing link. Laura had hoped that during that search, her father would run into the truth. For the missing time was well documented in another place. Rubin would know where to look. The only question was, would he dare to look and then dare to believe. The truth was there for Rubin to discern. It had taken Rubin 20 years to find it, and now this final tape would cement the truth into Rubin's mind and heart.

It had not been an accident that Carol had arrived at Rubin's doorstep today. Late the evening before, both she and her daughter, had a similar experience. Somehow, they both had understood that Rubin had finally found the truth and accepted it. For Carol, it had come as a thought, persistent and persuasive, that the time was now right to seek Rubin out. For Laura, it had been a dream.

Carol had told Laura about her father when she was old enough to understand. Laura had asked many times to go and meet this mysterious man, but Carol knew she needed to wait until the time was right. Eventually, Laura had also understood that there was something other than Carol's own desire, preventing the meeting. She accepted her mother's decision and waited suspecting that her mother was expecting something to happen.

After so many years Carol had begun to despair that the time would ever arrive. After Rubin had forced her out of his life, she had also left her position as his assistant. She could not bear the thought of working with him. She had known for over two months that she was pregnant. She had shared her condition with her friend Laura, that same evening she had read from the mysterious scrolls the first time.

Laura had not known what advise to give her. Both Carol and Laura spoke little about her situation. They continued to make their own discoveries about the scrolls, and the excitement had pushed back the need to deal with Carol's condition.

It would not be until the day of the fire, that Carol and Laura would talk extensively about Carol's condition. By then, both had come to a new understanding of reality. And both knew that unless Rubin also discovered the truth, Carol's condition would not aid Rubin's situation.

She had not found the right time to tell Rubin, and then with the events that had occurred, the time never came. When he had begun to force her out of his life, she had promised that she was not going to use her pregnancy to try and change his mind. She had been silent through the weeks of criticism. Instead, she had hoped and prayed that what she knew to be true would become obvious to Rubin as well.

Carol had taken a teaching position at a university four hours away from Rubin's university. She had kept an eye on Rubin, always watching from a distance. She still heard of his activities through her contacts at the university. Laura was born in the late spring of the year. Fortunately, the university had been very understanding of her situation, although no one knew who the father of her child was.

Rubin had never found out that Carol had a child, until the day she had arrived at his doorstep. Carol had built a life for herself and Laura, spending as much time with her daughter as possible. She had foregone the potential advancements with her career, opting instead for a junior position, always teaching undergraduates, and never reaching for the positions that would require more of her time and effort.

She had spent her time with her daughter, reading from the special gifts her friend had entrusted to her before her death. It was during these sessions that her Laura began to show that she had been given the same gift as her namesake. Carol was somehow, not surprised. She had come to a point in her life where she understood that there were forces at work, outside her understanding.

When she had left Rubin and started her life on her own, she had also started her own study of the ancient languages of the scrolls. While she knew she did not have her friend's gift, she wanted to be able to finish what her friend had entrusted to her. On many days she felt like giving up. The language was more difficult than anything she had ever tried to tackle in her life. She marveled anew at her friend's gift.

When her daughter began to display the gifts that her friend had, she understood that she had been provided the solution to her problem. She, her daughter and another had spent years together pouring over the problem left behind by Laura and had finally completed the task left for them…. almost.

The voice on the tape was clear and penetrating, all three sat and listened to her words:

"Jacob and Simon were healed. The impossible had become possible. The Feast of Booth's was approaching, and already, the crowds coming to the great city were increasing. The news of what had been happening filled everyone's discussion. For the first time in years, I did not ask for mercy, simply news. I clung to every word that was being said about this teacher and all that he was doing.

During the feast, my brother Jason came with the news that one of my sister's husband's many mistresses had been caught and dragged before the teachers. In our law, those who are not married who become physically involved are married regardless of their desires. Their fate, however, is much better than those who are already married and venture into this area of gratification. For someone to be married and commit these acts, the punishment is severe, and the law is clear, they must be put to death.

David, who had been with the woman at the time of discovery, had been released discretely. No one wanted to charge or embarrass such a wealthy benefactor much less kill him. But the woman was another story. Jason relayed that she had been dragged before a teacher who had mysteriously released her. I learned from my brother that this teacher was the same one that now both Simon and Jason followed. The mysterious teacher was close by. My anticipation grew. Would the teacher come this way? If he did pass by, what would I say? What would he do? I did not have long to wait to find out the answers to my questions.

It was a Sabbath day, only shortly after I had heard from Jason. That day found me at my normal spot along the path. Suddenly I heard coming up the road a large crowd of individuals. It was obvious from the sound of the feet that the crowd was following someone. It was the teacher. I thought what to say but heard a voice speak before I could. It was a voice I had not heard before that asked a question that had raged in my heart for years: He asked "Teacher, who sinned, this man or his parents, that he would be born blind?" By his question, I understood, that all one needed to do was look at me, to know that my condition was an occurrence of birth. He had not known me, and yet knew I had been like this from my mother's womb.

The question had been asked, one of many that sought an answer. I strained to hear the answer, perhaps now I would learn the reason. Certainly, either my parents or I must bear some responsibility. Then I heard his voice. My heart fluttered as my mind whirled. "It is him!" a voice shouted inside me. His voice was older now and bore the tone of authority and certainty that spoke of ageless wisdom and understanding. Yet, at the same time, the voice was filled with compassion and longing that drew all who would listen.

His response, while directed to the questioner, was clearly aimed at my heart. It was not the answer I expected. He said: "It was neither that this man sinned, nor his parents, but it was so that the works of God might be displayed in him."

My mind went back to another conversation and became aware of a glowing ember of anger in my mind that was being doused by his words. I was not at fault, and neither were my parents. The resentment I had harbored as well as the suspicion of guilt faded away. My mind reeled trying to come to grips with the truth of this statement. I had been born this way because God needed me to be this way. I still did not understand.

But the teacher was not finished, I heard him continue to say: "We must work the works of Him who sent Me as long as it is day; night is coming when no one can work. While I am in the world, I am the Light of the world."

I heard him spit on the ground and then felt his gentle hands applying a substance to my face. His voice was the same, gentle yet urgent. The hand that had guided me through the city brought me to the temple, rebuked my anger now touched my face with patience and love.

He spoke to me both a command and an urgent plea filled with longing for me: "Go, wash in the pool of Siloam." Then he released me from his gentle grasp. I was stunned. Both his grasp and his words had kindled sparks through my being. As before, I shuddered. A suspicion arising in my soul, a question drawing close to my lips, and yet the answer still allusive, waiting for the right time. I wanted to say, "Who are you," but my words were frozen in my mind and would not emerge from my lips.

My next thought was surely he would come with me. Yet I realized that he was not going to take me to the pool. Now, this pool he spoke of was well known by me, but it was at least a ten- minute walk for a seeing person. For me, it was much more than a Sabbath day walk. I knew the way, but many were the obstacles both mobile and fixed that I would need to transverse to get there. I stood reaching out for the teacher, but he had already moved beyond my reach, and the crowd was receding with him. Why was he leaving me to take this journey on my own? Slowly I turned and wrestled with the questions raging within. But finally, I remembered Simon and Jacob, and hope sprung up, a flame kindled within.

It has remained a great surprise to me that none from the crowd joined me in my journey. Were none quizzical about the outcome of my journey? Having heard his words and his charge, would no one desire to see the results of this strange action? Yet, no one followed. It was my journey to take. Only my silent prayers and my shuffling feet accompanied me on the journey. The doubts that flew through my mind are too numerous to mention. All the old nagging questions reemerged, but finally the thought "What do I have to lose?" kept urging me on. Thoughts of Simon and Jacob and their experiences filled me with hope. His gentle touch soothed my soul and helped guide me along the path.

Along the way, more than a few passersby bumped into me, and some not understanding my condition, or maybe because of my condition, were less than accepting of my apologies. Finally, I knew from the sound and the scent I had reached the steps that led down to the pool. I slowly descended the steps reaching the boundary that marked the pool. I took another step and felt the water on my feet.

It was here that the greatest battle in my soul occurred. What would be the outcome of such a foolish action? Yet, I knew his voice, he had called me before, he had told me my story. I heard in my mind his words and then heard his voice again clear and filled with compassion. He had not spoken the words before, but I heard them clearly. He said lovingly, "Trust me, Cain, for this is your time, for this reason, you have been blind until this day."

Kneeling, I felt the cool water in my hands, and placing my hands together, lifted the water towards my face.

The water had the familiar feel as I had washed my face many times before, but as the water touched my face, I felt the mud, that the teacher had applied to my face suddenly change. Instead of washing off, like dirt and mud, would normally do, this mud coalesced into two orbs. Suddenly the contours of my face were changed, and then in surprise, I sat back in the water and slowly removed my hands from my face.

How does one describe one's first sight? I remember seeing my hands, dark shadows suddenly taking on form, with water drops running along the fingers. With light streaming through the gaps in my fingers. Then, I saw the water beneath me, the ripples caused by the falling remnants of water from my hands, and then a figure of a face staring back at me from the pool still disturbed. I saw a man with a black beard, with black hair, tanned skin, and green eyes staring back. I saw myself.

How can I explain to you what happened next? Would you believe tears? The tears of a lifetime flooded from my eyes. The tears that had been denied me because of my condition now flooded through the lids I had just gained. Tears of sorrow, of abandonment, of hurt and of anger, and finally of love and wonder surged forward and replaced the water that I had used up only recently. I sat there crying and suddenly realized another emotion so seldom experienced, that of thankfulness.

Would you understand why I looked up into the sky, saw blue for the first time, and the white of clouds? Would you understand why I looked around quickly and saw for the first time two individuals who had come to the pool as well for washing? Then I saw the baked brown and white of the buildings surrounding the pool, and the gray of the stones of both the road and some of the other buildings. I know the people at the pool thought I was crazy. They were right. I splashed in the water, sat in the water, and stared up at the sky, and I wept. The tears once denied me were now running without aid. I was whole.

A shudder passed through my body, and I knew something else. There was something still missing. Looking again in the water, I examined my eyes closely. There was no mud left on my face, and where before there had only been hollowed cavities with missing orbs, there were two greenish pupils with whitish orbs. How can I explain to you what I looked like before? I cannot! I can only guess what I looked like before. But I can tell you that my face was not pretty to behold. Where my eyes were supposed to be were instead empty sockets. I had been born blind, but this was more than just blindness from lack of ability, it was blindness from lack. The teacher had made two eyes from spit and dirt, and now I beheld what I had not been given at birth. I know that my whole face had changed. Its shape and contours were more normal now, as the hollowed-out depressions were now filled in.

My doubt had been replaced with fact. The teacher not only could restore what was lost, like what he had done for Simon and Jacob, but he could also replace what had never been given. With that thought, I stood knowing that I needed to return quickly to the teacher. I needed to tell him what had happened and to thank him. I needed the answer to what was still lacking in my life. I needed to know the answer to the question I had not been able to ask. "Who are you, Teacher?" raged within my soul.

I needed to tell my friends and my family. My heart was bursting with need. I stood and rushed out of the pool area. But I was lost!

I knew how to get here blind, but now in the light, everything was so different. I had trusted the feel of my feet and hands before, but now with sight, it was as if those senses had ceased to exist. I stood confused as to which way to go. Finally, I forced myself to close my eyes. Fear welled up within me that perhaps I would not be able to open my eyes again, but when I did, the light continued to steam in. I closed my eyes and waited for my sense of direction to return. It finally did, and I opened my eyes and followed where my feet and hands directed.

Just how different I looked was confirmed as I rushed back to the area that had been my home for so long. Have you ever had the experience of talking to someone and knowing their voice but never having seen them? I do not know if I can explain this, but people's voices do not often match how they look. This was my experience. For years I had been a neighbor with many people, yet as I looked upon them for the first time, I was confused. I recognized their voices, but I did not know them.

There was a group of individuals standing close to the home of Clovis, a baker. Clovis was one of the few truly generous merchants that lived close by to my perch. Many a day I had counted his bread as a blessing, even if it were the older bread, he gave to me to meet my need. I heard his voice and turned to his shop. I had expected a small man with a round face, for his voice was high pitched, yet the man before me was taller than most, with a barrel chest and a square face. I almost laughed at my former misconception.

Like most shops, his was closed for the Sabbath, but he was outside speaking with a group of neighbors about the great disturbances that had been occurring with the arrival of this new teacher into town. I hesitated to stand on the other side of the group but finally walked up to him wanting to hear more clearly his comments. He realized I was standing there and turned to me, he started to say, "Hello C...." but then changed his mind as he looked at my face, and instead said, "Sorry Can I help you?"

"Do you not know me, Clovis? I asked. He stared at me, hearing my voice, but my voice and my face did not match in his mind. He said slowly, "Do I know you?" Suddenly another merchant, Levis, who was a wine dealer, said, "Is that, you Cain?" I turned to Levis, who had never been generous but had neither been abusive and said, "yes, it is I."

Silence and then the questions flew around me like flies attracted to food. I heard some say,

' It's not Cain, he just looks like him.' To these, I insisted, "It is I, I am he." Others asked, "Is this the one who was blind?" While still others asked, "How is that you now see?" To these questions, I explained what had happened. I told them honestly that the man that is called Jesus made clay, anointed my face where my eyes should have been, and told me to wash in Siloam. I had, and now I see.

The group of neighbors grew rapidly from the five or six it had started with until finally, over twenty local people were swarming around me. Finally, Clovis asked if he might touch my face, and I gave him permission. I knew what Clovis wanted to do, and I closed my eyes, feeling his hands running over what used to be missing. His hands fell back, and the conversations continued. He turned to Levis and said, "It sounds like him, but he sure does not look like him!" Levis asked me, "Where is this teacher, that gave you eyes to see?" I answered him that I did not know. He had left me to find my own way to the pool.

Together the crowd began to discuss everything that was occurring. Two of my small group of beggars had been watching the commotion from a distance. I turned, leaving Clovis and Levis to their discussions and walked over to where they stood, watching from a safe distance. The first was named Benjamin and had just recently joined our small group. The other was Enoch who had been with our group for several years. Both were whole men, but had fallen on tough times, and had found begging better than starving. As I walked towards them though, Clovis reached out and took my arm.

He turned me around and said, come with us. I looked back upon Benjamin and Enoch and promised myself that I would return to tell them what had happened. Clovis said, "We need to take you to the teachers, so you can explain what has happened. Perhaps they can then explain it to us." Perhaps they could. And maybe they could tell me who this teacher was. Surely, they would know.

The group led me along the street and then turned towards the local place where people gathered to worship and be taught on the Sabbath. As normal, there were several teachers still there. Like the neighbors I had returned to, the teachers were also discussing the events of the recent past as we approached. Upon seeing the crowd, the teachers had turned when we entered the building and watched our approach. I was placed in front by Clovis, but before he could speak the crowd burst into questions and demands.

While the argument surged around me, I was turning to look at where I stood. This was the first time I had seen the inside of such a building. I had never been permitted further than the back, but now I could see the colors and the contrast of this special place. The room had many candles and the special smell that I remembered so well from my youth.

There on the center wall was a special cabinet. Covered by a red cloth with gold fibers interwoven the cabinet contained the sacred writings. These were the scrolls that contained both the history of my people as well as the direction and revelation of the God that we served. The cloth, covering the cabinet, rippled as if by a breeze. Strangely, the candles showed no motion. The breeze was coming from within and around the cabinet. Within I sensed a great truth-seeking escape from the confines now restraining it.

As I looked, I was filled with longing, and I remembered the Samuel of old standing before the great Ark of the Covenant. I remembered the great desire to read for myself, the stories that I had only heard all of my life. To hear through the writings, the voices of those who had seen and heard, all that the writings revealed. The cloth responded again, fluttering even more as if the writing within recognized the great desire and desired to fulfill its purpose. I remember even amid the confusion a strange peace flooded over me, and I almost spoke aloud the words that were embedded in my mind, "Speak Lord, thy servant is listening."

I think one of the teachers saw my distraction and sensed a greater presence. Standing, he motioned for quiet. The strange breeze quieted as the longing ebbed, and my focus returned to those around me. He asked Clovis to explain why they were here. I knew his voice. This man had passed by my perch frequently, and surely knew who I was. He had never given any money to our small band, but I had often heard his voice discussing with those following him, the meaning and importance of the various aspects of our law. My mind told me not to expect too much from this man. I had never understood how someone so familiar with our traditions could be so unaware of our physical need.

He turned to me and stared at me. Then he said, "You are the blind man, who sits with the other beggars on the square?" It was more a statement than a question, but I answered: "Yes, you are right." He walked up closer to me, looking at my face. This was the closest he had ever gotten to me. I could smell his breath as he stared at my face. My heart beat rapidly as he reached out to touch my face only to withdraw his hand at the last minute as something in his mind seemed to prevent him from touching me. He asked me, "How did you receive your sight?"

I told him the story, now repeated for a new group of inspectors. I told them all that the man called Jesus "applied clay to my eyes, and I washed, and now I see." It was then that the arguments started among the teachers and my neighbors went silent as they listened to the discussion. All of the teachers took there turns in approaching me. Some were bolder than others, and unlike the first teacher, some even dared to touch my face, normally reacting as if they expected to feel something that would explain my new condition.

The argument seemed to center around what was permitted on the Sabbath. It was as if my healing was of secondary importance but instead that the weightier issue was whether this type of activity was permitted on the Sabbath. I was confused. I had come to them hoping for answers about who this teacher was but instead was listening to a discussion of why I should not have been healed on this day. Why I thought, did it matter about making clay from spit and dirt on the Sabbath Day if it had brought such miraculous healing? Surely healing was not included in the prohibition against work. I remembered then that there had been prophets in the past that had done many mighty works and healings. Of course, I also knew that none had done what this teacher had.

I tried to say something, but my words were drowned out by the argument surrounding me. Some finally began to talk about the issue that was close to my heart. The argument had proceeded from what was permitted on the Sabbath to who this Jesus was. I heard some say that since Jesus broke the Sabbath day ordinances that he could not be from God, while others asked the question that I also would have asked, "Then how can he do such amazing things?" Finally, one who I did not know turned to me and said, "What do you say about him, since He opened your eyes?" There was a hushed silence as the teachers and my neighbors waited for my response.

I had thought about this question and gave the answer that first came to my mind, "He is a prophet." I said. As soon as I said the words, my mind told me I was only half right. There was still something missing in my answer. "My answer did not satisfy the teachers and started another round of questions and arguments.

One group of the teachers, who did not know me, began to insist that I could not have been blind as I had stated. "Perhaps,"" they said, "He is a deceiver, like this teacher is a deceiver, and he is only here to throw us into more confusion?" Finally, one of the teachers who knew of me said, "I know this man's parents. They live not far from here and have always been faithful to our traditions and guidance. Why do we not bring them here and we can hear their testimony as to whether this man is their son or not? "To this, there was general agreement, and one of my neighbors was appointed to fetch my parents to this tribunal.

I had never seen my parents before. My father and mother entered the area, and as they did both looked upon me in astonishment. My mother moved quickly over to me, followed by my father. My mother was a small woman now compared to what I remembered. Her face was etched with the lines of age, and the wrinkles that come from a life of hard toil and concern.

Her hair was gray. I would never know the golden flax color that had been her great joy in her youth. Her eyes were deep and dark brown. She placed her hand tentatively on my face and said in a hushed voice, "Is that really you Cain? "My eyes filled with tears as I replied, "Yes, it is me, Mother."

Then I told her my story, and what had happened.

My father had stayed slightly back but had edged closer as I had spoken with my mother. When I had told the tale to my mother, I turned to the man I knew as my father, who had turned me over to my life as a beggar so many years ago. At first, there was a quiet silence between us, then I swept him up in a fierce embrace.

Little did my father understand that the teacher had done more than heal my eyes. My embrace would have been unthinkable if the teacher had not also touched the anger in my life. When I pulled back, I was moved to realize that my fathers' eyes were also leaking tears.

The teachers had allowed this brief exchange but then demanded the attention to the immediate problem at hand. The first teacher who knew me and my parents asked the first question. "Is this your son?" But before they could answer, another teacher added, "Who you say was born blind?" and then still another teacher jumped in demanding, "How does he now see?" The questions had happened in such rapid-fire, it was as if the three questions were but a single question. I watched as my mother and father looked at each other, at me and then at the teachers. It would be only later that I would learn that the decision had already been made to exclude from the community any who proclaimed any possibility that this new teacher might, in fact, be who I now believe and know he is.

I had never seen the look that came over my father, yet I understood the tone of his voice, having heard it many times as he had negotiated the price for his wares. It was the voice of a negotiator, who knew what could be said and what must not be said. I would confront him with his words later, but for now, I understood that my father desired to remain outside the fray that was clearly developing.

His first words were reaffirming and direct, "We know that this is our son and that he was born blind." The crowd murmured in excitement, "He is not a fraud" I heard some murmur. But then my father's voice changed tone, and I heard him say, "but how he now sees, we do not know, or who opened his eyes, we do not know."

It struck me that the questioners had asked the how but not the who. Now my father had drawn them back to the central question. No one could dispute that my eyes had been opened. The how was an interesting question but a mere diversion from the more immediate, Who? Everyone knew that it had been the man called Jesus. But who was Jesus?

And then my father returned the problem to me, "Ask him, he is of age, he will speak for himself." So, even after all these years, once again, I was to be abandoned by those, I loved the most. But this time I understood and was not bitter.

The teachers looked upon me again, and then the first teacher said, "Give glory to God, we know that this man is a sinner." The statement was odd. It was as if they wanted to create a two-headed coin. God was deserving of glory for my miraculous healing, yet the vehicle of that healing was not to be considered as good. "How could that be?" I wondered. For the first time, an internal voice began to tell me that there was great danger ahead. At the same time, another power began to surge through me, and I understood that the moment of testing had come, and I must not shy away from the truth.

I answered their statement saying, "Whether He is a sinner, I do not know; one thing I do know, that though I was blind, now I see." After the event some in the crowd that had brought me said for the first time they saw a spark in my eyes, as if a mighty flame lay just below the surface, waiting to *leap forth from the eyes that had been given me. Several of the teachers backed up a pace, while others closed in, like hornets demanding attention and unwilling to accept what they had already heard.*

Once again, the questions of how poured forth "what did he do to you? How did He open your eyes?" still others demanded. I could tell that though I had explained it already, they had chosen to believe something different from what I had told them. For the first time, a different type of anger began to form in my soul, not the anger of self-hurt, but the anger of being asked to deny what I knew to be the truth. My words were not skillfully chosen but were directed by a force that seemed alive in my soul. This force denied me any ability to think about pleasing words to calm the situation. Instead, they were blunt, direct, and designed to force the issue to a climax.

I said, "I told you already, and you did not listen; why do you want to hear it again?" Then from deep within the growing knowledge of what I must do leaped up and took the form of words, " You do not want to become his disciple too, do you?"

The question asked, had answered another question lurking beneath the surface of my own mind. I now knew that I must find the teacher, and like Simon and Jacob, I would follow him anywhere. No one had ever touched me as that teacher had. And who but a man blessed by God could do such great miracles. Even as I thought these words, I knew that there was still something lacking in my understanding of who this teacher was.

The response from my questioners was immediate and ferocious.

The cynicism was dripping from their words as they responded, "You are his disciple, but we are disciples of Moses. We know that God has spoken to Moses, but for this man, we do not know where he is from."

You need to understand the tone of their voice as they relayed this to me. Not only were their words cynical, but the way they said, "Disciples of Moses," it was as if they were expecting me to fall at their feet as Moses must have fallen at the burning bush. Their tone as they said, "God has spoken to Moses" was not the tone of acknowledgment of Moses' special connection to God but instead their claim of special connection to God for themselves.

I listened in amazement with the fire burning hotter in my soul every second. Their final statement, however, brought my soul to a full boil. And I responded in amazement and more than a little doubt as to their claims.

I said, "Well, here is an amazing thing that you do not know where he is from, and yet He opened my eyes." I looked around at these supposed teachers, the wisest of the wise of our community, and continued what I now understand was not obvious to them "We know that God does not hear sinners" …. (So much for their first stated fact about Jesus as being a sinner, I had just called them all liars), "but if anyone is God-fearing and does his will, He hears him" … (So much for their second stated claim of unique special relationship with God for themselves) , " Since the beginning of time, it has never been heard that anyone opened the eyes of a person born blind"… (So much for their obvious attempts to either downplay the scope or deny the relevance of the miracle I was part of) and then finally the truth that would break their backs and many others as well, "If this man were not from God, He could do nothing."

My final words brought a sucking sound, as those who had brought me to the teachers drew back, from the boiling over they knew must come. Later some would also tell me that as I spoke my last statement, green sparks had been seen leaping from my eyes, revealing a smoldering fire contained within waiting to leap forth. Once again, the cover of the special cabinet fluttered. The breeze had returned.

The twin angers, that of my questioners now accusers, and that of a force living inside me appeared ready to clash, and the crowd drew back.

I watched as even my parents appeared to cower before these teachers. I saw my father glance my way and suddenly froze riveted by what he saw within my eyes. The fire within me reached out and touched him. He would never be the same man again after this day.

The steam in the pot vented quickly. The faces of the teachers changed from the seemingly wizened faces of leaders to the flushed faces of spoiled children. They hurled back an insult that I knew to be false, claiming what I had once believed but now knew as untrue. They claimed that my original blind condition had been my fault. They said: "You were born entirely in sins, and are you teaching us?"

They had heard enough and taking hold of my arms they forcibly carried me from the building and deposited me with great effort and anger outside. As they turned to reenter their place, they warned all those who had been my neighbors, saying that I was even more unclean now than when I had been blind. With that, most started to withdraw from me.

Even as they did, a tearing noise was heard from inside the building. Later we would learn that even as they had ejected me from the building, the cloth covering the great cabinet had been torn from top to bottom and the scrolls had spilled out onto the floor, running as if to exit the building as well. This day would long be remembered by many.

My parents started to leave as well, but my father suddenly returned, reached down, and lifted me to my feet. "Son," he said, "let's go home."

I was surprised by his action, not yet realizing that the fire within had touched him as well. After all that I had heard before the teachers, this was the last action I expected from my father. I shook my head, and said softly, "Thank you father, but no. I must find the teacher first to thank him, and then I will come home." With that, I embraced this man who was my father and yet a stranger. His embrace in return told me he no longer wanted to be a stranger. I made another promise to myself that I would return home and learn what I did not know about my family.

My search for the teacher did not take long, for as it was, the teacher was also looking for me. He found me but a short distance from my former perch. I knew who it was from the crowd that still followed his every step. I think a smile was upon my face, and I knew there was a gleam in my eyes as I realized I had found the teacher. Reaching him, he looked upon me with warmth, turning me slightly so that he could examine the finished product. His smile was replaced with a look of compassion and concern, and before I could thank him, he asked me, "Do you believe in the Son of Man?" I understood the question, for this title was reserved for the savior that was to come into the world. Immediately I remembered the promise, I remembered the forerunner that was to come first. My spirit suddenly leaped for joy, He was here? The savior was here! The teacher both knew who He was and would point me to him. As soon as I thought the words, I somehow knew I had still missed the mark. Yet I said, "Who is He, Lord, that I may believe in him?" My question was asked in true faith. I knew this teacher would not lead me astray as those who had thrown me out of their presence such a short time ago.

Even as he responded to my question, the pieces were falling into place for me. He said, "You have both seen Him and He is the one who is talking with you now. "Falling to my knees, the final piece was in place. What I had not been able to solve was now plain, this teacher was the Lord, and this Lord was the Savior. My life had not been marred by accident; it had been blessed by direction. The privilege to be alive at this time, and to have seen with my eyes and touched with my hands the Lord... my dreams as a youth had been surpassed in reality. No longer would I be envious of Samuel's name and history, for I was experiencing in the light what he had seen in the shadows.

I had been born for this very purpose. What my soul had known for a long time, my mind simply had not been able to comprehend. Now I knew.

I had heard the voice of the Lord while blind. I had been rebuked by the Lord when angry. The Lord had healed me, both in body and in soul. I was finally what I had always dreamed of being and never thought possible. I was a whole person. My words echoed my soul, "I believe Lord!" and even as I spoke, I sank to my knees clutching his legs with my embrace. Joy and reverence surged through me.

The tape clicked off, and Laura stood to remove it from the machine. She replaced it in its cover and slid it into her pocket. She looked at her mother, who nodded her head almost imperceptibly.

With the same motion, Laura withdrew something else from her pocket and walked over to Rubin. She reached for Rubin's hand and turning it right side up waited for Rubin to open his palm. She then slid from her other hand and from the pouch it contained two gleaming green stones. The stones slid onto Rubin's hand. They were shining green gems, cool to the touch but filled with a fire that should burn all that they would touch. Rubin stared mesmerized by their sight. Only yesterday he would have howled in fear. Today he turned the stones slowly in his hands, and whispered to Carol saying, "There is more to the story." To this Carol nodded and said simply "Much. "

15

DECISION TIME

The lab staff and Carol had listened to Laura for over an hour as she had read from the first scroll. Finally reaching a spot where the scroll would once again need to be unrolled, Laura stopped. She stood back slowly from the hood and sank on a nearby chair.

For the first time, Carol realized that this amazing gift also took a toll on her friend. Carol had moved ahead to advance the scroll, but Laura shook her head and placed her hand on Carol's arm to stop her. Laura said, "I can't, I need a break for a moment." Looking around, she searched for Rubin, having been unaware of his earlier departure.

Before she could ask, Carol answered, "He left just after you started the second part. I think he was disturbed by your reading." Laura picked up in Carol's tone that there was something more, but she let it be for this time. Laura began to stand, and Carol aided her to her feet. Another assistant ran over with a cold drink and gave it to Laura and said for the entire staff, "That was truly amazing! We had heard that you had this ability but never truly comprehended it until we saw it today." Laura smiled weakly and said, "Normally I do not get wiped out like this, but I normally do not read for such an extensive period either."

Looking at Carol, she said, "I need to finish the reading, but first I want to find Professor Rubin and see what he is up to." With that, she headed to the door, with Carol in tow.

They did not find Rubin for over an hour. Finally, having searched the entire lab building, they had ventured across the campus and back to Rubin's office. They found him sitting behind his desk, his hands folded against his lips, with his eyes closed in meditation. On his desk, a book sat, one that Laura remembered but had seen out few times before. She turned it around to see what Rubin had been looking for but saw that the book had been opened, a marker placed in its pages, but she could not tell whether Rubin had read the pages or not.

Rubin still had his eyes closed and had not acknowledged their presence although they knew he had to be aware that they were there. Laura began to sit down, when Rubin spoke, still with his eyes closed. "Well, what do you think about my discovery?" The way he said "my discovery" left Laura uneasy, and Carol even more so.

Laura attempted lightheartedness, and replied, "It is an amazing discovery! From what I have seen, this may well rank as one of the greatest discoveries of this century! "Rubin's eyes opened, and Laura and Carol saw within his eyes the wildfire of sanity straddling a razor. He asked simply, "You think it may still be a fraud? "He asked the question in a tone void of hope and resigned to the expected answer. Laura looked at Rubin and did not answer. Instead, she asked, "What is wrong? Why did you not stay to hear the translation?"

To this, Rubin merely shook his head, saying, "I had something I had to do." No further elaboration or explanation was forthcoming. Rubin turned to Carol and asked, "What is everyone else doing?" Carol shook her head and shrugged, saying, "I guess they are continuing on the different tests you ordered. When Laura stopped reading, we went to look for you. Are you okay?" Laura recognized the true tone of worry that infiltrated Carol's voice. Both Carol and Laura sensed that something terrible was happening inside of Rubin, but they were unsure of what, or why it should be happening.

Rubin kept them locked out and pulled the blinds down on the windows they were trying to peer into. "I am fine," he said again. "I have some things to do now, so you two run off and do whatever you need to do." Neither Laura nor Carol budged. Laura looked at the book on her father's desk and asked, "Did you find anything there of interest? "To this Rubin looked first at the book and then at Laura, and said, "No." To this, Laura looked at the marker. She realized Rubin had not placed the marker there.

She remembered many years ago, another man, her grandfather, had placed this marker here and had told Laura that this was his favorite part of the entire book. That he should have picked this passage was a wonder to Laura now. She sat and read the passage. Looking up at her father, she asked, "Did you read this?" To which Rubin merely shook his head in the negative. He then added, "Why I got it out in the first place I do not know. A true historian never uses a book of fairy tales to examine the truthfulness of a discovery." To which Laura had thought to herself, "Unless the discovery points to the book as being less of fairy tales and more or less the truth."

Picking up the book, she looked at her father and said, "I am going back to the lab. When you are finished, please come back, and we can go to dinner." Trying to lighten the mood she added, "We can go to the Blackhorne, and have dinner there. The Blackhorne was Rubin's favorite pub. Rubin had often taken Laura there both to unwind and to enjoy the good food. It was a frequent place for both to enter either deeper or lighter discussions. She reasoned that perhaps some good food and a little drink would snap her father out of whatever mood had grabbed him. Rubin merely nodded but said nothing.

Laura carried the book with her, not asking permission, and Carol followed, looking back on Rubin before slowly closing the door and leaving him to his brooding.

After they had left, Rubin took out a pad and began making notes. There was much to do if he was to carry out his plan. It would be difficult, but if handled correctly, he reasoned, he could both accomplish his goal and still escape detection and exposure. The thought passed through his mind that Carol and Laura might be a problem, but as fast as the thought had entered, he dismissed it. After all, it was his discovery, and he could do with it what he wanted. Of course, that was a lie. At this moment, Rubin had already accepted many other lies that had been whispered to his mind. Thinking they were his own ideas; he did not realize either their true source or the truth that source did verify.

Carol and Laura slowly moved back towards the lab. At first, silence reigned between them, but then Carol asked what the book was that Laura had found opened on Rubin's desk. Laura handed the book to Carol, and when Carol looked at its binder, she stopped in her tracks. Laura also stopped, looked at Carol, and said, "It was my grandfathers. I did not realize that my father still had it. My grandfather used to read from it every day. It was the book that revealed my gift to him." Then taking the book back, Laura opened it to the pages that had been marked and read them to Carol. Carol's hand went up to her mouth in shock, and she said, "My God, that cannot be."

Laura shook her head and said. "Yes, it is, and I think we know who the writer of our discovery is supposed to be. Now the only question is, is the discovery real or not." Then she stopped and thought again, and said "No, that is not the only question, the real question is, if it is real then do, we believe that this," Laura pointed to the book, "is also real?"

They continued back to the lab, but instead of returning immediately to Rubin's lab, they found a quiet office, and Laura took the book, opened it to the beginning of the story, and for the next hour read aloud the entire account. When she had finished, she put the book down and waited for Carol's comments. They would not make it back to the lab that day, for their discussion lasted for hours. Rubin found them sitting in the office but did not ask them why they had not been in the lab or what they had been doing.

Their dinner at the Blackhorne was subdued, with little conversation. All three were lost in their thoughts and shared only brief pleasantries and ate their food in silence. After dinner, Carol had left Rubin and Laura alone.

Laura had waited while Rubin had drunk another pint of his favorite ale. Of the three, Rubin's appetite seemed the most unaffected by the day's events. When Rubin had placed the stein down, Laura pulled out her grandfather's book and laid it on the table. When Rubin said nothing, Laura said, "I think you know what is in here, and what it might mean to the discovery and what the discovery might mean to this book." Rubin still said nothing.

Laura looked again at her father and said, "Aren't you interested that we might be sitting on the type of discovery that can change the way we think about this document?" Her father looked at Laura again and finally said, "There is nothing that we could discover that would change my opinion about that book. All that we might discover is that there are multiple documents relating the same fairy tales and myths that have haunted us for too long. And I suspect, that when the search is over, we will find that this recent great hoax was spread by recent creation only to confuse matters more."

Laura replied, "What if it is genuine, and what if it is all true?" To this, Rubin shook his head and said, "A lot of "if's" It's not, and it's not true."

Laura looked at her father and finally said, "How can you be so sure? "Rubin had no answer, only the shaking of his head and he repeated aloud a recurring thought, "It would have been better that I never found this so-called discovery." Laura did not remind her father that he, in fact, had not discovered the find. She also chose not to tell him how excited she was that the discovery had been made. Picking the book up she wished her father a good night. But just before she turned to leave, she stopped, returned to the table and placed the book down softly in front of him. "I have my own copy, although it is hidden away on some dusty shelf, I am going home to find my own. You really should read it for yourself and keep that notoriously open mind, open. She turned and left the pub.

Rubin picked up the book. His first urge was to throw it in the trash, but then he slipped it in his pocket. Leaving the pub, he returned home. Carol was not there. Just as well he thought, he was not much in the mood for company this evening. Taking off his coat, he removed the book and crossed to his bookcase. He slid the book in, between two thick books of philosophy and speculation. If he had been a collector of comic books, he would have placed it with them. That thought brought a chuckle to his mind, and then the blackness returned.

As he reached to close the case door, he remembered another little book that was more of a pamphlet than a book. He had discovered it among his mothers' belongings.

The pages of the pamphlet were yellow and brittle. The writing was faded and smudged, written in ink not designed to weather the time. The writing was in Greek, but through the years other owners had penned other languages in. It was only six pages long. Rubin had read the notes that were in Latin, French, and Old English, and had realized that this document had traveled a great distance through many hands. He had discounted what he had learned from the document until now.

He picked it up and standing by the bookcase, read it again. His Greek was not of the caliber of Laura's, but he could make out the meaning all the same. The pamphlet started without introduction or preface. Rubin thought again, it would have been nice to have the original, but this copy certainly was very old and appeared to have been copied either from the original or from a very old copy of the original.

When he finished reading, he placed the little pamphlet beside Harry's book and closed the case. He thought again about the coincidence of the discovery coming to him and that he should also be the owner of this other manuscript. His mind whirled, and once again, a black mood filled his mind with an even darker cloud. What had started as a curious junction of events, now appeared as something directed. He once again rebelled at the thought that he should be included in a play he had not written.

He almost spoke aloud his thoughts, "I am the master of my life, and I am the captain of my own ship," he quoted from a favorite writer. And then he thought, "Superstition and fear should not be allowed to exist." He could not understand or tolerate the fear that was building in his mind. With a shudder, he left the room.

Feeling chilled, he grabbed a sweater. He retired to his study and retrieved his notes and continued writing out the events that needed to occur. He did not notice that the room was quite warm and that the chill had nothing to do with the temperature.

Carol did not come home that evening. Rubin never realized that fact and could honestly say that he had not missed her. He was too busy, scheming.

Carol had waited for Laura to exit from the pub. Laura had seen her appear from under the light post outside the pub and waited for her to approach. "Well," she asked, "did you figure out what is bothering him, or did he tell you?" Laura only nodded negatively but then looked at Carol and said, "I suspect that we both suspect but we do not know for sure."

Their discussion picked up where it had left off when Rubin had found them in the office. It was well after 3 AM in the morning before they had both retired to get some sleep. Just shortly before they had gone to bed, Carol had shared her other news with Laura. Laura had listened, but when Carol asked her for advice, she had simply shaken her head while saying, "That is one I need to think about. I do not have any advice to give right now. Does my father know?" To this, Carol shook her head negatively.

Both Laura and Carol were wired but tired. Carol crashed on Laura's couch. She had decided that she neither wanted to be alone in her apartment or with Rubin. Laura merely shook her head, provided her with a blanket and pillow, and then retired herself.

They slept but a few hours and were back in discussion by 7 AM that morning. Laura had found three versions of the book that Rubin had hidden in his bookcase. One was in Greek and had been given to her by her grandfather. It had been this very book that had started her on her chosen profession. Carol and Laura took notes for several hours and then returned to the lab on the campus.

The lab was empty, as most of the assistants chose not to work on Saturday. Laura returned to the hood that contained the top with the stones and stared once again at the green stones contained there. As she watched, she saw what she thought was a water drop run along the edge of one of the stones. Carol also noticed the movement and watched in amazement as well. A steady flow of drops ran from the stones to the tabletop on which the cover rested. Carol ran to get a cloth and placed the cloth into the transfer case. Then sticking her hand through the openings and into the gloves, she opened the transfer case began to dab the liquid with the cloth. No sooner had she touched the cloth to the liquid than the entire towel had burst into flame.

Both Laura and Carol at first panicked, but then settled down as it became obvious that the only thing that was burning was the cloth. The fan for the hood removed the smoke quickly and efficiently, keeping ahead of the decaying towel. Once the towel was gone, so was the liquid. The towel had been consumed completely, without even any ash remaining. Both Laura and Carol looked at one another, not knowing what to say. They stared intently at the stones, but the earlier phenomenon did not reoccur.

They had no proof of what they had witnessed. There were no remains to be examined. The fire had occurred, consumed the entire towel, but left neither ash, burn mark or scar to show what had occurred. If Laura and Carol had not witnessed it, no one would ever know it had happened. No hard evidence remained to indicate it had happened.

Laura had a sudden thought and switched off the fan and reached for the filter casing through which the air of the hood was filtered.

Opening the filter, she removed the filter carefully so as not to disturb what should be there. The filter was clean. In fact, it appeared to be even cleaner than what a new filter would look like. With the smoke the towel had given off, the filter should have been clogged with evidence. Instead, it appeared that the smoke had purged whatever dirt and dust should have been there. Laura careful replaced the filter with a new one and placed the original filter in a disposable bag that she then sealed. She knew enough about forensic science to know that she needed to be able to keep the filter as original as possible. She would have one of the research assistants look at the filter on Monday for an explanation.

After about an hour of searching for a reason, they had returned to the case where the first scroll still lay. Carol opened the scroll to a new section and set up the tape recorder to capture what Laura would read. Laura looked at the scroll and for the first time, felt a tingle of fear, spread through her body. The destroyed towel was vividly in her mind. She looked down on the scroll, wondering exactly what she had gotten into and wondered if her father had been partially right about this discovery. Was she going to regret that it had ever been found?

Looking at the scroll, she waited for her gift. It took a little longer than normal, but then as in the past it finally kicked in, and her voice once again took on its melodic trance-like quality as she read. The tape caught her words, and Carol listened on.

"I followed the teacher for the rest of that day. There were many discussions with many different people about what happened to me. At the end of the day, I discovered that many people desired to be close to the teacher as well. I spotted two men, who were keenly observing me from a distance. They kept pointing at me and then beckoning me to come over to them. As I turned to go to these two strangers, I saw the teacher observing me. I looked at him, and he smiled and nodded. He then returned to the

discussions that were raging around him and the questions of those who pressed in upon him.

Reaching the two men, I looked upon them and asked first, "Do I know you?" Their joyful laughs and voices gave their identities away. Jacob and Simon.

I saw for the first time both their faces and their smiles. Our embraces were wild and filled with excitement beyond anything I had experienced before. This time it was my turn to share what had happened. The last light of my first seeing day was concluding when I finished my story. Looking up, I saw that the teacher was still surrounded by people and still was talking and teaching. Simon and Jacob smiled as they saw the question in my eyes. Without me asking they answered,

"Yes, sometimes he stays up all night speaking to any who have questions for him. Normally he gets just a few hours of sleep, and then it seems to be a habit that he finds a lonely place and prays."

I looked at my friends and then again at the teacher. I remembered my earlier promises to myself, and I stood. I told my friends that I needed to return home, but that I would come back in the morning.

It was Jacob who suggested that he and Simon might also go with me.

Together we stood and began to walk along the path and back towards the village. Three friends, brought together in tragedy and sorrow, now united in a common joy.

It was a clear night, and for the first time, I saw the stars and the moon. Every new sight filled me with awe. I stopped and starred. My friends stood silently appreciating without really understanding what I was experiencing. Their smiles caught my eye as I stopped looking up.: "I cannot believe it! It seems almost as if I am in a dream." We continued our walk towards my father's house. From time to time, I got confused as to the direction, and then Simon would take over for us. He was very familiar with where my family lived.

We approached the house and the shop. The tree that I remembered from my youth was still in the yard, but somehow its size now appeared diminished to my eyes. My memory was of a mighty tree, yet the tree was little more than eight-foot tall. As I approached the door of the house, I suddenly was filled with fear. I stopped walking, but both Simon and Jacob gave me a gentle nudge, and I continued forward.

The door opened before I arrived at it. In the door, backlit with light from the inside stood me. Except this person had the dark brown eyes of my mother and father. It was then that I realized that for the first time I looked upon my brother Jason. My twin.

Jason cried out, "He's here!" and rushed forward and swept me off my feet and lifted me in the air in a bear hug. After he set me down again, I realized for the first time that the house was full of strangers. My whole family had gathered together. I recognized my father and mother, but though I knew the rest were family, I could not have told you who was who.

Jason quickly drew a young woman and two children to himself and introduced his family to me. Jason introduced Ruth to me first. I had heard Ruth's voice many times, for Jason had brought her to visit me whenever possible. Her face was round with sparkling brown eyes and long black hair. She had a slightly pointy nose, but her mouth was full. She had the biggest smile filled with the largest white teeth I had ever seen. Her children were a boy and a girl. The boy was already nine, and like a sapling was already clearly sprouting up. He would be taller than his mother shortly and would most likely surpass his father only a short time later. The young girl was two years her brother's junior. She looked like her mother and had the deep dark eyes that I was sure would capture many a man's attention in the future.

Ruth said, "Rubin and Leah, this is your Uncle, Cain." Then from behind Ruth, a young man, came out and approached me. I heard a much older voice call out saying "Samuel wait." I turned and watched as my brother, Samuel. And a woman I knew must be his wife, Gaila, stepped past Ruth and her children. Unlike Jason, my brother Samuel chose to look at me from a distance. I recognized his voice and sensed the uneasiness in his tone. His son, Samuel, was already a young man. He obeyed his father's voice, but I could tell that he wanted to see up close the one he had heard about but never seen. His curiosity got the better of him, and he asked straight up, " Were you really blind?" To this, I answered yes, and then as I was drawn into the house, I turned and introduced both Simon and Jacob to my family.

Once in the house, I realized it was much smaller than I remembered. With all the people present, it was even tighter. Yet, everyone sat wherever possible. Once again, Samuel spoke up, much to the displeasure of his father. But he asked the question that I had hoped would be asked. The story of what had happened to me was repeated in the hearing of my entire family, except that now I added my belief that this Jesus of Nazareth was the promised Messiah.

I realized after I had told my story that the eyes around me revealed the opinion of their bearers. It was obvious that both Jason and his wife Ruth not only believed my story but also already had come to grips with the claims of the teacher. My father's and mother's eyes betrayed uncertainty but openness. Samuel's eyes spoke of outright disbelief and hostility, while Gaila's eyes hid their internal struggle, but her grasp upon her husband indicated her support for her husband. Their son. Samuel's eyes betrayed curiosity, and an obvious lack of understanding of the gravity of my claims.

As I had related my story, I realized that the two other women in the house must be two of my three sisters. The older one's eyes spoke of

CHARLES A. DE ANDRADE

uncertainty but joy at having her brother back. Sarah reached around her cousin and placed her hand gently on my arm. She looked up into my face and with tears in her eyes, welcomed me home. Naomi, the youngest, stood back, examining me from the corner. In her eyes, I saw a keen intellect, understanding what she was seeing and yet hesitant to accept what she saw on face value.

I said to her, "You must be Naomi?" She nodded her head and then looked over to my two friends. Her eyes locked on Simon's, and she said aloud, "You are Simon, and then she added, "the leper?" The room went terribly silent, and I could feel the coldness in the air suddenly increasing. My friend's laugh broke the frost. "Yes, it's me! But you can now say, I am Simon the 'Used to Be' Leper. "His self-abasing tone and light voice immediately reclaimed the air, and the opening brought forth his story.

He finished his story and not to be outdone, Jacob immediately introduced himself and began his story. I noticed while Jacob was telling his story that Simon had walked over to Naomi and had presented himself for closer inspection. Their quiet conversation did not detract from Jacob's tale, but it was obvious to me that Simon was of real interest to Naomi.

After Jacob had finished telling his tale, there was a knock at the door, and another woman entered the already packed room. I turned to see a beautiful woman enter, with her head adorned with the trappings of obvious wealth, and the scent of expensive perfume proceeding her. Her clothes were the rich colors of clothing only worn by the very rich. Yet her eyes betrayed loneliness and hurt that was of incredible depth. She looked upon me, her eyes wide with wonder, and said, "Hello Cain." My sister Rachel stood awkwardly at the door. Sarah reached out to my sister and drew her in. It was obvious from the reaction of most of the family that she now was the least accepted here. Before this day, I thought that I had been the outcast, but know I understood that my sister's shame was even greater than my own former condition. Her husband, David, was not with her.

As the conversations began among the groups that were beginning to form, I found myself drawn to Rachel. My mother, father, Jason and Ruth and their children, and the young Samuel were drawn to Jacob. Naomi and Simon continued their intimate discussion, while my brother Samuel and his wife Gaila continued to stand apart and aloof from the rest of the family. When Rachel had entered the room, I saw that Samuel and Gaila took even a further step back, as if to distance themselves from her even more.

I turned to Rachel and found her talking softly with Sarah. I walked over to where they were and found that despite my miraculous healing, Sarah and Rachel were lost in quiet conversation about her husband David, and what she was going through. I listened quietly to their discussion, and when it became obvious that they had reached the point of uncertainty that I said softly to them, "You should come with me and ask the teacher about what to do."

Rachel looked at me, and for the first time, I saw the flame of anger that was quickly hidden again behind the shame and sorrow of her life. "Why should I do that, Cain? He released the woman that they caught with David, and now I am twice the outcast as I was before." I had never thought about what the effect of the release of the woman by the teacher might be on her. I also knew that there was mercy at work within the teacher that spoke of his role as the Messiah. I told Rachel this but saw immediately that her heart was going to require more than my words. I walked up to her, took her hands, closed my eyes, and placed her hands on my face. The room had gone strangely quiet again, as all eyes watched what I was doing. With her hands on my face, I said, "If he can do this, he can explain to you why he did what he did, and what you should do as well."

I felt her hands and fingers searching my face, and when I opened my eyes again, I saw her eyes full of tears and heard her voice sobbing. "I am so ashamed," then breaking away from Sarah and me, she left the house. After she had left, I heard my brother, Samuel, make a comment about it being good she was gone. I think something in my eyes must have flared, for when I looked at him, he took a step back. Simon would tell me later, that when I had looked upon Samuel, my green eyes had glowed brilliantly, and that for the first time everyone had seen a side of the gift that was frightening.

I turned to the door and followed Rachel out quickly. I caught up to her at the end of the path, at the tree that had stopped my progress so many years before. Like my former position, she sat at the base of the tree, hugging it as well, and weeping. I sat down beside her, and despite her turning away, put my arms around her and whispered, "Come back, with me." She turned to me, and then throwing her arms around me, she continued to weep..

When her energy was spent, she finally stopped and then looked at me in the light of the stars. She once again, placed her hands on my face, this time of her own accord. After she had once again examined the changes, she asked, "What is it like? To be whole, I mean and no longer an object of disdain?" It was then that I understood that there were conditions far worse than physical deformity. The anguish of a soul broken and lonely could exist even in the most perfect of bodies.

I told her about my confusion and the struggles in my own life. And then I shared once again what the teacher had done for me. Slowly standing, I placed my arm around her and led her back to my father's house. When we arrived there, she once again hesitated at the door, but Sarah opened the door to us instinctively. And we walked back into the house.

Samuel, his wife, and their son were no longer in the house. Sarah threw her arms around Rachel in a mighty hug, and soon, all of the family that was left also had swept her into its embrace. We talked well into the early hours of the morning.

The next morning, I awoke, well before the sun had risen. I stood and quietly exited the house, desiring both solitude and a new experience. My first sunrise would find me back at my perch of so many years, while I awaited the arrival of the family of beggars that were the family that had supported me for so many years. Just as the sun was beginning to peak over the horizon, I realized I was not alone. Turning, I saw a woman watching me from a short distance away.

This woman's hair was long and full, and though still not light, her hair appeared as a dark main. She was a tall woman, with strong bronze arms that showed they were used to hard work. Her face was slightly curved and thin and contained bright gray eyes. Her eyes betrayed a depth of intellect and purpose. There was a strength to her that instantly attracted me to her. She wore no adornment in her hair, and from her dress, I assumed that she must be one of the poorer local merchant wives'.

She continued to examine me without any comment. I stood and walked slowly over to her. When I was only a few feet away, my heart fluttered, and I knew. It was Mary.

I think my eyes betrayed my heart, for she spoke before I could. "Cain, it is true what they say?" To this, I nodded and then turning so that she would not see the tears and emotion welling up in my eyes. I watched the sun as it broke over the horizon. Mary moved and stood beside me. After the sun had broken the spell, I turned and looked upon this woman that had been such a blessing in my life. I saw in her eyes, her desire and took her hands gently closing my eyes and allowing her to feel my face.

When her curiosity had been fulfilled, I reopened my eyes. She asked the obvious question, and I told her everything that had happened in the last twenty-four hours. It was just as I had finished my story that Benjamin and Enoch approached. Seeing Mary and me together they hesitated, but I motioned them over, and the questions began again.

Simon and Jacob found us together an hour later. I was still describing and answering questions when they arrived. Rachel, Naom, and Sarah were with them as well. Together we all set off to find the teacher. There were many questions already answered, and more to be asked."

Laura stopped her reading and looked at Carol again. Their discussion for the next hour had little to do with the text. Their growing suspicion at how this discovery was going to be received was their focal point.

It was already close to lunchtime, but neither Carol nor Laura was hungry. They heard the key in the lock of the lab and turned as Rubin walked in. He looked startled to find both Carol and Laura there. They could tell from his eyes that he also had not slept much the prior evening.

Rubin saw the tape recorder and asked, "Have you discovered anything important?" Laura answered, "I think every word we read of this document is important, but nothing more significant than what we already heard before. It is obvious to anyone who would read this document which the author claims to be, the only real question is do we believe his claim." Rubin answered back, somewhat heatedly, "No, I think the real question is, is this document real? If it is not, then it does not matter who the person claims to be."

Having said that, Laura realized Rubin was carrying his large briefcase that appeared to be quite packed. "You have work with you today?" she inquired. To this, he answered that indeed he did and that he was looking for a quiet spot where he could spread out and do what he needed to do. Looking at the two women, he said: "Perhaps one of the other offices would be better," and before either could challenge him, he left the lab.

In the hall, Rubin's heart was still galloping. He had not expected to find anyone in the lab, although now he wondered why he was so surprised to find them there. He walked quickly up the hall, taking the stairs rapidly. He hoped that no one would follow him or question him further about his burden. He now realized he would have to wait to a later time, or perhaps even another day before he could complete his mission.

He grasped the briefcase to his middle, not wanting that the contents be shaken any more than they already had been. He thought again and decided to return to the lab he had left before coming to this lab. It would be best to return the contents there and then wait for a better time.

After Rubin left Carol and Laura, they had both looked at one another, and the same thought had occurred to both. Carol said it first, "He's going to do something stupid." Turning around, they walked back to hoods and the different pieces of the discovery. Their discussion now turned to what they should do to protect the discovery.

16

PATHS CHOSEN

Rubin stared at the two green stones in the palm of his hand. Looking at Carol and then at Laura, he gently placed the stones back in Laura's palm. Reaching inside his shirt neck, he slowly lifted out the pouch that had been there for many years. Lifting it over his head, he then opened the pouch and produced a single golden coin, tarnished but still identifiable. He held the coin in his hand looked at Carol and Laura and said quietly, "I thought this was all that remained of the discovery."

Carol and Laura looked at each other and then realized that the time of sharing the rest of the story had arrived. Carol slowly removed a similar pouch from around her neck and slid into his hand another coin. They were identical.

Rubin looked at the stones in Laura's palm and the two coins in his own. "I never did understand why nothing of the discovery remained. I expected that some remnant of either the box or the documents would remain to testify to its former existence. I actually thought that the eyes," he called them what they really were for the first time, " might be found among the ashes. When they were not, I was relieved but also suspicious. They did not go through the fire, did they?"

Carol looked at Rubin and said, "No, they did not."

He looked at the two coins in his hand and at the small book resting on the table and shook his head in amazement. "It has all been planned and designed to happen." Rubin's comment was both a question and a statement. Carol sat, and her eyes misted over as her mind traveled back to another time, and another life. She began with the day that changed her life.

Carol and Laura sat after Rubin had left the lab and pondered how they could protect the discovery against the very one charged with its protection. They had quickly discounted sharing their suspicions with anyone else. Professional jealousy was widely known and accepted as happening. Despite Laura's own credibility, and the fact that she was Rubin's daughter, did not mean that the authorities would not suspect an internal squabble between two experts within the same family.

Laura also did not want to widen the breach that the discovery had already made between herself and Rubin. Their normal close relationship was obviously under a great strain since the discovery occurred. Laura also knew that her growing understanding and belief challenged Rubin in an area that he was just not ready to be confronted with.

As they stood by the case that housed the top of the box and the stones, both Laura and Carol's eyes were drawn once again to apparent movement within the case. The eyes were crying again.

As Carol watched, Laura's mind was whirling. She turned to Carol and directed, "stay here and watch. I'll be right back" Carol started to ask where she was going, but Laura was already at the door.

Laura raced up the stairs and out the front door. She remembered that her father maintained a small lab, where his curiosity in Chemistry could be stroked. As a tenured full professor and department chair, Rubin's interest in more than just historical discoveries, allowed him to maintain a modest lab at University expense.

Laura entered Rubin's lab and looked for the vials she knew were here. As she searched, she realized that several sheets of notepaper lay on the counter of the largest preparation table in the room. She walked over and recognized her father's scribbling. Picking the sheets up, she began to read. Her heart froze. It was her father's plan.

Having read the list, she heard an internal voice telling her she must get what she came for and leave quickly. She carefully returned the pages to their original order and tried to place them back in the same position that they had been in before her discovery. She found the empty containers she had been seeking as well as the pipettes she would need.

Just as she was preparing to leave, she spied Rubin's overstuffed briefcase, stuck in the corner of the room. Reaching it, she opened it slowly and seeing its contents removed one of the smaller containers and slipped it into her pocket as well. She closed the case, stood, and as quickly as possible, left the room. Her internal voice had reached nearly a panic level by the time she had finally left the room.

She would never know how close she had come to discovery. The door she had passed through had just stopped its motion when Rubin had entered in from another door. Shaking his head at his own stupidity, he had quickly retrieved his notes that were out in the open for any to see. Although no one else was supposed to use this lab, nonetheless, he could not believe that he had left the notes out and visible.

He turned, looked at his briefcase, and seeing nothing out of place, left the room.

Laura's heart was racing. She hurried back to the lab where the discovery was contained and realized that not only was her father planning to do something stupid, he was much further along in his plan than she would have ever realized. If she and Carol had not been in the lab today, it might have already been too late.

Returning to the lab, she found Carol still standing and looking down on the case with the top and the eyes. When Carol saw Laura, she got up and once again asked where she had gone. Carol saw the vials in Laura's hands and the long thin pipettes and began to understand what Laura's intent was, although for what end, Carol was still at a loss to guess.

"When you left the tears stopped," Carol said. Together they walked over to the hood and looked down upon the lid top. No sooner had they looked down, and the earlier phenomenon started again. Carol took the vial and one of the pipettes and passed them through the access panel. She then carefully used the pipette as a slide and placed one end in the vile and another into the liquid pooling on the top. The liquid slowly ran down the pipette and into the vile. As soon as one vial was full, she inserted another and continued the process until the five vials she had taken from Rubin's lab were full. The tears from the stones stopped once the final vial was filled.

She removed the vials carefully and after sealing them removed them to the top of one of the stainless-steel sinks. She then removed the other small vial she had taken from Rubin's briefcase and then told Carol what she had discovered about Rubin's plans.

"What are we going to do?" she asked Laura. At first, Laura only stood still, searching for the answer to that question as well. And then remembering the unusual fact that the tears had not damaged the box top, a plan began to form. Taking Rubin's compound, she placed a small drop on the steel countertop. She and Carol both stood back and watched. It took well over a half an hour, but suddenly the small droplet appeared to dry and just as soon as it had, a bright flash occurred, and a one inch perfectly round hole penetrated the quarter-inch, thick stainless-steel board. Rubin's plan was clear. If a small drop of his compound could do so much damage to a supposedly indestructible steel sink, what would it do to the discovery?

Laura took another small drop of Rubin's compound and placed it on the sink again. Then using the pipette, she placed an even smaller drop from the tear vial. The teardrop no sooner hit the other drop than it flared up and disappeared totally. So too, Rubin's compound had also vanished. In contrast to the hole produced by the former drop, the stainless-steel sink still gleamed with a brightness that spoke of a recent polishing, and not the recent destruction they had both witnessed.

Together they began to talk about how they would accomplish what Rubin desired, without it including the destruction of the discovery. The discovery must disappear and should be made to disappear in the destruction that Rubin was planning. Slowly their plan took form.

After several hours, with many of the details remaining unclear, both women sat back and were silent. The problem was that one of them would always have to be either in the lab or with Rubin. Until they had figured out exactly how to control the timing of the events, they would need to be sure that the events did not start before they were ready. They both suspected that the event timing would be controlled to a great extent by the stability or instability of the compound Rubin was using. Laura had continually swirled the vial containing Rubin's compound. She did not want any of it to solidify; as she suspected that it was when it turned solid that it became truly dangerous. How long did they have?

She felt her internal voice once again tell her that the time was very short. With all the planning yet to be done, Laura felt overwhelmed. It was the first time she had felt out of control. It was also the first time in over twenty years that she felt the need to pray. She stumbled in her mind attempting to form the words, her spirit knowing anguish of words not able to be spoken. She was surprised when she realized that her friend, beside her, was speaking out loud, but not to her. Carol was also praying.

Her prayer, like Laura's, came out in spurts and false starts. The basic components were there, but it was far from orderly or eloquent. In later years Carol would remember this prayer and the amazing fact that everything she had petitioned for had been granted in a very short period.

After the prayer, Laura had ventured over to the hood with the first scroll. She reached in and unrolled another piece, and as she stared at the new passage, she wondered aloud whether she would ever get to finish the translation. Carol walked over to her friend, looked down as well on the writing behind the glass, and said,

"someone will." Laura looked at her and then shook her head and said, "I have the same feeling, but I do not think it will be me." A shudder passed through her and looking at Carol, she said, "Promise me that whatever happens, if at all possible, the translation needs to be completed, so the world can have this testimony and the others."

Laura glanced down again at the document, and then at the tape recorder. A feeling of urgency passed over her, and she reached over and pressed the record button. She needed to read, she wanted to know the rest of this man's story. Something told her she would learn his story, but not from the scroll. Her gift kicked in, and she began again, with the sense of urgency pursuing her.

Her voice returned to the melodic chant that her gift produced when it possessed her. Carol sat and listened. Neither heard the door slightly open, and neither knew that the eyes that looked in upon them were filled with concern, but for a different reason. They were still there and still reading from the discovery. Rubin knew that the compound he had created did have a shelf life, but he also knew he had thrown it together in less than ideal circumstances. When were they going to take a break and go home? He lifted his bag again and started back to his other lab one more time. He needed another plan to get them out of the way. He pondered what that should be.

If he had stayed, he would have heard the next section of the testimony. If it was possible, it was even more amazing than the last section. Laura's voice was captured on the tape, and Carol was the sole beneficiary of the first reading. She heard Laura say:

"We found the teacher, and finally had the opportunity to speak with him about so many of the concerns that were on our hearts. He listened quietly and then spoke to each of us individually. After he was through, he stood and announced that he and his close disciples were going to the other side of the Jordan. Mary, who had sat close to the teacher's feet, could not go. Her place was with her brother and her sister. Jacob and Simon stood to follow him as well. Surprisingly, my sister Naomi stood with Simon. Turning to Sarah, she asked her to let our parents know that she was okay, but that she was going with Simon as well. I looked at Simon, whose admiration of Naomi was obvious. He looked over at me, and his eyes told me that he would make sure that nothing would happen to her.

The teacher was already moving, and the crowd of followers was also. I felt torn between staying and going. I saw the same emotion etched on Mary's face, yet she stood still, and so did I.

Turning to her, I said, "I must return home with Sarah, but perhaps I can see you again, soon?" Mary looked at me and shook her head, saying, "I would like that." And then she turned and departed for her home.

It would be several months before I would see my friends again, or my sister Sarah. The event that brought the teacher back was the last thing I would have expected. But then I would come to learn that his presence often followed the breaking of many hearts. He was, after all, the great physician, who came to heal not only the physically sick but even more so the broken-hearted.

During the preceding months, I spent a great deal of time with my family, except for my brother Simon, whose disdain for my new belief and condition, was beyond my comprehension.

It was during this period that my parents and I, as well as most of my remaining brothers and sisters, made peace with my past. While I waited for word about the teacher, I also now began to draw into my parents' home, many of those who were like my former self. They came to hear my story, and most stayed for a meal, and then some just stayed. My parents had never been overly hospitable before. But something had changed, and suddenly their home took on the feeling of a communal shelter. Even my father stopped his work early every evening so that he could help with all of the work needing to be done to prepare for the usual crowd at dinner.

Jason, Ruth, Naomi, and even Rachel joined in the work. One day my brother Samuel, who had been working more as a partner with my father, exploded when he saw what was happening at the house. He parted ways with my father, and we would not see him or his family again for many years. He moved his family and set up his own business in a town several days journey from Bethany.

Rachel no longer wore the clothes that spoke of her wealth. Instead, she took on the more modest dress of a working merchant's wife. We did not speak about her husband. It turned out that David had left Bethany on a business trip and did not return when originally expected. Rachel was working among our guests when one of the local elders knocked at our door. Seeing the crowd and judging the nature of the visitors, he stood outside until Rachel was called to him. He handed her a scroll and spoke with her briefly. I saw her head bow, and her cheek flush, but then a peace returned to her, and she nodded and returned to her work.

Later that evening, we learned that the elder had delivered a certificate of divorce to her. Her husband David had found a cleric that for the right price had no problem in releasing him from his earlier commitment. Rachel would not speak of the event privately or publicly for many years until a new love had filled her heart and mind.

I had seen Mary several times since my first healing. I found that I desired to be with her more often, but I could tell that she was distracted, and I was uncertain as to why. Finally, I learned the truth. Her brother Lazarus was sick.

He had been growing weaker and frailer ever since the teacher had left the area almost five months ago. Despite all of her and Martha's efforts, they could not determine what was wrong with him. He still managed the shop where he continued his father's trade in olive oil and perfumes but had not been out to find new sources or supplies in almost a year. His failing health had not dampened his humor or his spirit, yet when I finally saw him, I was shocked at how far his condition had deteriorated.

It was when he took to bed for a week and did not get up, that I knew something was terribly wrong and that something needed to be done. It was

I who suggested to Mary and Martha that they should send for the teacher. Surely, if he were able to heal me, this illness would be nothing for him to deal with. Both Mary and Martha spoke with me together about it, and I did not understand their reluctance at first. It was Jason who explained their hesitancy to me.

I had known that there was much discussion about his ministry among the leaders, and I also knew that some were even denied entry into the worship congregation for those who followed him. It was Jason that shared that there was now a large contingent of the leaders and their followers who desired to silence the teacher. Our brother Samuel was among them as well.

Lazarus continued to get worse. Finally, Mary and Martha had decided to send a short note to the teacher. They wrote: "Lord, behold he whom you love is sick" and gave the note to a trusted servant who left immediately to find the teacher. I spent much time with Lazarus. It became obvious that if the teacher did not hurry, he would be too late.

Lazarus died four days before the teacher arrived.

It was early in the morning, and I had slept just outside Lazarus' shop, on the porch that had served as my resting spot for many years. It was Martha that had come and woken me before the sun had risen and brought me back to the house. Entering, I found Mary at the foot of the bed, weeping. "He is gone," is all she could say. And then her tears returned. Her grief tore at my heart as no grief ever had. I looked upon Lazarus and realized that he had shrunk even more. His spirit had left. What remained was so much less than what was there before, even in his former sickly state. It was the first time I had seen what death looked like.

I did not know what to do, but then remembered Lazarus' prayer when his parents had been taken from them so many years before. I spoke the words softly and realized that the words that had brought anger to my heart years before only seemed to deepen the wound in Mary's heart. My heart broke at the thought that I had caused more grief for this woman that I loved.

Martha helped Mary out of the room. My father and my brother Jason found me kneeling at the base of the bed, in grief as well. They had come to see me and had learned of Lazarus death. Together they had helped me to my feet and then listened as I poured out my wonder and grief. "Why had the teacher not come?" I wondered out loud. And then I shared quietly with them, "I had prayed that God would take back the sight the teacher had given me, and instead restore Lazarus to his family. But I still see, and Lazarus is gone." It was my father that displayed how far he had come in the past few months when he reminded me, "Only God has the right to give or take away. Do you accept only what appears as good and reject that which appears as bad even though both come from the same God?"

His rebuke lifted my spirit, and I set out with them to prepare what was needed. Late in the afternoon, my father, Jason, I and two friends, who had been blessed by Lazarus' generosity, carried his body on the makeshift stretcher to the tomb that also contained the remains of his father and mother.

I could not enter the tomb. I stood back with Mary and the large crowd of weeping women and other townsfolks as my father, Jason, and my friends carried Lazarus' body in and laid it to rest in its own place. I could not bring myself to help roll the stone back in place after they had exited the tomb. As I watched the stone roll into place across the mouth of the cave, I held the small gold coin in my hand and remembered both Lazarus' father and the teacher.

I stayed behind after the crowd had started to walk back to the village. I picked up another stone and moved slowly to the tomb and placed my stone upon the door-stone. Mine was the first witness to the goodness of the man that was buried within. I slowly sat on the ground with my back against the door, and I watched as the sun began to disappear behind the hills. I struggled with my own battle for, but a short time, for once again as the sun set, I pondered the glory of the creation, and the fact, that like Lazarus, I too would face death. I wondered what it was like to die, and what happened after the spirit left the body. I also wondered whether, like Lazarus, I would be able to face death with a heart filled with joy. The last time I had sat at this door, my heart had been filled with anger. Today, it was sad but also expectant. The teacher truly had changed me in so many ways.

The teacher arrived three days later. I had been staying as close to Mary's house as possible. The times I had seen her, I realized that she was involved in a mighty struggle with sorrow. Try as I may, I soon knew that I was incapable of supplying the relief she needed. At times I suspect that my presence even added to her grief. I was a visible reminder of what the teacher could do and had not done for her. I found that I was forced into prayer, and I prayed that she would not abandon her strength to let this grief overwhelm her. It was the first time I realized that even Mary, my bastion of strength, bravery, and encouragement, had limits.

The message that the teacher had come reached us as so much information often did. A traveler coming into the village informed a friend, who then informed Martha. Mary was still sequestered inside and did not hear the exchange or witness Martha's rapid departure. I saw Martha leave but chose to stay within earshot of Mary. Just in case she would need me.

About two hours had passed, and suddenly I saw Martha returning up the path. She entered the house, and soon she and Mary followed by the crowd of mourners who had joined Mary in her grief, exited the house. I followed close behind the crowd, desiring to be nearer to Mary but still afraid that my presence would be too much for her to bear.

The teacher and his traveling followers were about a fifteen-minute walk, just outside the village. I saw the teacher rise as he saw the gathering crowd and I watched as Mary fell at his feet. I heard her cry out both in sadness but also with a note of accusation in her words as she said: "Lord if you had been here, my brother would not have died!"

Along with her words came the weeping of so many of Lazarus's friends and others who loved Mary as well. The tears fell freely from my eyes as well. I heard the teacher's voice, filled with emotion and sadness, and remembered another time when I heard his voice in a similar state. He spoke saying, "Where have you laid him?" To that, a number of people pointed the way and said: "Lord, come and see." Then for the first time, I saw his tears. He wept openly, but I suddenly realized his grief was deeper than any of those around him. His grief would have shaken the ground I stood on; I believe if he had allowed it. Suddenly I was aware that in my grief was still a measure of selfishness, but in his was none.

It was then I heard some of the comments of some of the others who had come with the crowd. I heard some remarking on his tears "See how he loved him", and then still others having have seen me, and knowing my story, mocked him with the question that still tore at my heart "Could not this man, who opened the eyes of the blind man, have kept this man also from dying?" Hearing the tone of their question, I was ashamed of my earlier doubt. Nothing the teacher had done deserved such mocking.

I prayed silently, "Lord, forgive my doubt." Yet even as I prayed, I still wondered why he had blessed me with my sight, and yet had chosen not to be present to prevent Lazarus' death.

We reached the tomb after a short walk. The stone blocking the entrance was now covered with the small stones, placed there by others, who had been touched by Lazarus's life.

It was then that the teacher said something that startled everyone. I heard him say, "Remove the stone." The entire crowd gasped. To be exposed to such a great uncleanness was beyond any of our understanding. In our culture, there is nothing considered more unclean than a dead body. Plus, this was a dead body that was already well into decomposition. I heard Martha speak up, saying the words the rest of us could but think: "Lord, by this time, there will be a stench, for he has been dead four days!"

The teacher looked at Martha with eyes full of compassion. His eyes communicated so much more than even his words did. He said to her, "Did I not tell you that if you believe, you will see the glory of God?" It would be only later that I would hear of the earlier discussion Martha had with the teacher before she came to get Mary.

I moved forward to do as he had requested. I removed the stones of witness that had been placed on top of the stone. Together with several other men from the village, I helped push the stone back. Mary was right, there was a stench. The odor of decaying flesh is one never forgotten. I could not imagine what the teacher intended. Two of the other men were already pale and left the door area quickly. There was no denying the presence of death here.

I looked at the teacher, concerned. But his eyes were elsewhere. He was looking up, but his voice was strong, and firm and he was speaking to someone, that try as I might, I could not see. But I heard the teacher's words clearly, "Father" the teacher began " I thank You that You have heard Me. I knew that You always hear Me; but because of the people standing around, I said it, so that they may believe that You sent Me." He was praying a prayer that indicated that something had already occurred. His verbal prayer had been proceeded by a nonverbal prayer, and he was giving thanks for the answer to his first petition.

As he finished these words, a breeze swept around us, and suddenly I realized that the breeze was blowing out from the tomb. The air that was once rancid, suddenly had a sweetness to it, like the air after a recent rain shower. The wind continued to blow, and then I heard the teacher again as he said: "Lazarus, come forth."

How can I describe my heart? It leaped. For even before I saw the man, I knew what was happening. He who made eyes from clay was the same one, who made the whole man from the dust of the ground. I knew now that this teacher was no ordinary man. He was the savior and something even more. I watched as Lazarus emerged from the tomb, still wrapped in the grave shroud, I had helped with my own hands to wrap him in. The shroud bore the marks of the decomposition that had started, but there was no longer the odor of death on the shroud.

I heard the teacher's command, "Unbind him, and let him go." I helped release Lazarus, who looked upon me with a greatly puzzled look, as I removed the face cloth. His face spoke of bewilderment. Mine spoke of incredible joy. I stood back as both Mary and Martha rushed to their brother and flung their arms around him. He looked at me over their embrace, and his eyes spoke his question, "What is all the fuss about?" And yet, as he began to understand where he stood, suddenly I saw his face turn white. He looked up, saw the teacher, and understood. He turned slightly to look at the grave, looked again at me, and I nodded. It was then that his knees buckled a little, but his sisters were supporting him, and he did not fall.

The crowd that had followed Mary and Martha now were beside themselves. The commotion was unlike anything I had ever heard or seen up to that day. Some were throwing dust into the air, in distress, others were shouting Hosanna and praising God. Still, others were already racing away, back to the village, to tell what they had seen.

Lazarus walked slowly past me, and over to the Lord. What they said to one another is in Lazarus' testimony and not for me to share. I can tell you that the Lord placed his hands-on Lazarus' shoulders, and then they embraced one another. Lazarus and the teacher began the walk back to the village. Not only was Lazarus not dead, his current condition was nothing like his condition when he had been sick. He walked beside the teacher, lost in conversation, while both Mary and Martha clung to his side as well. I followed at a distance.

I walked that path where I had carried an empty dead shell, but four days ago, and now followed the living man back from the tomb. I had known since I had received my sight, that nothing was ever going to be the same. My heart now exploded in joy, and for the first time in my memory I sang quietly at first but then with a gusto that spoke to all around, I did not care what they thought, nothing would ever be the same. I do not know where the words came from, but I knew what I wanted to say, the words were simple,

"He has conquered death, he has set the prisoner free, Hosanna to the Son of David, Hosanna and Blessed Is He." I was told later by others, that Mary turned and looked at me, a smile upon her face. I did not see her look as I was lost in ecstasy.

As we entered the village, I did not follow the teacher back to Lazarus' home. Instead, I turned off and ran all the way to my parents' home. Bursting in the door, I found Simon and Naomi already there sitting with my parents. They had not stayed with the teacher when he had arrived at the village but had instead returned to my parents' home, to fill them in on everything that had been happening. It would be later that I would discover that Simon had also come to my father to ask permission to marry my sister.

While normally a go-between would have arranged this, these were strange times. Simon's father no longer lived close to the village, and from what Simon said, he had yet to reconcile with his father for having abandoned him in his former condition. Both my father and mother were more than delighted with this turn of events. They already knew how good a person Simon was. It was also clear that Naomi was in love and not to be denied.

Rachel, Jason, and Ruth were there as well. The look on my face caused their discussion to stop, and I poured out the news. Compared to my healing, the news I bore left that event as minor. At first, they could not understand my words, and when they did, shock was the first response. It was my father again who led, saying, "Let us go see this mighty thing that has been done." With that, they all stood, and I led the way out the door.

The cassette clicked off, and Laura looked up from the manuscript. She was unaware of the passage of time. This time instead of feeling worn out by her gift, Carol saw both tears and joy in Laura's eyes. "It is true," Laura said. Carol knew that this day would be like no other in their lifetimes, for on the same day, both Laura and Carol, came to faith in the teacher. The evidence had overwhelmed them.

They both also knew that the evidence had always been there for them to acknowledge. The testimony had only caused them to finally acknowledge the evidence they had ignored. Like Lazarus and the Lord, the two friends embraced and wept for joy. Just as suddenly, what needed to be done was finally clear to both. What had been overwhelming just a few hours ago, now appeared possible, for now, they no longer were relying on their own strength or timing.

17

NOT BY POWER OR BY MIGHT

Carol stopped her explanation, but Rubin knew there was much more. Once again, he looked at his newest daughter and at the stones her palm supported. He looked into her eyes and saw the glint of fire from the stones reflected within them. Rubin knew now that the rest of their story was important but that the truly significant story lay embedded and preserved in the book that lay open on the table.

As he pondered, this, Laura moved to the recorder, slipped the stones back into their pouch, and produced yet another tape. This tape she slid into the recorder and pressed the button. The story continued to unfold:

"A few weeks later, Lazarus and his family decided to give a meal in honor of the teacher. Many were invited, and I was as well. For the first time, I got to experience what a celebration meal truly was like. It was but six days before the time of the great Passover feast would be celebrated. Lazarus invited everyone he could think of.

Among the crowd were all the teacher's own close followers. The teacher had appointed twelve to walk with him at all times. I was happy for them, for they truly were blessed. At first, I even had another pang of envy, but later as I understood the great cost of that calling, I also better appreciated my own gifts and their price. It has always struck me as telling that I would compare so often my gifts with others. I now understand my nature and the effect of my sin that would cause me to ever feel anything but gratefulness for my own gifts and my own calling. I have struggled my whole life with gratefulness and even today still must put down the pangs of envy. I often wonder what there is that anyone else might have that is worth the price of envy.

The day of the meal approached quickly, and both Mary and Martha were extremely busy with the preparations. My family and I helped draw the water, set the tables, and organize the food. My sister Rachel was particularly helpful. Although she no longer had the status of a rich person, she understood how the meal should be arranged having directed many such meals before, when married to David.

As the meal started, it found the teacher reclining next to Lazarus, in the place of honor. Beside him were his disciples and then many of the leading men of our community and even some from the great city. I found a spot removed from the center of activity but from where I had both a good view and an even better listening post to all that was occurring.

I overheard the discussion by several from the great city, who while invited were obviously not pleased by all that was occurring. It was amazing to me as I heard one speak of the plans of the leaders not only to do away with the teacher but also with Lazarus. I could not understand why anyone would want to destroy the evidence that pointed clearly to who this teacher was. What was there to fear? How could anything but joy be the result of seeing and speaking with Lazarus? Why did they fear the teacher? What had he ever done but good?

The meal was continuing nicely, with much talk and laughter when Mary entered. While there were other women present, most were acting as servers, and none were a part of the meal. The tradition was simple; this was a man's affair. Mary stole quickly to the Lord with a vial in her hand. I recognized it as one of the perfume vials that my father often made for those who could afford such extravagance. It held enough perfume to last most people for many years.

She approached the teacher, and a quiet hush fell on the immediate group who were aware of her presence. Mary knelt at the teacher's feet, opened the vial, and poured out the contents on the teacher's feet. The fragrance filled the room quickly. I gasped. The perfume was spikenard. It was one of the costliest perfumes known. Even for Mary and her family, this was a tremendous expense. But just as I gasped, I also understood. What was of more value than her brother. My heart filled with joy because she had judged correctly. What expense was too great to give for such a gift and for such a teacher. My surprise turned to praise for Mary. Then she surprised everyone again, letting loose her long main mane of dark hair, and then using it she began both to wipe and kiss the feet of the teacher.

My heart jumped. Once again, a voice I did not know but had heard often said, "see, she loves him." For the first time, I understood this voice that desired to replace my joy with envy, and maybe even something worse. I shook my head silently and said to the voice within, "Go Away! She loves him, and so do I." In that instant, I gave up any claim on her and was filled with joy and pride for her that I cannot explain. My desire and hope were still there, but they no longer competed with either envy or jealousy. She had every right to love the teacher. Who could but love him? I wondered to myself.

It was then that I heard the voice of one of the twelve. His words were like a branding iron, destroying the earlier peace and joy that had swelled from my heart. His words were mirrored in the opinion of others around the table as well. As he spoke, I saw the heads bobbing in agreement. He said,

"Why was this ointment not sold for three hundred denarii and given to poor people?" His question was a hot poker, proclaiming both the great waste that had occurred and the tremendous good that could have been done.

Once again, my heart pounded. The words caught in my throat. How could he say such a thing? Was it not Mary's money? Did she not have the right to do with it what she might want? Did he not understand her joy over having her brother back? Yet, he was one of the twelve, one who knew the teacher better than either I or Mary. Was Mary wrong? Had I been wrong in my pride for her action?

Then I heard the teacher and his rebuke of his disciple. His words were spoken without anger or sarcasm but were filled with deep sadness. He had turned to look at the disciple who had issued the challenge, and he said: "Leave her alone." Turning he had placed his hands upon Mary's bowed head, he raised her eyes to meet his and continued saying, "She has done this to prepare me for the day of my burial." Resting his hand upon her raised head, I understood the position of benediction. He was blessing both her activity and her for having performed it. Then he looked around at those around him and finished saying, "The poor you will always have, but you will not always have me."

It would only be later that I would understand why his voice had such a sound of sadness. It was not only the fact of his death but the role the challenging disciple would have in that death. I often have wondered if this rebuke was not the lighting of the wick in the disciples' life that would lead to his betrayal.

Mary stood slowly, still gazing at the teacher and then turned and left the room. I did not hear or see the rest of the meal, as I followed her out of the room. I found her with her sister Martha weeping bitterly upon Martha's shoulder. I did not understand. Had not the teacher vindicated *her action? Why then was she weeping? Martha saw me, and in her eyes, I saw her beckoning me to come over. I could tell that Martha was confused by her sisters' actions. She had not heard the teacher, having been busy with the final aspect of the meal. She had not been told of either Mary's action or the teachers' response.*

I approached Mary, not knowing what to say. I finally asked, "Why do you cry, Mary?" She turned her streaked face to me and seeing my eyes both filled with hope and yet worry; she removed her arms from Martha and threw them around me continuing to weep.

Through her sobs, I heard her exclaim, "He is going to die." For the first time, his words took on meaning for me. I understood her sorrow and her tears. My arms encircled this woman I loved, and now the full impact of both her sorrow and the teacher's words flooded my soul, and the tears leaked freely from my eyes as well. We stood together weeping while Martha looked on.

After a period, her sobbing stopped, and then she realized that my arms were around her. I expected her to withdraw, now that her sadness was less, but instead, she laid her head upon my shoulder and gripped me all the tighter. I was confused. After what I had seen earlier, I expected that she would always be a good friend to me, but that was all. The aroma of the perfume still scented her hair and her hands.

Her embrace now spoke of something more. Something I had only dreamed of but never expected. I slowly disentangled and slowly held her at arm's length. I think she saw the confusion mingled with hope in my eyes. For the first time, I saw a small smile creep across her face in response to the confusion in mine. She forced my arms down and then wrapped hers around me again.

Her words made my knees weak, and I looked for a place to sit down. She said: "I have loved you since that first time you stood up to the bullies that tormented the beggars so many years ago. I have waited so long to know whether you could ever love me in return."

The tears that leaked from my eyes now were hot with wonder and joy. She had loved me when I was ugly when I was so self-absorbed that she could not breakthrough. The words I thought she had meant for another; she had meant for me. That which I had only dreamed of was now real. We spent the rest of the evening and night talking.

The pieces of my life were falling into place. I shared my dreams and my hope, watching her smile broaden and break forth like the sun. I questioned her in wonder, as to what it was that would have caused her to ever even consider the likes of me. Her words were ones of infinite wisdom, she said: "I do not think that we control who we fall in love with, only how that love will be displayed and worked out." Together we spoke of our failings and our feelings. Together we shared our worries and our fears. Our discussion finally turned to the teacher.

Her love for the teacher was the same as mine, one of a grateful servant and friend. She believed that the love she felt for me reflected the love of the teacher for us. We continued speaking about the teacher and finally returned to the fears that had filled her heart after the events of the evening before. Once again, she said, "I do not think the teacher will be with us much longer." I shared with her what I had overheard at the meal the evening before as well.

We saw the teacher emerge from the house, just as the sun broke behind the hill upon which the great city sat. We saw his smile as he inclined his head and motioned that we stay where we were. He slipped around the corner of the house, away from view. We knew that he had gone to pray, as was his pattern.

Together we were lost in thought and prayer as the sun rose in the morning. Neither of us had slept, neither of us was tired. We watched the sun come up outside her home, still lost in the wonder of the last few months. We spoke in hushed tones now, both as we wondered what the next few days would bring. We knew that something was about to happen.

An hour after the teacher emerged, Mary's brother joined us. I sheepishly released her hand as he approached my mind racing of how to ask what I was about to ask of Lazarus. He looked at his sister and then at me. Once again, I was to be surprised. "Finally!" he exclaimed. "You have finally told him?", he asked his sister. Mary nodded in the affirmative. "Well, what did he say?", he asked Mary but looked at me. I asked my own question, now quite amazed that he knew what I had been oblivious of. "You mean you have known all along? "Lazarus smile was contagious. "She has loved you for so long I cannot remember a time she has not been in love with you!", was his reply. "Well?" he asked, still looking at me. The fact that he did not know filled me with wonder. I thought most of my life that my feelings for Mary had been all too painfully obvious.

I felt myself straightening up, and then I asked my question. His answer was a bear hug and a joyful laugh. I once again took Mary's hand, now that I had permission. Mary was smiling, and I was beaming.

I wanted to run home, to tell everyone the news but other events would delay this happy announcement. The teacher had returned and still smiling at us; he had drawn Lazarus away. They stood out of earshot, deep in discussion. I saw Lazarus nod and then watched as the teacher's other disciples emerged from the house. I heard Lazarus' farewell and watched as the teacher and the disciples began their trek towards the great city. I looked at Mary, and we both began to follow, but Lazarus intercepted us both. He said, "We need to stay here."

Lazarus shared his conversation, and we understood. We later would hear of the triumphal entry the teacher made into the great city and the joy of the people and the disciples that followed him. It was a gathering fit for a *coronation. In my mind's eye, I still hear the joyful voices and the praises that were uttered that day. Those same voices would in, but a few days be filled with anger and curses."*

The tape clicked off, and Rubin's eyes met Carol's and then Laura's. His eyes were lit with understanding. The voice on the tape was not his first daughters' but the Laura that stood before him. This part of the story he had never heard before. He also understood that his first daughter also had never had the chance to read this part either. He looked at Carol, again and with dawning appreciation saying, "The testimonies were not destroyed! You have them!" Laura ejected the tape, and Carol nodded.

She picked up the story where she had left off.

She spoke of the strange occurrence of the tears and of Laura's discovery of her father's plans. Rubin's eyes went wide when he realized that he had been found out so many years before.

"Laura and I spoke for hours as to what to do, and we were at a loss until suddenly, we were swept into prayer and then found ourselves strangely at peace with what we must do. We knew you meant to destroy the discovery, and we knew from your papers that you intended to use the hoods in the lab to disperse the chemical as an aerosol spray that would dry and then combust. We had seen the destructive nature of the chemical after Laura had taken a sample from your briefcase in the lab." Once again, Rubin's eyes lit up as another piece fell into place. The missing vial was now explained. He had searched in vain and had worried endlessly as to what had happened to the vial. Now he knew.

His mind returned to the past and to the events of that fateful day.

18

A Plan Foiled with Success

Rubin had returned to his lab, placing once again his case by the wall. He returned to his office and was racking his brain as to how to get Carol and Laura out of the lab. He was at the moment of despair when both Carol and Laura had appeared in his office. Both seemed strangely subdued but announced to Rubin that they were done for the day and were going to grab a bite to eat. They inquired, "do you want to come along?" Rubin did not know that they had expected his answer, "No, I still have a few things to get done here, perhaps later?"

Laura and Carol both had agreed that they were too tired to do anything more and were heading back to Laura's flat after they had grabbed some food. They said that they would both be back on Monday, having decided to take a day off from their labors. Rubin breathed a great relief as they left. Laura had turned back briefly, almost catching Rubin in a moment of pure joy, and hugged him and said, "I love you, dad." With that, she was gone, as was Carol. It would be the last words he would ever hear from Laura.

Rubin waited until he saw Laura's car pull out of the lot and disappear around the curve away from his office, before he would venture out again. Picking up his case, he once more made his way back to the other lab and the testimonies that lay in wait for him.

The lab lights were still on, but the room was deserted. The tape recorder was gone from its stand, and Rubin figured that Laura or Carol must have removed it when they left. No matter he thought, for after the fire, all that would remain were the pictures in the vault and the tapes that Laura and Carol had made. These would be of no issue once the destruction of the originals was complete.

He went about the task immediately. Into each hood, he placed a vial that he then opened. The circulating air would start the drying process. Once the crystals began to form it would only take one to shake loose and fall and the conflagration would begin. He had placed a vial in each hood where the different testimonies lay. He approached the final hood, the one with the lid and the eyes, and suddenly realized he was short one vial. He looked through his briefcase again and searched each of the hoods thinking that he may have accidentally placed an extra in one of the hoods. He looked at his watch and realized he did not have time to return to the lab to either search for the missing vial or to create another.

Looking around the room, he saw a small dish on one of the tables. Taking it, he went to one of the hoods and gently spilled some of the contents of one of the vials into the dish. He then removed the dish and carefully moved it to the hood with the box top. As he placed the dish in that hood, he looked for the last time at the stones in the lid. They were just stones. For a short moment, he wondered about what he was doing. Did he really want to destroy these testimonies? Then he looked at the stones again and watched as they suddenly appeared to glow. He had his answer as fear crept up his spine. The sooner, the better was the voice that echoed in his head.

He turned to leave and picked up his briefcase. It was as he turned that he saw the pouch that contained the coin on the small tray in the last hood. He stopped briefly, debated, and he reached in and took the pouch. He left the lab, turned out the lights, and locked the door. He had about an hour, maybe less, before it would start. He wanted to be far away before it began, preferably in his favorite pub, drinking his favorite ale, among people who would vouch for his time this day.

He jumped in his car, placing the now empty briefcase on the seat. He thought about the missing vial and ran again to his other lab, briefly surveying the area for it. It was nowhere to be found. Wherever it was, Rubin knew that it would create a horrendous fire when it finally began to dry. It would raise issues, but he would be safely away. No one knew of his abilities or knowledge related to this compound. Even the invoices for the different chemicals were gone. Besides they had been purchased over many years. It had only been in a short span of time that he had realized that he had everything he needed to make the compound.

Laura and Carol watched as Rubin's car raced out of the campus. They had strategically placed the car so that they would see his departure, but he would never see them watching. As soon as it was obvious that he was gone and not coming back, they returned to the lab, pulling the car as close as possible to the entrance of the lab.

Then began the process of removing from the lab the testimonies. Before they had entered the lab, they had checked the surveillance room to be sure that Rubin had shut off the automatic taping of the activities going on in the lab. He had. They then moved quickly to the lab and began to remove from each hood the various scrolls and other items. These they lugged up the stairs and to the car where they were carefully placed in the trunk and on the back seat of the car. The campus was strangely quiet as they worked. Their great fear was that someone would see their activity. Throughout it all, no one had approached them or even taken notice of what was happening.

Finally, they were done. It was Carol that noticed that the coin was gone, but so was their time. Laura had placed in each hood next to her fathers' compound a vial with the tears as well. She did not know for sure what this would do, but she felt that this is what she needed to do. She still had one small vial left that she placed back in her purse as she and Carol left the building. She did not know how much time they had left.

Both Carol and Laura had decided that Carol's flat was the best place for testimonies for the time being. After the fire, they had reasoned that they would again make further plans on what was to happen next. Like Rubin before them, they exited the Campus as rapidly as possible and made their way for Carol's flat.

When they reached Carol's flat, they turned on the radio, listening for the first reports of what they were sure was about to happen. Carol's flat was on a level with the parking deck for the flat. It enabled them to transport the cargo without anyone seeing what they were doing. By six o'clock, the transfer was complete, and still, no news was forthcoming about the university. Both were exhausted with the day's events taking their toll.

Laura decided that she should drive back to her own residence. After all, this is what she had told her father she was going to do. It would be easy enough to explain that Carol had decided to go home as well.

She also wanted to be sure that all suspicions were diverted elsewhere. Carol agreed that they would meet the next morning to make the next plans. Before she left, Laura shared her thoughts related to

Carol's pregnancy. Carol had almost forgotten that problem midst all the other items demanding attention. Then as with some foreboding Laura had once again asked for assurance that Carol would protect the testimonies if anything were to happen to herself. After Laura left, Carol fell into a deep sleep, Laura's parting words still ringing in her mind. Carol would never know for sure what had happened at Laura's. What she did remember later was the dream, or at least she thought it had been a dream.

In the dream, she had seen Laura arrive home and lay her purse down. Laura had gone to take a shower. It was during the shower, that Laura had suddenly remembered something, and wrapping a towel around her left the shower and ran to her purse. She opened her purse and saw two vials still within. One was the tears, the other, the small sample of Rubin's compound. As she looked on, she saw the crystals in Rubin's compound begin to settle out, and then the brilliant flash of light followed by a second even more brilliant flash.

At that same moment two hours away, another twin set of flashes lit up the campus that had housed Rubin's lab. The building was almost instantly reduced to a wall of flames as the temperature leaped to thousands of degrees. Even the brick that comprised the building's exterior walls evaporated midst the heat. The old granite building that had been the labs neighbor received a flash burn that etched the picture of the former lab building on its side.

Laura's building faired a little better. One of her neighbors saw the flash through the window and had raced across the lot to find Laura lying on the grass outside the window she had been in front of. The blast had hurled her through the window. The tears had evaporated the compound, and nothing would remain to speak of the compound that started the fire. But the damage to Laura was done. The compound was gone, but the burn was present. Nothing Rubin's friend, Louis, could do would change the events that were unfolding.

Laura watched from a distance as medical help arrived and started their futile efforts to save her. She watched as her father arrived at the hospital, having received the twin reports of the fire at the university and the damage to his daughter. He had been at the pub where he had gone for an alibi and for forgetfulness. She watched as her friend Carol had arrived and held her hand gently and whispered the promises that they had made to each other related to the testimonies.

She had seen the tears of both her father and her friend. And she had watched with detachment as Louis' team had fought to save her life. As her life slipped away, she had turned to the voice, and she saw the teacher. His hands still bore the scars of ancient wounds, and she wondered if her face would bear the scars she had last seen as well. But then she realized that was not the case, for only he needed to bear such scars. In joy, she held this hand that had touched her life so recently. Then she saw her mother. Beside her mother, she saw her grandfather, and then beside him, she saw another, one with shining green emerald eyes. He was smiling as was a great host of others, all welcoming her home.

19
STARTING OVER

Rubin listened to Carol as his own mind replayed the events as he remembered them. He thought of his efforts to destroy the testimonies and now was strangely relieved that he had failed. The old sadness related to his daughter's death began to creep back into his mind, but his new daughter's voice drove the cloud back.

"Mom," she said, "it is getting late." Her words snapped Rubin back to the present. Looking at the table, he suddenly realized that the lunch he had prepared for himself still sat on the table. Four hours had passed by. Where he had earlier been hungry, all thoughts of food had departed when Carol and Laura had arrived.

He suddenly realized that he had offered his guests neither drink nor food. He stood up, saying, "I am so sorry. I have some food here; I guess I have completely lost my bearings. You have been the first visitors I have had in a long time."

Standing, he moved over to the kitchen, remembering as he moved his earlier review of the meager provisions in the refrigerator. Before he could get there, Carol said: "There is no need." Laura continued, "Do you want me to drive back home and come back and pick you up in the morning? I know that you have a lot of catching up to do with him. Rubin understood why she could not bring herself to call him either father or dad yet.

Carol looked at Rubin and thought. Finally, she turned to her daughter and said, "No, I am going with you." To Rubin, she said, "We have an extra bedroom at home, would you like to come back with us? We can catch a bite to eat on the way, and we will bring you back in the morning." Carol looked at Laura, and Laura nodded approval for the offer.

Rubin did not ponder his answer at all. He shook his head, enthusiastically. There was so much more he wanted to ask and to know. He also knew that he wanted to look again upon the discovery that had so altered his life. He went to gather his coat. He found it behind the door underneath Carol's own coat. It was the shabby condition of his coat compared to Carol's that started his hesitation. He held her coat and saw compared to its rich brown color and soft texture his was drab.

He looked down at his trousers and for the first time, realized that his coat was not the only part of his wardrobe that was dingy compared to his guests own attire. His mind whirled. He asked himself the question that had been lurking just below the surface: "Is it too late for me?" Another voice, familiar but somewhat faded from just several days ago leaped alive. It argued with his newest desire telling him both that he was old and decrepit. It answered saying: "Yes, yes, you know it is too late for you."

He was about to turn and announce his change of mind when Laura laid her hand on his shoulder. He turned to look at her. It was the first time he really had seen her eyes and realized that unlike her mother, the blue was more light green. Her eyes suddenly sparkled in intensity and Rubin heard the internal voice cry out in pain, and then it was gone.

The doubt and worry that was flooding over him was obvious to her. She reached out for his hand and then placed a small pouch in his hand. It was the pouch with the coin in it. Her eyes never left his, and she said: "Remember," and then she added, "It will be okay." Her eyes once again flamed with that strange sparkle and the voice that had driven Rubin close to despair did not answer.

He handed Laura her coat and stepped back to give Carol hers. He then put his own on and slipped into the small hall washroom where he pocketed his toothbrush and a disposable razor. He thought only briefly about his clothes again, but a new voice told him it did not matter. He smiled, knowing that he was so accustomed to wearing the same clothes he did not even need to give it a second thought.

He considered what else to bring, and finally just walked over to the table and picked up both the small pamphlet and the other book that lay there. These too, he slid into his coat pocket. He looked at the tapes spread on the table and once again decided to leave them where they were. He looked at his sandwich and taking hold of it placed it in a plastic bag and then placed it in the refrigerator. Looking at Carol and Laura, he smiled and said, "I am ready."

Feeling the youngest he had in many years, he followed Carol and Laura out, turned and locked his door, and continued following them to Carol's car. Carol's car was no longer the small white Saab he had remembered but was now a mid-sized Toyota wagon. Laura slipped into the back seat while he held the door for Carol and then walked around the other side, jumping into the passenger side seat. They fell back into conversation as they started the trip. He realized he knew little about what had happened to Carol and knew nothing about

Laura. The testimonies were forgotten, and for the next six hours, Carol shared what had happened to her since she had left Rubin some twenty years earlier.

They had stopped a few hours into their drive at one of the few old pubs that had not been replaced by the rash of new fast-food restaurants. Over dinner, Carol had continued her story, and from time to time, Laura would add a salient part related to her own life. Rubin discovered that Carol was still teaching at a university where she had been since leaving Rubin. Rubin asked many questions but finally got to the one that had been bothering him since he had realized that he had a daughter he did not know. He asked quietly during one lull, "Why did you not tell me about Laura?" To this Carol had bowed her head but then looked up at him and said equally as softly,

"Because you would not have wanted her, and you would have tried to keep her from the truth. I could not let that happen." He nodded both his understanding and agreement with her observation.

He then asked two questions intertwined that had also been bothering him, "Why did you come back now, how did you know? "To this, both Carol and Laura shared similar experiences the day before. Both sensed that not only had the barrier preventing them from returning been removed. Now both were filled with an urgency requiring action. The sensation became overwhelming. Rubin sat in awe. He understood that forces were at work that he had long held in disdain. He no longer could deny what he knew to be true. Strangely both a sense of joy and a sense of peace flooded his mind and soul.

The rest of their trip continued in discussion. Rubin found himself drawn more and more to Laura and her story. At one point, he had turned almost completely around and was looking and listening to Laura's story. Carol had shared her first understanding of the unique gift that both her friend and now her daughter shared. Laura had listened quietly as her mother described the early evidence of the gift and her surprise as her own daughter began to excel in the work that her friend had left for them. Rubin looked at Laura. He once again saw the strange green flash within her eyes. He blurted out, not able to help himself his observation that left both Laura and Carol strangely silent. "Your eyes, they sparkle at times. They are truly beautiful. "The quiet in the car made Rubin for the first time uncomfortable. Carol pulled the car over to the side of the road, and Rubin understood that there was a part of the story that demanded Carol's full attention.

Carol looked at Laura, who silently nodded her head, asking her mother to tell this part of the story. Carol looked at Rubin and then, with a faltering voice began. "Rubin, when Laura was born, she was born blind." For thirty minutes, Carol shared the portion of Laura's life that only she could remember. Carol told Rubin of the normal delivery and the first indication of problems related to Laura's eyesight. As was normal in most deliveries the nurse applied a solution of silver nitrate to her eyes to destroy any of the bacteria that remained from the birth process. It was during that first application and examination that the nurse had called the doctor over to examine her eyes.

As they looked at Laura's eyes, it was obvious to both that something was wrong with the iris of her eyes. It would not be for several days before the doctors would confirm their fears to Carol. They had first told Carol they needed to keep Laura for an extra day based on some minor complications that had arisen. Carol remembered her fear and her questions, but they assured her that it was nothing life-threatening and that they just wanted to be sure that everything was okay before they sent her home with Carol. Three days after the birth, the nurse had brought Laura to Carol saying it was okay for her to take her home. It was also when they had finally told her the truth.

Laura's condition was rare. The iris is a very complex organization of specialized nerves and cells. For whatever reason, something had gone wrong in their formation, and Laura's eyes, while fully formed, lacked several key components that were required for sight. Laura, they informed Carol, would never see.

Carol had taken her six-month leave of absence granted to her by the school for the delivery. Laura had developed normally during those months and by the end of the first month was already tracking her mothers' movements based on the location of her voice. Carol noted that by the time that Laura was three months old, she would respond to her mothers' voice with the same smile that so many normal children would also give. But unlike most normal children, it never made any difference to Laura whether it was dark or light. She also noted that Laura would track her motions using her hearing, and that would often require her turning her head, where a normal child would have just moved her eyes.

Probably the biggest problem for Carol was that Laura's lack of sight also meant that Laura had no understanding of night or day. It took Carol almost the entire six months to finally get Laura in the habit of sleeping at night.

Carol had spent many hours anguishing over what to do with Laura for the long term. During the entire period that Carol was off, the testimonies laid untouched and unnoticed. Carol had not had time to consider them. Laura had needed every moment of Carol's attention. They remained undisturbed in the extra room where Carol had placed them after her move to the university area. As Carol's six months ended, she knew that she was going to need to make provisions for Laura, so she could return to her work. Carol had spoken with many different social agencies trying to scope out what she could do. Finally, she had decided to look for a nanny that could stay with Laura while she worked.

It was during her anguish that Carol also found herself drawn back to prayer. Carol remarked to Rubin how strange it was to her now, that it had taken her so long to finally draw on this activity for guidance and hope. She shared that it was only when she had struggled with her friend Laura as to what to do with the testimonies, and then when her friend lay dying in the hospital that she had been drawn as fervently to prayer. Rubin only smiled, realizing that in his former condition, his response to Carol's comment would have been completely different than it was now.

During this same period, Carol found and joined a small church congregation in the area where she lived. Like so many of these congregations, this one had few men, and a smattering of middle age and older women and only the children brought by the women. The pastor name was Charles Brown, and his wife was Cindy. Both he and his wife had taken a special interest in Carol and her little child. They had never had any children of their own. Carol had explained her situation one day in the church, hoping that perhaps someone in the church might need some additional money and would be willing to care for someone with Laura's special needs. "I do not have much, but I will pay everything I can," Carol had said. Not knowing what to expect from her plea, Carol found Cindy waiting for her the next Sunday after church.

Cindy had invited Carol over for lunch. The pastor and Cindy greeted her warmly as they received her into their modest home. Unlike many other pastors, their house was not part of the church property. In fact, given their small congregation, both had found it necessary to work other jobs whenever possible. Cindy was interested in providing the care for Laura while Carol worked. It was a heavy load removed from Carol's heart.

Charles and Cindy became the grandparents Laura would never know. Carol dropped Laura off to Cindy in the morning and usually was able to pick her up in the early afternoon. Carol made sure that the classes that she taught were never scheduled for the late afternoon. She also refused any additional assignments that might interfere with the schedule that she had worked out for Laura.

One afternoon she had arrived at the pastor's home and found Laura, now two, sitting next to Charles as he worked on his sermon. He was talking to her, much as she remembered her friend Laura had told her about her grandfather speaking to her. She was startled at the similarity although she knew that unlike her namesake, her Laura was not seeing what the pastor was pointing to.

Carol shared, that like the writer of the first testimony, Laura too had learned her way around both the pastor's home as well as their own small flat. It was when Laura was two that Carol also started the laborious task of finishing the translation that her friend had been unable to complete. She had not mentioned the testimonies to anyone. They were a secret and a burden Carol was convinced she must bear alone.

Carol had equipped herself with the best reference materials she could find, using up much of her already meager remaining savings. Normally at night, after both Laura was down for sleep and Carol's schoolwork was complete, she would open the additional room and spend several hours pouring over the first manuscript that her friend had only three quarters finished. Carol had become convinced that it would take her the rest of her own life just to finish the first scroll, much less do anything on the other testimonies that still lay unopened. There were times that depression started to set in, but Carol remembered her friend and her promise and continued.

During this time, the strange occurrences that had accompanied the original finding and readings had disappeared. No further tears ever appeared from the stones on the lid. Every evening before Carol would go to bed, she would carefully lock the door to the room before retiring to her own bed. The pattern of Carol's life took hold, and the years began to slip by.

Like other children her age, Laura had begun to speak as well. Although she was slightly slower in identifying items with the words that described them, by the time she was three, she already had amassed a considerable vocabulary. Also, her ability in moving around the two homes that were her fence, increased every day, as did her curiosity. It was when she was four, that she became aware of the locked room in her home. It was this room that her mother would disappear into many evenings after she had gone to bed.

One evening, after Carol thought Laura was asleep, and as she worked with the first testimony, she discovered Laura standing next to her elbow in the secret room. Carol had left the door slightly ajar and had not thought anything about it. Somehow, Laura managed to find her mother in the room, without producing any noise to alert Carol of her transit through the room. Carol was so intent on the translation, which for her was a word-by-word affair, that she was unaware of Laura's presence.

Her heart had jumped when she turned, and her elbow came in contact with her daughter's cheek knocking Laura over. Laura did not cry, simply sat on the floor and listened as her mother first hyperventilated in surprise and then bent over in concern to check on her daughter.

Carol's first impulse was anger, but then, as she thought about it, she realized that Laura would have no understanding of this room or its contents. Laura said nothing as her mother picked her up and carried her back to her room. It was only as she was re-tucking her daughter into bed that Laura asked the question.

"Mommy," she said, "can I sit with you?" Carol thought about the question and wondered why her daughter would want to do such a thing. But then she remembered all the times she had found Laura sitting quietly beside Charles Brown, never disturbing him, but simply listening as he went about his already quiet work.

Carol rubbed her daughter's head and whispered, "Not tonight, honey, it is time for you to go to sleep." At first, Carol expected the normal childhood response of "but mommy I am not tired," instead Laura said, "goodnight mommy" and rolled over and fell asleep. Carol watched her daughter for several minutes after it was obvious that she had fallen asleep.

Carol's tears came, leaking through her eyelids and running down her face. Carol thought about all that her daughter would never experience because of her lack of sight. Carol did not go back to her work that evening. Instead, she retired to her own room, where she wrestled again with the sorrow and despair that welled up within her. Her wrestling finally took on form. She spoke with the one she could not see. She was convinced that He heard everything and had the power to bring her the peace she so desperately needed.

Carol did not remember falling to sleep that evening. Her tears and grief had accompanied her all the way to the final minute of awareness. She had fallen into a dreamless sleep.

The crash woke her up. She felt the shudder more than heard the noise. Leaping from her bed, she ran to her daughter's room only to find the room and the bed empty.

She looked down the short hall and saw the door to the secret room ajar. She had forgotten to lock the room. In fear, she ran to the room, expecting to find her daughter hurt. She entered the room and looked around for her daughter.

Her daughter was lying beside the table on which the top of the box had lain. The box lid was now lying on the floor and on top of her daughter. Carol ran to her daughter lifting the box lid without concern and all but throwing it aside, reaching for her daughter. Picking her daughter up she had cried out, "Laura, Laura, are you, okay sweetie!" She held her daughter close with tears streaming down her face. Finally, she heard her daughters' small voice saying, "I'm okay mommy," and she felt her daughter's little hands patting her own head trying to comfort her distraught mother.

Finally, Carol had stood Laura back from her and looked at her. She began to say, "Why did you come back in here?" but the words stuck in her throat. Laura's hands slowly guided themselves around Carol's face, and a smile broke forth on Laura's face as she said, "Mommy, you are beautiful!" Green fire-filled Laura's once silent eyes.

On the floor where Carol had flung it, the lid rested. As Carol turned, she saw the writing and remembered its promise. The green stones shone, and Carol saw through her own tears a final drop sliding off the lid and onto the floor where it disappeared harmlessly.

20

A New Beginning

Carol looked at Rubin, the memory still flooding her mind, and fresh tears still dripping from her eyes. She smiled. laughed, and then wiped the tears from her eyes. It seemed she could not remember the event without bursting into tears. They were not tears of sorrow, though. "It is funny," she said, "that now I cry more from joy than from sorrow!" The promise had not been that she would not cry, only that the tears of sorrow would be wiped away.

Rubin looked at Carol but then turned and looked at Laura. Her light green eyes sparkled with excitement but not with the fire that he had witnessed several times already. He was filled with wonder as he looked at these two women, and then the cloud of sorrow once again enveloped him. He whispered quietly, "I am so sorry."

Both Carol and Laura understood. Rubin was feeling the lost years and now counting them as wasted. It was Laura's voice again that drove the sorrow back. "We cannot reclaim the past, only try to make sense of it. It is the present that we can rejoice in, and future that we look towards in hope. The one who allowed us the past also gives us the future."

Rubin marveled at her words. They were spoken with a maturity that far outstripped her years.

His sorrow subsided, and he nodded his agreement. Through the tears, he felt Carol's hand on his shoulder and her words as well, "I am just so thankful that now I know there is a future for you," and then she added, "and for us." Rubin looked up at Carol and saw in her eyes what he had not dared to hope for. His heart, so recently pierced with sorrow and regret, swam in wonder.

Carol turned back to the driver's wheel, and once again turned the car back onto the road. In the brief time they had stopped the light of day had faded into twilight. Carol turned on the headlights as they continued their journey. The rest of the journey was spent answering the numerous questions that seem to burst forth from Rubin. There was so much of the past that he did not know, much less understand. Carol and Laura continued their story through the answering of Rubin's questions. Often the details still left Rubin struggling to come to grips with all that had occurred.

"How did you keep Laura's change from becoming a sensation? I would have expected that the doctors would have been abuzz, and your friends also would have exposed what had occurred," Rubin asked.

Carol thought and then continued the story. "After Laura was given her sight, I was faced with a number of problems. As you can imagine, I did not want to have to explain to anyone how the change had occurred. I was not ready to admit that Laura had been the beneficiary of such a strange occurrence. I also had no desire to reveal the set of documents that I had hidden away. I was pretty sure, after I thought about it, that I had broken some law somewhere by taking the documents. I also could not see me explaining that I had taken them to keep them from being destroyed. Also, how was I to explain the fires, if the documents were discovered in my possession?" To this, Rubin nodded his head. He also was glad that he had not learned of the deception earlier. He shuddered to think what his reaction would have been years ago.

"All those questions flew around me after I understood what had happened to Laura. I asked her again, Why she had gone into the room?" Carol went silent for a moment, the memory still difficult for her to relay. Laura filled in the gap. "I heard a voice call my name, and I followed it back to the room. I followed until I bumped into the lid, and it fell on me. I felt the liquid dripping onto my face, and then the light slowly appeared before me. It was the most incredible sensation I have ever experienced. And then my mom was there, and I saw her face. It was the most amazing." Laura stopped speaking, and Carol picked up the story.

"Laura finally fell asleep in my arms later that morning. After I put her back into bed, I found myself outlining my options. I took the day off from school to try and figure out what to do. I decided to take Laura to a doctor who had never seen her before. I needed to know for sure that the change was real. I needed to know if they would discover anything different about Laura, other than her ability to see now.

I just asked the doctors to see if she would need glasses, not telling them what her former condition had been. The doctor never asked any questions, and I did not volunteer anything. Her tests came back normal, and he assured me that Laura's eyesight was fine.

The doctors' office was close to my home, and I started taking her to them from that day forward. They have now cared for her for over 16 years and have never picked up on the change. I learned later that they had called her former doctor for her medical records but had never spoken with Laura's earlier physician. The receptionist did not know us and relayed to the new doctor that her records had been lost in a freak accident at the former doctor's office. Apparently, the standpipe to the fire extinguisher system had burst, and the resulting flood had destroyed a group of records that included Laura's. Fortunately, the new doctor had never sought out the other doctor for any memories related to Laura.

The real challenge was what to tell the pastor and Cindy when I brought her back. They were the only ones who really understood the scope of Laura's former blindness. I spent a very restless night trying to decide what to tell them. The next morning, I thought about taking Laura with me to school but then realized that I could not hide what had happened forever. While the circle of people who knew Laura was very small, none-the-less there were some people that I was just not going to be able to hide the change from. I thought about moving but then realized that would only create other problems and questions. Besides, I had a job that fit our needs, and a church that I now felt was a good home for us.

I left early for their home, expecting that I might need a lot more time to explain what had happened. I had bought Laura some colored glasses before the cure, and she wore them that first morning back. I struggled what to say, but Laura had jumped into Cindy's arms and handled the announcement on her own.

"Guess what Miss Cindy," Laura said after leaping into her arms. "What, honey?" Cindy answered in her jovial manner, not suspecting the change. Laura was always jumping into her arms and announcing different exciting discoveries she had made. Before Carol could say anything, Laura duplicated her activity with Carol the evening before and ran her hands over Cindy's face. She smiled sweetly and then said in her same voice, "You are beautiful too!" To this, Cindy had laughed but then caught herself. She suddenly understood that this was more than an innocent blind child's game. Cindy had slowly lifted off Laura's glasses and saw the light sparkling in Laura's eyes. Cindy's eyes had filled with tears, and she had hugged Laura closely saying, "So are you honey. So are you."

"It was then I knew how much Cindy and Charles really did love Laura. I also knew that the secret would be safe with them. The pastor reacted similarly, although he had more questions for me than Cindy had voiced. Finally, Cindy had told her husband, "Shush dear, if she can tell us she will otherwise let us just be grateful for whatever has happened."

I did not make it to class that day either. I finally knew that I had to share my burden with someone. I spent the entire day with Cindy and Charles and told them as much of the story as I felt I could." Carol could tell that this news had raised both concern and questions in Rubin's mind. "I left out your role in what had happened or the fact that you were Laura's father." But I think they pieced that together on their own, although even after all these years they have never mentioned it to me or anyone else. After all, both the fire, the loss of the discovery, and Laura's death had made it into the news. It had been front-page news for over a week, and the press had carried extensive coverage related to Laura's surprising and mysterious death. As with all such headlines as time passed it slipped from view and became merely another footnote.

"Charles did come over to my home that afternoon, and he surveyed my secret. The lid was still on the floor where I had thrown it. I watched as he picked it up and returned it to the table. His language skills were better than mine, and he read aloud the inscription on the lid. I watched as he had run his hand over the stones and then slowly set the lid down. He looked at the lid from a short distance. His eyes opened in wonder as he saw the similarity. He slowly stepped back further, looked at me, and smiled a shy smile. His words were "I see," and then he moved on.

He listened to the part of the translation that I had and saw the little bit I had accomplished on my own. He quietly removed his glasses and chewed on one of the earpieces. Finally, he said, "I understand why you did not tell anyone about these. Even if they believed you, these would create quite an uproar. I suspect that many would focus on either destroying them or at best discrediting them. Also, if anyone ever suspected what had occurred with Laura, she would become an object instead of a person. No, it is much better that these things remain hidden."

Then he asked me another question that filled my heart with joy, "Carol, I know that these are your burden, but I would relish the opportunity to help you with the translation work, in the evenings or whenever you can allow me to. I promise that I will not tell anyone about these."

It was an offer that answered another of my prayers and concerns. For the next few years, he and Cindy came over as many evenings as they could spare. They became my closest friends. It was during those times that Laura, now fully seeing and still sitting quietly next to us as we worked on the translation, began to display the gift. By the time Laura was seven, I had left the translation work for Charles and Laura. I never really enjoyed it and discovered that I was no longer needed for the work. They finished the remainder of the first testimony translation when Laura was eight. It had taken us four years to finish the first translation.

Carol pulled into a short drive that led into a small village. They passed Carol's university entrance on the way into the village. Carol pointed out the entrance and mentioned that perhaps he could accompany her tomorrow and sit in on a few of the classes she would be teaching. Carol did not see the smile that swept over Rubin's face. She did hear his, "I would really like to do that."

Rubin appreciated the seclusion yet closeness of her home to the university. The small village radiated out in a circle from the center plaza to the farmland that surrounded the village. Carol's home was on one of the side streets. The street appeared as a spoke of the central plaza. They passed the small gray church that she attended. A little later, she pointed out the pastor's home. About a block further, she made a sharp left onto another side street and pulled up in front of the small gray stone house that Carol and Laura called home.

The lights were on in the house. As she had pulled up, two individuals stood waiting to greet them on her porch. Laura reached them before either Rubin or Carol and immediately hugged both. Rubin was surprised to see a twenty-year-old hugging anyone. At the same time, he realized a surge of a feeling that bordered on jealousy. He only hoped that eventually, he would have a similar experience.

Both greeted Carol with similar hugs and then looked on as Carol introduced Rubin. "Pastor, Cindy, this is Laura's father, Professor Rubin James. Charles and Cindy Brown were in their late sixties. To Rubin, Cindy looked like the model grandmother. Her gray hair, round face, and happy smile reminded him of a different age when people still cared about each other. In the poor light, he had not been able to make out the features of Charles. As he approached Charles, the light finally exposed his face. Rubin stopped a look of surprise leaping over his face. His mind went back, now more than fifty years ago, and he remembered another face, of another minister. The resemblance must be more than a coincidence, Rubin thought.

The pastor smiled as he realized Rubin had made the connection. He reached out his hand, taking Rubin's and shook it. "It is good to see you again, professor." Turning to a surprised Carol and Laura, the pastor explained, "My uncle was Harry Brown. The professor's first wife was my uncle's daughter. I was only eighteen when they were married some fifty years ago. I attended their wedding and decided that day to follow my uncle into the ministry. I had not met Cindy yet, so she would have no memory of those events. As I have grown older, I realize that I look more like my uncle every day. Hopefully, I have also been half the pastor he was."

Looking at Carol, he admitted, "I suspected that the professor was Laura's father. She is so like Anita's Laura. I thought that our paths might once again cross, although I never imagined the way." He continued now looking at Rubin, "I saw Anita's Laura often at my uncle's home, normally during my breaks from school when I would come over to get help from my uncle on some of my lessons."

Rubin realized he had never seen the pastor at Harry's house. Outside of his vague memory of the reception immediately after the wedding, he did not remember the pastor, but his resemblance to his uncle left no doubt. He also remembered both Harry and Laura having mentioned the visits of a relative, also pursuing the ministry, but never realized that the circle of events would intertwine them all again. Taking Rubin's arm, the pastor led the startled group into Carol's house.

Once inside Rubin was immediately drawn by the light feminine texture of the house. It was clear to Rubin that the house had not ever had the presence of a man in it. Unlike his own, with the heavy bookcases, and heavier chairs and sofa, this living room was filled with furniture that only a female hand would have chosen.

The study desk with its small adjoining bookcase in the corner of the room was the only hint of Carol's profession and background. The walls were the light creamy texture that spoke of constant care and of Carol's love of light. Rubin immediately contrasted it with his own dark and dreary habitat that had only seen the light in the last few days. How different his life would have been if he had chosen differently, he thought again. An old familiar pull on his heart was quickly released when the thought hit him: no-where in the room was there any hint of the gifts that were housed within these walls.

Rubin sat slowly into one of the larger chairs, his coat still on and his hat still on his head, as he took in his new surroundings. Carol had been speaking with the pastor but now turned her attention again to Rubin. *How strange he looked*, she thought. Even sitting in her largest chair, he still dwarfed its frame. She saw him studying the room, and pain of regret pierced her soul as she realized how out of place he must feel. She moved over to the chair and asked, "Can I take your coat and your hat?"

Rubin very quickly got up and removed his coverings. He handed them to her, a smile crossing his face, and warming Carol's soul. He looked down the hall, past the kitchen and the small dining area, and could make out four doors all coming off the same hallway. He could see the bath at the end of the hall. Carol had turned and moved to place his coat and hat on the pegs behind her entry door. She had seen his glance down the hall and understood the longing and the fear that must already be playing in Rubin.

By the time she had returned, she had found that the pastor, his wife, and Laura had all taken seats in the living room. Even Rubin was once again seated, no longer looking so out of place or so large with his coverings gone. He still looked uncomfortable in his chair. There was no way to hide the functionality of the chair related to his size.

Carol entered the kitchen and placed the teakettle on the stove for heating. She selected a grouping of teas and found a few biscuits to which she added a serving of jelly on the side. Laura joined her to help carry in the items. Laura carried the hot water and tea while Carol handled the biscuits and jelly. After serving everyone, they placed the remaining items on the tray and laid it down on the study desk. Carol moved the chair from the desk over next to Rubin. The discussion began as the pastor handed around a set of pictures that he had taken from the pocket of the sweater he wore.

Laura had seen the photographs before, but she never knew their significance until now. Laura remembered after gaining her sight of how the pastor had explained some of his own heritage to her. She had heard the name of Anita and Laura before and had seen one very old picture of Anita's husband Rubin, but never understood her own relationship to these pictures until now. She realized that the pastor had shown these pictures to her before, half expecting Laura to make the connection. She never had.

The pastor spoke of the strange gift that Anita's Laura had displayed. It was this gift that cemented his belief of the relationship to Carol's Laura once she had started to display a similar tendency. Laura also realized that it had been the pastor's careful attention to her that had also spurred that gift's unveiling.

The pastor concluded with, "Now you all know my part of the story. I cannot begin to tell you how happy I am to finally be able to share this with you. I am sorry not to have shared it before, but I just could not know what the impact would be. At least now, we all know the truth."

The discussion continued unabated for more than two hours, as each shared both memories and asked question spurring even further memories, discussion, and questions. It was past eleven when the pastor finally stood and announced that he needed to return home. "Kept you folks up long enough and we can talk more tomorrow!" He and Cindy made it to the door, but not before receiving a parting hug from Laura and Carol.

The pastor shook Rubin's hand. Looking him in the eyes, he said, "Get some rest before you try to tackle what resides here. There is too much to take in when you are already tired." And then they left, leaving promises of an early return the next day. "Not too early," Cindy reminded her husband. "Carol has to teach, Laura has school. We will see you around dinner!"

After the door had closed and the pastor was safely on his way, Rubin suddenly realized just how tired he really was. The day had been an emotional roller coaster for him. Carol had guided him to the small guest bedroom down the narrow hall. She pointed out both her own room and Laura's. What was behind the other door, need not be mentioned.

To his own surprise, after he entered his room, having said goodnight, he closed the door and found himself drawn to sleep. He had trouble keeping his eyes open long enough to permit him to take off his few clothes. His clothes he laid on the chair at the base of the bed, but by the time he had his socks off, he merely threw them towards the chair. Under the covers in his underwear, he was asleep before his head hit the pillow. The dream started sometime in the night. He awoke the next morning rested, but now with a renewed sense of purpose. He knew that everything was happening with design. He still had a role to play. Instead of fear, he was grateful for the dream. He was also grateful that he had recognized the voice. He realized that even in the twilight of sleep, the purpose of the journey could be made clear. He greeted the first light of morning with one of his first true prayers, "Lord, this day, let all I do bring your name honor."

A new day stirred to life. An old man sat up in bed with eyes ablaze.

21

Morning Has Broken

Carol stirred under the covers of her bed. The aroma of fresh coffee and fresh bread filled her head and her thoughts. Opening her eyes, she realized it was not a dream. There truly were those delightful smells filling her home. She smiled, thinking that Laura must have beat her awake and was even now preparing for the day ahead of them. Carol sat up in bed. The light outside was still dim, so she turned on her bedside lamp. She reached for the book that she kept by her bed and for the next few minutes tried to concentrate on her normal routine. Finally, she realized that there was nothing normal about this day, and she whispered a silent prayer for herself, for her daughter and for Rubin. Slipping out of bed, she wrapped herself in her robe and was moving towards her door when she heard a soft rapping at her door. She opened the door to find Laura, the sleep still fresh in her eyes, her own robe only recently put on as well.

Carol looked at Laura, and they exchanged a similar unspoken question. If it was not them, then who was creating all the delicious smells coming from the kitchen? Rubin? "*It cannot be,*" thought Carol. In all the years she had been with Rubin, he had never cooked a meal. It had been a standing comedy between them that Rubin could not even boil water well. Most of their meals had either been eaten out, or Carol had been the cook. But it had been twenty years thought Carol. Everyone can change in that time. But Rubin?

Both Carol and Laura made their way to the kitchen. As they rounded the corner, they saw Rubin, seated with his back towards them, at the kitchen table. His already gray and thinning hair bore a light white powder, evidence of his earlier activity. They saw that he was reading and was unaware of their approach. They also realized he was crying, although quietly.

Carol cleared her throat, attempting to alert Rubin of their presence. He turned in his chair, facing them, the tears still streaming down his cheeks. In his hands, he held a book that both Carol and Laura recognized immediately. On the table, before Rubin was a stack of papers, still organized neatly but obviously recently read. A simple piece of twine lay beside the papers on the table.

Rubin looked at Carol and said, "I never understood death before today. Now seeing His death, hearing his words, I understand." Carol crossed the final distance between them and wrapped her arms around Rubin as he buried his face in her robe and continued to cry.

So it was that Rubin finally had come to the spot not only where he accepted his Lord but also met his Savior. All other moments and hopes had finally led to this single spot in time. All the events of the past week, indeed of his entire life, had drawn him to this single moment in time. Rubin would remember this day, but only as one of many in the process that had finally drawn him to the truth. But in another realm, there was singing that he could not hear this day. Many never realized the day of their own change, but that day was marked indelibly both upon their own souls and in the great book where their name had resided from eternity.

After a short period, Rubin pulled away. The tears were ending, the traces of their paths still cut through the powdery remains of his efforts. He said with a smile. "I made biscuits for breakfast." Carol and Laura surveyed the kitchen and the evidence of that activity. Carol laughed and smiled, saying, "I see." Her smile warmed Rubin's heart. Her eyes sparkled with the mirth that comes from seeing a small child, making his first steps of independence. For Carol, the moment was doubly special. She suspected what had finally occurred but also realized that the effects of the change were already starting in his life. Rubin, who had for the most part, never attempted to serve anyone, other than himself, had reached out to serve, in the most unusual of ways.

Laura went to the refrigerator, removing the jam and butter. Returning to the table, she set them down. Soon Carol, Laura, and Rubin were holding hands, each seated in their chair, as Laura said, "Lord bless this food and this day to your service we pray," to which they all added 'Amen."

The biscuits were good. The coffee was fresh. Rubin began to explain the papers before him on the table.

"I woke early, started the biscuits and coffee, and found that the house was so quiet and peaceful that I needed to do something. I found your book, he nodded to the book laying on the table, and opened it to the passage you had marked." Carol interrupted him only briefly. "Not I, Rubin, but Laura so many years ago marked this passage." Rubin nodded his understanding and continued. "I finished reading the section but then found I could not stop."

In Rubin's mind, the images of his early morning were fresh in his mind. Walking down the hall, he hesitated as he placed his hand on the doorknob, old fears and worries springing up yet disappearing as they came into the light of his greater desire. He opened the door to that extra room, surprised in finding it unlocked. He did not realize that Carol's last act before retiring herself the night before, was to unlock the door. Something told her that she needed to do that.

Inside the room, Rubin discovered the five testimonies lying wrapped as if never opened and resting beside the box that had borne them. The box he saw was still in the pieces that his staff had created as they had removed the bottom so many years ago. The sand and the salt were in a large clear plastic bag, also beside the box. On a second table lay the box lid, the green stones missing, the openings appearing strangely empty. The small pouch that contained the stones now resided with Laura and hung as a necklace around her neck.

Surveying the table Rubin felt a strange tug on his mind. All the pieces were here.

A task remained to be completed, not of destruction but of preservation. The thought that reached out to him startled him. The voice was clear in his mind. It said, "The testimonies must be passed to another generation. They have completed their purpose for this generation." "Completed?" Rubin asked almost aloud. Surely not he thought, for they were still all but unknown. Only a few were aware of their existence. Surely there must be a much greater circulation of these. The voice in Rubin's mind remained silent, leaving Rubin wondering about the strange thought.

Beside the lid, Rubin found ten boxes. The boxes were arranged in two parallel rows. The vertical presentation made it obvious that each set of two boxes were organized as if to create a unit. Five of the boxes were of loose-leaf paper size while five other boxes clearly bore cassette-sized tapes. Each box bore on its lid a simple label. Stooping down in the dim light Rubin read the first cover. On the cover of the first box, in a familiar script was written, Eyewitness - The Tears of the Saints – The First Testimony. Moving to the second box lid, he read the next script. It also bore a single sentence: Eyewitness - The Risen Saints – The Second Testimony. Moving along the table he looked down and found the next title Eyewitness - The Healed Saints – The Third Testimony, and then the next Eyewitness - The Saints Changed– The Fourth Testimony and finally the box which held the thinnest of the five testimonies and its title Eyewitness - The Rest of the Saints – The Fifth and Final Testimony.

Returning to the first box, Rubin gently removed the lid from the box. Inside he found a sheaf of papers joined by a simple twine wrapped around the papers and tied in a simple bow. The first page bore the same title that the cover of the box did. It also bore a second line that stated: The testimony of Restitutus known as The Restored One, who was blind but was given eyes by the Lord. Opening the second box, he looked down, saw the title but scanned for the next line. There it said: The testimony of Lazarus, brother of Mary, wife of Restitutus, who died but was raised, Rubin returned the cover to the box and lifted the third. The second line read: The testimony of Jacob the lame and Simon the leper two of many who were healed. He continued to the fourth box after he had returned the cover to the third and repeated his action. He read "The testimony of Joseph of Arimathea, The Owner of the Empty Tomb. Finally, he reached the smallest of the boxes and lifted its cover. It read "The Rest of the Saints: a testimony by Joseph, son of Cain who was also known as Restitutus.

Returning to the first box, Rubin lifted its lid again and surveyed its contents.

The paper was not bound as a book. Reaching in, he lifted the enclosed papers as a unit and held them in his hands. It was then that twin thoughts hit him: "*The translations were complete, and these were the original and only copies.*" The thought caused his hands to shake slightly. He marveled at the lifetime of work that these five simple boxes held. He also wondered in surprise at the wisdom of keeping all of these in the same room, without copies. If something happened, all this work could be so easily lost. Just as soon as that thought had occurred, Rubin also realized that for the second time, he was concerned about the preservation of these items instead of their destruction. He understood he had been changed in the last week. He was no longer the man that he had been. He now had different desires and changed priorities.

Rubin looked on the table with wonder. The translation was complete. He was astounded at the simplicity of what lay before him. He looked down at his hands. There within his hands lay the translation of the first scroll. His first urge was to place the sheaf back into the box. It was as if he had stumbled onto something sacred that he dare not touch, yet even as he thought this thought, he knew clearly that this was not sacred, and it had been given so that it could be read. Turning slightly, he saw another book, of much more modern printing and binding. He looked at it and knew that like the testimonies, it too was of ancient origin. He also understood, where the testimonies he was holding were not sacred, what was contained within that single book, was.

Strange, he thought, that something so sacred was widely available to everyone. What he had held in contempt for so many years now caused Rubin to tremble at what it contained. Laying the sheaf of papers down, he touched the book and opened it to where a simple marker had been placed. He read the passage that was marked. The voice returned thundering in his heart and mind, "He who believes in Me, does not believe in Me but in Him who sent Me. He who sees Me sees the one who sent Me. I have come as Light into the world so that everyone who believes in Me will not remain in darkness."

Rubin gripped the edge of the table as the world spun before his eyes. Suddenly he was aware that he was not alone in the room. For a brief instant, gleaming beings of light and majesty surrounded him, and their song-filled every portion of his being.

Just as suddenly, Rubin found himself once again standing alone with the sheaf of papers resting before him. The book still clasped in his one hand Rubin replaced the marker and slowly closed it. The house was still quiet, although the biscuits and coffee aroma were beginning to permeate the house. Rubin picked up the sheaf of papers and the book and retreated to the kitchen.

Returning to the kitchen, Rubin placed the book and the sheaf on the table and then sat down. Taking first the sheaf of papers, he carefully untied the twine that held it together. Turning to the first page, he recognized immediately the text of what his first Laura had read into that first tape so many years ago.

It took him but a brief time to find where he had left off in his listening to the tape version of the testimony. He picked up reading the account there.

The words echoed in his mind. His daughter's voice absent from hearing yet clearly seen in the writing. He heard her voice in his head as he read.

"After the teacher had directed that we not follow, Lazarus and I spent time speaking about all that had happened. With the day of the great feast approaching, we soon agreed that we would join together to celebrate this first feast remembering both my first sight of the Passover and Lazarus first

since being returned from the grave. I returned to my parents' home with Mary. Taking my father aside, I shared with him what had occurred in the last few hours. His smile and hug filled my being with joy. Truly we were all changing and growing at rates unimaginable before.

The few days before the feast passed rapidly. My father still worked at his business, while many still came to visit me and check on the great healing they had heard had been accomplished for me. It was only to be expected that many more visited Lazarus for what had occurred to him was of even greater interest.

During these days, we continued to hear bits of events in the great city. While we had heard of the great reception and entry of the teacher into the city, we only learned later of his entry into the temple area and his driving out of the merchants. As normal that news traveled with people that left the city.

Finally, the day of the celebration arrived. My family had agreed that we would gather with Lazarus' family at their home. Only my brother, Samuel, and his wife and children were not present with us. He had not returned to my father's home even after the news about Lazarus had finally reached him.

Together that evening, we remembered the great events upon which the feast was based. As the cups of memory were filled, and the great story of our people and our God were told, tears filled my eyes. For the first time, I saw the great feast and its many aspects. Lazarus led us through the reading of the account. Even Martha, normally busy with the preparations sat with us, listening and remembering what God had done in the past. It was Mary, who brought us back to the present saying

"Not since the time of Moses and the prophets has God been so obviously at work as in our time." Then looking at her brother, her smile grew tempered as she finished her comment. " I feel like something is about to break, and yet do not know what it is or what to do."

My family and I took our leave late that evening and returned to my father's house. I found sleep difficult that night, my thoughts were drawn frequently to Mary's fear and my own apprehension. Yet after a while, the joy of the day, the great blessing of sight and life filled my mind. The joy of a realized love and the wonders of the possibilities closed out the cares, and I slept soundly.

The next day was the day before the Sabbath. I arrived at Mary's home early, having promised to go with her to the market. It was more an excuse for us to spend more time together, still marveling. Walking together through our village, I now was becoming more aware of the smallness of our village. We spent time speaking of the future but more time speaking of all of the experiences of the past few months. I was still an object of conversation as we walked among the shops. Yet as with most curiosities, after the first visit, the interest was already waning among many. The news of my betrothal to Mary had raised some speculation, but even that too was passing.

We returned to her home to find that Lazarus had a visitor from the great city. The news that the visitor brought froze my heart. The visitor spoke of the teacher. During the night, our leaders had arrested the teacher. Early this very morning, he had been condemned by our leaders and brought to the Roman governor, who had agreed to his death. Even as we spoke, his death was underway.

Looking at Mary, I saw in her eyes the thoughts that were flooding my mind. How was it possible that anyone could wish this teacher's death? Lazarus stood, but I was already moving towards the door. I looked towards the great city and the path that would take me there. I looked back at Mary and she nodded her understanding. I began to run.

Even as I started up the path, I noted that a strange grayness had begun to fill the sky. The sky remained cloudless, but the formerly bright day was quickly dissolving into dimness. If I hurried, I would make the city within a couple of hours. Looking back, I saw that Mary, Martha and Lazarus stood looking as well at the sky. Soon I passed from their sight as I rounded the sharp curve in the path that took me from Bethany to the great city. Before long, the darkness increased. As I raced towards the city, I noticed that more and more of the travelers on the path were stopping in small groups discussing the strange darkness that was falling. Soon as I passed by houses, the lamps of the night were being lit. But even their light seemed to be swallowed by the increasing darkness.

Running became impossible. Even walking was becoming difficult. At one point, I stepped into a hole and went sprawling on the path. I was forced to slow my pace even more. Without a torch, the path was fading from view. It was then that I remembered and closing my eyes I slowed until other senses took control. Soon I was walking guiding myself with the sense that had developed through years of blindness. For the first time, I thought of a reason to give thanks for those years.

I had been walking for nearly an hour when the ground heaved, and a great rumble passed through the earth. I stopped and found myself resting against what appeared to be a small stone wall on the side of the path. I was just a few minutes from the great city. A final great sigh seemed to be uttered by the ground and a great breeze rose and then diminished. While this occurred the blackness that had fallen upon the earth started to fade. The strange stillness that filled the land began to be lifted. It was the sound of a bird that made me realize that the normal sounds of animals had also disappeared for more than an hour. I opened my eyes and watched as the blackness faded back to gray and then slowly returned to a late afternoon sky.

I finally approached the crest of the hill that would now bring me to look down upon the great city. The Valley of the Kidron stretched before me. Approaching the city from this direction, I could see the path that approached the temple area and passed into the city through the gate known as "The Beautiful Gate." I choose the path that would lead me into the city slightly above that gate.

As I approached the city, I listened closely to the comments of the few travelers leaving the city. With the Sabbath so close, few people would dare to venture forth. Even I was uncertain what I would do for the evening, but other greater needs drove me. As I walked, I overheard one of the few travelers mention the execution of several criminals by the Romans this day. Listening, I learned what I needed.

The place of execution was little more than a twenty-minute walk after passing through the city wall on one side. Passing through the city walls on the other side I began the climb up the short path that led up the hill. As I reached a curve in the path my heart froze again. Against the pale sky stood three crosses at a distance. Against one already rested a ladder, and it was obvious that someone was being removed from the cross. I picked up my pace, fear filling my heart.

How does one describe the scene that I discovered? Near each of the crosses were people who knew those who had suffered this execution. The crosses on both the left and the right still had bodies upon them with soldiers still guarding the area. I could tell from the body's strange angle that the legs of both had been broken as the bodies were now slumped down and the bones jutted out of the flesh where the bones had torn through.

Gathered around each of those crosses were just a couple of people. Obviously, either parents or friends who had come to witness the final hours of someone they had cared for. On the center cross, hung the teacher.

As I approached the person on the ladder just freed the final nails that had held the teacher to the horizontal beam. He carefully passed the body down to a man below who held the body against his own chest. There was a small circle of women and a few men there. I watched as one woman slowly sat on a small wooden bench and the body was lowered so that his head rested on her lap. My heart broke and my eyes flooded. Over his head was pressed a cap of thorns. The woman holding his head seemed oblivious to the thorns. Even as I looked on, I realized that the thorns that had pierced his brow were certainly piercing her lap where his head lay.

It was the first time that I had thought about the teacher having a family. Surely this woman was the teacher's mother. I recognized the man standing just to the side of the woman holding the teacher's head. He was one of the disciples of the teacher. I stood frozen, taking in the scene. As I watched one of the other men had taken a piece of material and covered the teacher's middle, restoring in death the dignity robbed from him while dying.

My eyes burned. The thought passed through my mind that it would have been better had I never have been given sight than to witness this. Yet even that thought faded quickly as the word froze in my mind: Witness.

The two men that had been involved in taking the teacher's body down turned to me. I had seen one man before, although only briefly. His name was Joseph, and he was a member of the elders of the nation. He motioned me over, and I walked slowly closer. I stood within a few feet and looked down upon the teacher. His feet and arms were covered with blood from where the nails had pierced his body. The feet were brutalized. The nail that had held his feet fixed to the cross had torn the flesh more than the original puncture. It was obvious that the teacher had strained against the nail, raising himself often to take those final few breaths of air he had been allowed.

After a few minutes, Joseph had spoken softly to the woman holding the teacher's head. She had merely nodded, and then Joseph had slowly lifted the head and placed it carefully on the ground as well. He then used great care as he removed the cap of thorns that had been placed on the teacher's head. It had been a difficult task, and I know that his hands would bear the pricks as well from those thorns. Anger surged through me. They had tortured the teacher before they had killed him. The amount of torture became even more obvious after Joseph had freed the cap of thorns. He had slightly turned the teacher on his side, and it was then that I saw the teacher's back.

The skin was laid open and the flesh underneath had deep gashes in it. The anger gave way to horror as I realized the pain that the teacher had been forced to experience. It was when the teacher's body was placed on a stretcher that I saw the hole where a spear had been jabbed under the arm area and into his heart. The mark of an expert, familiar with the method of ensuring death, there was to be no doubt. The teacher was dead."

Rubin had stopped reading the testimony placing the sheaf of papers back together on the table. No tears had fallen from his eyes. Something was missing. Turning to the book he had brought with him from the room as well, he opened it and read. He heard the teacher's voice and listened. It was the teacher's care for his mother that had started the tears flowing. It was the final words that broke Rubin's heart. "It is finished!" At that very instant understanding flashed through Rubin's soul. As the impact of "It is finished" rushed through Rubin, the tears of sorrow and joy flowed freely from Rubin's eyes.

He read until he was unable to continue reading. The tears streamed down his cheeks. He closed his eyes and prayed for forgiveness. It was while he was praying that Carol and Laura had discovered him. A new heartbeat within his breast.

22

THE LIFE OF A WITNESS

Rubin looked up and smiled. Both Laura and Carol had finished their first biscuits. Rubin was sure that their gracious praise for his efforts was more than what the effort deserved, but he was happy all the same.

Both Laura and Carol returned to their rooms, the morning routine and preparations demanding their attention. Rubin also stood from the table and picked up the sheaf of papers. Returning to the room, he carefully placed them back in their box. The twine that had held them together remained untied, and he placed it on top of the papers. He hoped he would be able to finish reading the first testimony soon. Anticipation filled him as he looked at the others as well. But first, he had other tasks to finish.

He returned to his room. Within thirty minutes, he was fully dressed. The remains of his early cooking experience were brushed from his hair, and from his shirt. He waited quietly in the kitchen as Carol and Laura also finished their preparations.

Laura emerged first, her backpack stuffed with books, and her slacks and shirt mirroring the student persona she now adopted. Rubin

CHARLES A. DE ANDRADE

spoke with her while they both waited for Carol. Rubin had learned a little about Laura's education the evening before. He had discovered that Laura was majoring in economics and media communication. This had surprised him. With her obvious gifts in language, he found it odd that she was not pursuing the linguistic degrees she was so obviously capable of.

He asked, "What made you choose the majors you have selected? I would have expected you to major in languages." Laura's eyes sparkled. Her smile showed that she had expected this question at some point. She said, "I wanted to be viewed as normal, not anything special. Few people know of my gift, and I desired to keep it that way."

"Besides, I am interested in both how the economic systems in the world work and the place of communication in society. I believe that all human history has been shaped and molded by communication and economics. In my generation, the advances in both areas will reshape much of our world. I wanted…she hesitated briefly, "No, I felt I needed to be fluent in the skills that will be shaping our society during my lifetime. I want to be able to talk with the people that will be shaping this future in their terms, so I can expose them to the truth that I know. In order to do this, I knew I needed to be credible, and my degrees will help me build that credibility."

As Laura finished her last statement, Carol arrived in the kitchen as well. Her brown tailored jacket and matching pants had transformed her into the assistant professor of literature she was. Her hair had been returned to the tight bun Rubin remembered. She looked very proper, and her intelligence still sparkled in her eyes as well. "We have to get going, my first class starts in less than an hour," Carol said. With that, they all headed for Carol's car.

The trip to the campus was uneventful. For the first time since Carol had arrived on his doorsteps, Rubin rode in silence, taking in both the scenery and processing what had occurred over the past day. Turning up the hill that led to the campus of Woodstede University, the path was lined by the gray flagstone that was common to the area and used in so many of the homes and in the walls that lined the roads. As they drove, Rubin remembered that it was this abundance of stone that had allowed the Romans to build the wall that had hidden the testimonies for so many years.

Reaching the university grounds, Rubin was struck by the similarities and differences to the university he had spent most of his life at. Carol parked in a gravel area that bore the sign "Faculty Only." From this area, Rubin looked down at the seven large buildings that comprised the greater campus. The buildings all appeared to be of similar age except for one. Most of the buildings were constructed of the same gray stone that lined the roads, although the one brick building created an unexpected and unwanted contrast in Rubin's mind. As Rubin looked, he realized that like his own campus, this one too had symmetry. All the buildings appeared to radiate around the brick building that was now the center of the campus. A two-car wide lane wound around the campus, touching each building before continuing its meandering to the next area. In at least two areas, far from any of the major buildings, were the larger parking areas. It was quite a hike from those to any of the education buildings thought Rubin.

It was to the brick building that Laura now sprinted. Waving at both Rubin and Carol, she was off, saying only, "see you around four Mom." Rubin watched as she departed. Carol pointed out to Rubin each of the buildings, giving him their names and the departments they contained. Carol pointed to the brick building where Laura was already entering with a group of other arriving students and said, "that's the new computer science, communication, and economics building. There are days that Laura disappears into that building and does not emerge until the day is over." Carol and Rubin made their way much more slowly down the little incline and headed towards one of the stone and granite buildings that were closer to their parking area.

As they entered the building, Rubin was aware of the smell of the building. He smiled as he recognized the universal scent of a building of higher education. It was one of the great stable experiences that bound all such schools together. Like the smell of a new car, educational buildings also were identifiable by their aroma.

Carol and Rubin entered through the same door that students were also filing through. A few of the students greeted Carol and Rubin listened as Carol returned their greetings. Once inside, Carol guided Rubin to a flight of steps that they both ascended. Reaching the next foyer, Carol led the way down the wide hall and approached a small room, whose door bore her name and title.

She opened the room, which to Rubin's surprise, had been unlocked. The room was only 10' x 12' and held an ancient metal desk, three stuffed bookcases, and a small tweed covered couch that had seen better days. Two chairs and a small coat and hat rack made up the rest of the décor. Unlike Carol's home, this room held neither the light feminine touch nor the bright light that Rubin would have expected. What little of the walls could be seen, were bare except for a single framed diploma that jutted out from behind one of the bookcases. The single window and a fluorescent light fixture provided the light for the room. The desk had several stacks of paper, and Rubin could see that the papers were reports or assignments that Carol was in the process of reviewing.

Carol took off her coat and hung it on the coat rack. Rubin followed suit. Carol watched as Rubin surveyed the room and then said simply, "I stay here as little as possible. I keep it as drab as possible to remind myself that this is not where I want to be. I fear that if I started to dress this place up, I would start to find reasons to stay here longer. When Laura was young, I could not allow it, and now I see no reason to change."

Rubin surveyed the bookcases and froze. One entire shelf of the largest of the bookcases contained familiar volumes. He looked down the row and realized that Carol had a copy of every book he had written during his career. His final book, written already ten years ago, was the last book on the shelf. Altogether he had published more than twenty books, and Carol had them all. He reached out and picked out his last work.

Titled "The Increase of Knowledge and the Demise of Superstition," it had been a best-seller and had kept Rubin busy both on the speaking circuit and even on several radio and television programs. It had been hailed as a masterpiece of intellectual achievement. He looked at the book now and shook his head sadly. He had been so blind....

"I read them all," Carol said behind him. He turned to look at her. She continued, "Of course I could not agree with much of what you said, and some of your arguments left me lost, but I needed to know what you were doing and what you were thinking." Rubin returned the book to the shelf. Carol picked up a stack of her papers. The briefcase she had carried from the car she picked up in her other hand. Rubin offered to carry something for her, but she only smiled and said, "Catch the door and the light if you would." Together they left the room.

Carol once again led the way, and they climbed another set of wide stairs, mingling with the students also climbing the stairs. On the next landing, the hallway became even larger with classrooms and lecture halls on either side of the hall. As they walked down the hall, Rubin looked at each placard that identified the subject or lecture being conducted within. Halfway down the hall, Rubin stopped, riveted by the placard.

Carol sensed his stopping and turned to look at Rubin. She looked at the placard and understood. There on the placard stood the title of the book he had so recently returned to Carol's bookcase. Carol came up beside Rubin and said, "Your book has been the basis for many courses and is in many circles, mandatory reading for many students. It is considered a breakthrough in Philosophy although you wrote it as much as a study in the advancement of English literature. "Carol quoted an accolade that Rubin was familiar with. Underneath the placard was the name "Professor Willard Dillington."

Rubin looked at Carol, but he sensed an internal prompting that was similar to a voice issuing a demand. Rubin knew he must obey. He looked at Carol and said simply, "I must go here," to which Carol had nodded and said, I will see you back here in about two hours." She turned and continued on her way. Rubin looked with some trepidation at the closed door and wondered if he would be disturbing the lecture that was obviously already underway. But the internal voice would not be dissuaded.

As quietly as possible Rubin opened the door and slipped inside.

The room was a theater-style lecture hall. Two hundred seats were three quarters filled. This class and the lecture were obviously popular or required. Since the class was an upper-level class, Rubin assumed it was popularity and not a requirement that brought so many to it. Rubin slipped into the back row, hoping to escape detection. He failed.

While most of the students did not turn to witness the late arrival, the professor who stood below and was speaking noted his entry and stopped in mid-sentence. Looking up, he recognized Rubin at the same time that Rubin realized both, that he had not escaped detection and that he knew the speaker. The professor's broad smile filled Rubin's heart with dread. Professor Dillington had been one of Rubin's star pupils. Like so many other students over the years, Rubin had sponsored and helped usher Mr. Dillington through his own assent in academia. For a brief moment, Rubin acknowledged his former student with a nod and then sat still hoping that was all that would be required. Once again, Rubin would be disappointed.

The professor was a thin man, of a keen eye and sharper tongue. His sparkling blue eyes and short blondish hair spoke of his German heritage. His proud stance reminded Rubin of the self-confident, slightly arrogant student he had guided years ago. Now Professor Dillington showed the approach of middle age but hid its effects well.

Rubin remembered that the professor was particularly fond of ridicule as a device for discrediting opposing views and had exercised that device with the skill of a surgeon. Rubin thought wryly that Professor Dillington had learned the technique from the best. His student had only met his match in one other person, the one he had learned it from. Rubin now regretted having been his teacher and mentor. Rubin realized he had led many astray. He also knew now why he had been required to enter. It was now time to begin to set things right. Rubin prayed silently that the trial might be delayed. Even as he prayed, Rubin heard the answer. It was a resounding: "No."

Professor Dillington still smiling suddenly seemed to stand even taller, and he made an announcement to his lecture hall. "I have spoken to you all fondly of the man who has been a champion of enlightenment and who I credit with single-handedly leading much of academia to the correct understanding of reality. I had not expected to ever be able to introduce him to you personally, but I am pleased to tell you that I was wrong. Smiling broadly he said, "Ladies and Gentlemen, I give you Professor Rubin James, without whom neither this class nor my own professorship would have been likely." Rubin desired to disappear, as the faces of so many students turned to look at him and the Professor's own clapping started a crescendo of acknowledgment. Rubin's own legs felt like rubber. He felt a new emotion wavering between shame and fear as he slowly stood to acknowledge the welcome that he neither desired nor wished he had earned.

Finally, the clapping subsided, and Rubin slowly began to return to his seat. Rubin never got the chance to fully sit down. The professor invited Rubin to the front to address the students. Rubin looked at all the beaming faces looking up at him and whispered a silent prayer once again to give him the strength needed. As soon as he had thought the prayer, he heard a louder voice echo in his mind words he had not read in many years, "Be not afraid, for I am with you and you will be my witness."

Slowly Rubin descended the stairs and entered the dais where the professor stood. The professor's smile was still broad and genuine. As Rubin approached the professor, his outstretched hand acquired Rubin's reluctantly offered hand. The professor shook his hand and then gave Rubin a hug saying to Rubin, "It is such an honor to have you here."

Rubin smiled sheepishly and then turned and looked up at the expectant faces that once would fill him with energy but now filled him with dread. The hall grew quiet as the students waited to hear from the master himself. Rubin saw the professor's smile through the corner of his eye, and Rubin once again whispered a quiet plea for help. Closing his eyes briefly, his mind whirled, and then he knew. His plea had been answered, and he began without further introduction.

He asked the eager faces a question, "How many of you believe in God?" He continued to look up at the faces. More than a few nervous laughs but no hands or voices raised to answer his question. He then asked his next question beginning as a statement: "Let me ask the question in a different way, "Why do you not believe in God?" To this, several hands did rise.

Looking up, Rubin seized on a young woman who appeared to be Laura's age and seemed eager to make an impression on both the master and on her own professor. Her black hair appeared as a strange combination of a pixy and a slanted slash. The highlights of purple and orange accented the oddity of the haircut. But what Rubin found most disquieting was the numerous silver rings and balls that punctuated both her ear lobes and several other facial locations. Her dress, if it could be called that, hung loosely from her fame, yet hid neither the fact that she had a well-proportioned body nor that little other than the thin fabric stood between her and the rest of the world.

Rubin could not help but stare at this apparition and wonder what had led her to both such self-mutilation and public display. Yet, her voice was strangely out of place with her appearance. After acknowledging her raised hand, it graced the hall with a musical and pleasant tone. Her eyes sparkled with an intelligence that also seemed out of place with the rest of the visage. She said, "I do not believe because all things have natural explanations and besides most brilliant men like you do not believe." She stood waiting for his praise.

Rubin smiled and nodded, looking every bit like an approving father who had just received back the appropriate reply. He then looked up at her, locking eyes with her and spoke to the person he saw hiding within her eyes saying: "What if you are wrong on both accounts?" The sudden quiet and the sudden inhaling of air told Rubin he had their full attention now. Through the corner of his eye, he also realized that the Professor's smile was still there but now was strangely frozen, the warmth beginning to fade, and his eyes bore the light of confusion.

Rubin pointed quickly to another young student that had raised his hand in response to the question and asked him again, "Why do you not believe in God?" The young man rose to the question without the same enthusiasm of the first student, yet still seemingly convinced that in the end his view would be vindicated. The student said, "I agree with Molly, whose answer you already have, but I would add to hers that the level of suffering in this life speaks against the presence of God and that logic dictates that we are but a cosmic accident. Everything that we are learning today about ourselves clearly points to a natural explanation for our existence. The belief in a God or gods was mankind's attempt to deal with experiences that had no natural explanation or understanding in that time.

Now that we understand the structure of matter, the relationship of energy to matter and have the ability to detect the natural forces at work, we no longer need to cling to this former substitute as the explanation, we now know the real explanation. I would also point out that your own works professor has pointed clearly to the absurdity of any belief in the supernatural with our own advancing understanding of the natural world. To quote your work, 'Our knowledge has so increased that it has forced out any room for entertaining the former speculation. We now know the truth, and this truth has set us free from the bonds of the former superstition. We are now free to explore all areas of life and experience much that was considered off-limits or taboo under the former views. With our knowledge, we are building a tower that we can climb and see past the former limitations placed upon us by the outmoded beliefs. We, in fact, are now in place of God for only our own inability sets the current boundaries of our potential. I believe that as our knowledge continues to grow, we will rapidly approach a time when nothing we choose to do or think will be beyond our ability to accomplish.'"

He had quoted Rubin's work verbatim. Rubin recognized that the young faces that looked down at him were filled with the self-assurance and self-knowledge that would lead many to pride. He remembered all too vividly how he had nurtured this development in the past. So much needed to be corrected.

The student continued to stand, waiting for Rubin's response. Once again, Rubin's nodding head and presence gave everyone the expectation that the former answer had been but a ruse to cause alarm among the gathering. Rubin looked up at the student and nodded again and motioned for him to sit down.

"I see that you have all learned the lessons well." His smile seemed to reassure the students again. But then Rubin asked his next questions, "Have any of you experienced something that has no natural explanation, or do you know someone who has had such an experience? Do any of you know of any reason why I was wrong in my former statements?"

No hands went up, once again the voice of the first student returned, and Rubin turned to look at her. She said, "If we had such an experience, our logic tells us that the fact that we have no natural explanation does not mean that we should accept a supernatural explanation. It just means we have not had enough time to figure out the natural cause of the experience. "She too, had quoted from one of his works although not with the accuracy of the other student. But she had captured the kernel of his argument. Rubin realized that he was fighting his most fearsome opponent…. himself.

Once again, Rubin was nodding his head. Then Rubin began: "Let me tell you a couple of stories."

So, it began.

Carol returned to the hall outside the lecture hall, where she had left Rubin almost two hours ago. The hall was empty. She knew that the lecture was supposed to have concluded over a half-hour prior to her arrival. She looked up and down the hall and saw only a few lingering students but no Rubin. A couple of students slid past her deep in conversation and headed towards the lecture hall door. As the door opened and quickly closed, she heard his voice. She made her way to the lecture hall door and opened it slowly. As soon as she opened it, she heard Rubin's voice clearly. His words swirled around her.

Like Rubin before her, she made her entry quietly and sought a seat in the rear. There was none available. The lecture hall was filled. Carol recognized that some other professors had also slipped into the hall as well and now sat listening intently. She stood in the back and realized that students were still slipping into the hall and were now sitting on the steps and listening to all that was occurring. Rubin was speaking: "As they opened the grave, the stench of death held heavy in the air. Some who were there turned pale and fled from the area, their stomachs reacting to the odor within. Then a man spoke and called the one who was rotting to come out. What had been dead and decaying instantaneously was alive and whole. He came out from the tomb and was received back by his family. This dead man was known to be dead by many, was seen dead by some, smelled dead by others. Yet, he was now alive.

As he finished the account, Rubin asked, "faced with the evidence I have just relayed how would logic allow you to accept anything but a supernatural explanation?"

Rubin's former student, now the professor, took up his challenge. Carol could tell by the tone that the words dripped with skepticism. She looked with fear at Rubin but then relaxed as she saw Rubin's peaceful smile and demeanor. She now knew Rubin was no longer working under his own power, someone else was at work. She listened to the professor's answers and Rubin's questions. The professor's answers were so like the old Rubin but the questions that came forth from Rubin had confidence and power that took her breath away.

The exchange continued. Finally, after Rubin had asked another set of questions, the Professor had finally stood silent. Looking at Rubin, he finally said, "I never would have expected this of you!" Rubin had smiled and shook his head and said: "Neither would I, but in the face of such overwhelming evidence and a nudge that I can only explain as supernatural, I have no option but to believe as I now do. To do anything else would be both intellectually dishonest and experientially false."

He looked at his former student who appeared both flustered and at a point of intellectual befuddlement. As he watched, he saw an idea flicker to life within his former student, and the wry smile spread across the face of his student Rubin had the sense of the jaws of a trap being spread. Looking up at his students Professor Dillington said, "Well, today certainly has turned out differently than I expected."

Then turning to Rubin, he said. "Perhaps you would be willing to return again next Thursday when we would look forward to continuing this discussion?"

Rubin had bowed his head, and then looked up at his former student and said, "I would be honored to once again come and discuss this with you and your class." The professor nodded his smile breaking forth. To his class, he said, "I am changing your assignment for this week. You will all prepare arguments and questions, focusing on the correct view of reality. You will each be graded on your ability to discredit the superstitions you heard today." Turning to Rubin, the professor smiled and said, "I look forward to seeing you next week."

The professor had turned and walked off the dais without any further greeting or departing comments. Rubin looked up at the expectant faces, many of which were already packing their own books and once again shrouded behind their own masks.

But more than a few sat riveted to their seats still looking down upon Rubin. Included in their group were some of the late-arriving professors who had gathered to witness the strange exchange that had been taking place.

One of the students raised his hand, seeking Rubin's attention. Rubin saw his hand and acknowledged him with a "Yes?" The student asked, "Professor, this room is empty for the next period, could you stay and answer some more questions for us?"

The next two hours passed quickly as the remaining students and professors stayed and plied Rubin with more questions. Often Rubin was answering the questions with "I do not know," or "I will need to think about that question some more." Rubin realized that while he had prided himself in the past with having answers for all questions, now he was freely admitting that he did not have all the answers.

It was as the questions continued that Rubin saw Laura enter and seek out a seat next to her mother. Carol had moved from her step position to a vacated seat left empty after the first class had been dismissed. Even at this angle, Rubin could see Laura's eyes. As he continued to answer and ask questions of the remaining students, he saw the fire in Laura's eyes. For the first time, he also saw something else there as well. His heart skipped a beat after he had answered a particularly difficult question and saw both her smile and the glint in her eyes that spoke of approval and respect. Rubin experienced a new emotion. He knew now that he both craved and needed his daughter's respect. He also understood he needed her love as well.

Finally, Rubin had waved off the remaining questions and asked their forbearance. He said to the remaining students and professors, "Folks, I am old, and I am tired. Please forgive me if I say I need to stop now. Besides, my ride is here, and I must not keep them waiting. I look forward to seeing you all again next week." With that, Rubin had found a seat where he sat down, obviously exhausted. Both Carol and Laura made their way down to him, as did two of the remaining students.

Rubin looked up at Laura and Carol and smiled. He looked at the gathering of others and prayed another silent prayer for strength. Once again, his prayer was answered, and the fatigue disappeared. Beside Laura stood both Molly, the young lady that had been so brave to take the first question, and the young man who had followed with the verbatim quote from his work.

Rubin looked shyly at Laura and Carol and then turned his attention to Molly and her companion. Molly's companion was heavy set and similar in physique and statue to what Rubin remembered himself being at his age. He stuck out his hand and introduced himself. "Professor, I am Arnold Andrews, and this is Molly Costen." Rubin shook Arnold's hand and then turned to Molly to apologize for having chosen her to begin the day's events. Molly merely shook her head and exclaimed. "No need, it was incredible."

Rubin's surprised look was greeted with another grin. Molly turned to Laura and said, "Hi Laura, do you know the professor? I am certain he would be interested in hearing your views as well!" Laura smiled and then explained the mystery to Rubin.

"Molly has been attending a little study that I hold with some of the students here every week," she said. Arnold asked a question that started a whole new chapter in Rubin's life. "Where are you staying?"

Carol and Rubin sat alone in Carol's car as they headed back towards Carol's home. In the rear-view mirror, Carol saw the other car bearing Laura, Molly and Andrew were following. Rubin was lost in thought. "What had he started?" he asked himself. "And would he be up to the task of finishing the race now before him?" He shook his head in amazement at what had occurred.

He looked at Carol and asked, "How much did you get to hear?" "About the last two hours," was her response. He shook his head in amazement. "What have I done!" he exclaimed. To this, Carol turned her head and said, "I suspect only what you were meant to do." Her gentle laugh returned Rubin to the present. His fears poured out of him, and Carol listened quietly.

After he was done, Carol had summed it up with a question of her own. "When you were talking, did you feel anything unusual?" To this, Rubin nodded and said: "I knew I was answering the questions and asking the questions, but at times the answers came to me as if directed from somewhere not totally of myself?" He answered with the raised voice of a question and saw Carol's head nodding. "So now you know, there is more going on than either you or I can discern."

Carol turned into the small path leading to her house. Once again, the light was on in her house, and on the steps, the Pastor and Cindy were waiting. This evening the small group had grown by two.

It was far too early to bring Arnold or Molly into the circle with knowledge of the testimonies. After a light dinner, the questions that had never stopped during the entire drive or preparation of dinner continued. The evening was passed, answering both Molly's and Arnold's questions and filling in more of the blanks for them. Rubin was glad that the pastor and Laura were there. Many of the questions that Arnold and Molly asked, Rubin himself wanted answers for. Together they listened, probed, and learned from the pastor.

Rubin marveled at the insights that Laura also had into the questions. Carol sat down beside Rubin and listened in on the discussion as well.

Within a few minutes after dinner, the pastor had pulled a well-worn book from his pocket and continued to answer the questions, often quoting from the book. By the time Arnold and Molly left, Rubin's eyes were already having trouble staying open. It was already approaching midnight. He stood and said goodnight to Carol, Laura, Cindy, and the pastor. He retired to his room, forgetting how the morning had started but thinking more about the afternoon and the evening. He fell asleep quickly, but not before he said silently a thank you for the day.

No dreams interfered with his sleep.

The aroma of coffee stirred him back to consciousness. The voices outside his door brought him surprise. He had neither robe nor nightgown, so he was forced to put his clothes back on, looking more rumpled than the day before. He opened his door and walked into the kitchen. At the table sat Molly, Arnold, two other young people Rubin did not recognize and Laura. The clock above the stove said it was but 5:30 AM. Rubin thought back and was sure that Molly and Arnold had left the night before. Yet here they were barely a few hours since they left. Laura looked up from the book she had been reading aloud and said: "Good morning professor, I hope that we did not wake you." Rubin could tell from the twinkle in Laura's eyes that she knew both that they had, and that is what she had hoped for.

Immediately, Molly introduced the two newest additions. To Rubin's obvious surprise, she said: "We could not sleep and had so many questions; we found our friends and drove right back." It was then that Rubin understood that while he had slept, Laura had not. They had been at it all night. Then the pastor approached from the stove with a cup of coffee in his hand and extended it to Rubin. The pastor's eyes were tired but sparkled with mirth that matched Laura's eyes. The pastor had been at it all night as well.

Rubin thought, "It must be nice to be young" but realized that the pastor was not.

He accepted the cup from the pastor and sat in the last available chair. Laura smiled broadly at him and then said, "Let's see, where were we?" Then she began reading again from the book in her hands.

Rubin listened. After Laura stopped, the questions, answers, and more passages swirled around him. His tiredness fell away. He started taking part in the discussion. Before long, he was sharing his own story. He was unaware of Carol's entry behind him. He shared his own unbelief and the many years of stubborn insistence on his independence and self-reliance. He shared his foolishness at driving away the woman he loved, the years of loneliness while a family he did not know existed grew, and the great discovery of a person who brought both peace and joy to his own soul. He spoke openly of the teacher and the effect that his words had upon him. He spoke freely of the blind man and his testimony and the effect of that testimony on himself.

It was as he spoke about the blind man that Molly interrupted him and said, "Professor, you sound like you know this man, yet all we have is a brief mention of him. If he lived, he lived two thousand years ago. How can you speak in such first-person terms? You never met the man much less ever heard him speak?"

The professor bowed his head, both fear and desire swirled in his mind. Taking Laura's book from her hands, he turned the pages to the passage he desired. He said. "Listen." And he read. The passage was short, poignant, and complete. His voice was not his own, but that of the man remembered in the passage.

As he finished reading, he felt the tears running from his eyes and realized that the students all were looking at him in awe. Even the pastor and Laura were gazing at him with both surprise and appreciation. And then he felt Carol's arms slowly encircling his neck and her lips gently brushing his cheek as she whispered, "so you have met them both." He knew exactly whom she was referring too.

23

FINISHING THE RACE

The old man looked down on his writing. As he knew, he was running out of scroll, yet only a fraction of his story had been told. He remembered the words of another witness who had said that there did not exist enough books in the world to tell all that had been done. He understood that truth now. Each person, touched by the teacher, had his or her own story to tell. Thinking back and trying to organize what still needed to be told of his own story, he searched his memory, looking for only the most important parts.

Laying the stylus down, he stood and looked out the tiny cell window. The dim light was his only connection with the outside world. He knew it would not be long now. He must complete the task.

He sat down again after this brief stretch. His sparkling green eyes looked down on the scroll, and the memories swirled around him. He read the last sentence he had written and then relived the events that followed immediately after.

Joseph of Arimathea removed the cap of thorns. I saw the terrible wounds and the scope of the teacher's last suffering. Another man arrived, also from the council. This man, Nicodemus, brought some spices and perfume with him. Unlike Joseph, Nicodemus did not appear to be moved by compassion but by necessity. It was as if he was completing an obligation. But none the less, I was glad that someone else was there to help with what must be done.

I heard Joseph tell the one close disciple that he should take the teacher's mother away. "She does not need to see this," he said simply. Before he left, I touched the disciple's shoulder and asked, "Where are the others?" His only response was to blush and then I watched as he vainly tried to prevent the tears from escaping his eyes. He turned quickly without having answered my question. I would learn the answer later.

I watched as he slowly guided the teacher's mother away from the scene. Her frame was bent as if weighed down by a heavy load. She rested on the shoulder of the disciple; her grief still unspent. I grimaced at the thought of the sword that was piercing her heart. I knew the sadness that weighed on mine, and I had known him for such a short time.

What needed to be done was best left for Joseph and Nicodemus. I watched as they quickly wiped the teacher's body of as much of the blood and fluids as possible. Then they picked his body up, laying it back down on a sheet of cloth that Nicodemus had brought. Taking the remaining cloth, they covered the teacher. Now they were able to use the cloth to lift the teacher onto the mat that Nicodemus had also brought.

Joseph motioned to me. He gave me the jars of perfume and spices that Nicodemus had brought and asked that I carry them. After I picked these up, Joseph and Nicodemus picked up the mat and the teacher's body.

Together I followed the two men with several women also following at a distance. We went down the short path from the mount and followed a path that soon drew us away from the hill. I turned one last time to look up at the mount, the silent and now empty cross standing as a mute testimony to what had occurred and the two other crosses still bearing their own grisly witnesses. I followed in silence, not knowing where we were going. Finally, Joseph, who had been leading, came to a path that ascended slightly and entered a small grotto where I saw the tomb. The location of both the grotto and the tomb so close to the great city made it obvious that this tomb belonged to someone with both power and wealth. Not just anyone would be allowed to locate a tomb here.

Joseph did not say anything but entered the tomb with Nicodemus, the teacher's body still between them. I followed but stopped just inside the door. The fading afternoon light provided a dim light for the inside. Immediately inside and to the left of the door stood a single shelf. I had only seen one other tomb in my short experience and that one I had not entered. I noted that there were several other shelves for bodies in the tomb, but all the shelves were empty. The tomb had never been used before. Joseph and Nicodemus laid the teacher's body on the solitary shelf that stood separate from the others.

Nicodemus took the spices and perfumes from me and then helped Joseph briefly uncover the teacher's body again. Together they sparingly anointed his body and then placed a single thin sheet of clothe over his face. Then they returned the shroud over the body and prepared to leave the tomb. The sun was rapidly setting, and the Sabbath was approaching. Leaving the tomb, I helped them roll the large stone that was the cover for the tomb. The stone was set on a small incline and positioned above a groove in the stone floor in front of the tomb. The stone rolled easily into place; it would be much more difficult to reopen the tomb. It was just as we had finished that a group of soldiers arrived. They spoke briefly with Joseph. I saw Joseph shake his head in wonder but then nod.

Joseph grasped Nicodemus' hand and then gave him a hug. They exchanged words that I did not hear. Nicodemus left, leaving me to wonder what I should do. Joseph looked at me, and then came over and put his arm around me and said, "You should stay with me tonight. You can go home after the Sabbath." It was as we walked towards his home, that I learned that the tomb was his own and that the guard was there at the request of our religious leaders. Even in death, they still feared the teacher, or more so what the teacher's followers might do.

Joseph's hospitality was not lacking, although tempered by the recent events. I learned from Joseph that his actions had already brought him scorn from other leaders in the community. But Joseph did not care any longer. His words to me were "I had hoped that the teacher was the one promised. I am old now, and I will not live to see another like him." I saw Joseph looking intently at my face, and I realized he had heard my story but never from me. I told him what the teacher had done for me.

The Sabbath arrived as the sun set. Together Joseph and his family greeted the first Sabbath after the great feast with the prayers that were required. Joseph stayed at home this Sabbath. Having just handled the teacher's dead body, he felt unclean. He chose to stay with his family and me, but he did not forsake his prayers. Yet as he prayed, I could not help but notice both his tears and the faltering in his voice. Much to my surprise, I discovered that he owned several scrolls of the sacred writings. He opened one and then slowly read, "Who has believed your message? And to whom has the arm of the Lord been revealed. For He grew up before Him like a tender shoot, and like a root out of the parched ground. He had no stately form or majesty that we should look on him, nor appearance that we should be attracted to Him, He was despised and forsaken of men, "Joseph continued reading. I heard the words, suspicion growing within me that these words were speaking of the teacher, yet confusion and sorrow were the only conclusion.

I slept fitfully that evening for even in my sleep the vision of the wounds and the agony keep returning. Even in my dreams, I longed to hear his voice. But silence only increased my sorrow-strewn dreams.

The next day passed slowly. I spent much time with Joseph, as we shared our different experiences. Joseph was filled with deep sadness. His hope in the teacher, coupled with what had happened, had shattered much of his desires. His hollow eyes spoke of the despair that defined the day.

The sunset and the Sabbath came to an end. The day of rest had been a day of sorrow.

I decided that I would return to my family in the morning. I slept, but dreams continued to haunt my rest. The sun had barely broken the horizon when the first visitor arrived at Joseph's home. I recognized the disciple who had led the teacher's mother away. He spoke urgently with Joseph and then left. It was obvious that something had happened. I wondered what more could possibly go wrong.

Joseph turned to me, his eyes full of worry and said, "Something has happened, the disciples are all gathering together." Joseph told me the message the disciple had brought.

The room where the disciples had gathered was a large room over the top of a home. The room had held many large gatherings and was accessed from stairs behind the home. When we reached the room, there were already more than fifty people, both men and women, there. As we entered, I saw Mary. She, Martha, and Lazarus had made their way into the city at the break of the day. Lazarus had known of this room and found the disciples there. Mary came over to me, her eyes full of wonder and fear. Together we found a corner where I sat and told her everything I had seen and heard.

I had just finished my description of the day when another disciple arrived. I recognized him, as he, like my friend Jacob, was a fisherman. The disciples gathered around him. His eyes full of wonder I heard him exclaim,,

" He is alive!" He continued his story saying, "After John and I ran to the tomb and found it empty, I walked away in a daze. I was lost in thought, going over all that had occurred and been done. I did not know what to believe, as the story the women told this morning sounded like nonsense to me. Yet, the grave was empty, the soldiers were gone, and the stone was rolled away. I must have walked for an hour, just wandering the streets, thinking. I found myself near the spot where he had been killed. I sat down and was looking up at the spot where the cross once stood. I had closed my eyes to pray, to ask forgiveness for having denied, and for abandoning him. I was crying when I felt a hand gently rest on my shoulder, and I heard his voice, "Why do you weep?"

I looked up, and he stood before me. I fell at his feet still weeping, and then I covered my head and remember saying again, "Depart from me, Lord, for I am a sinful man!" I thought I was dreaming, but then he lifted me up from the ground. I looked at him; he smiled and said, "Remember, I told you that all these things must happen. I also have told you that I have prayed for you, and now you must return to your brothers and tell them that I am alive, just as I told you I would be." Then he was gone.

I marveled at his words. I had seen the teacher dead. There was no doubt in my mind. There was no possible way I could have been wrong. It was as I thought these things that the women who had gone to the tomb first and found it empty retold their story now, for the benefit of those who had not heard it before. The hours slipped by, as we remembered all that the teacher had said and done. We remembered some of the teacher's sayings that we now began to understand but still could not believe.

The sun had already set. While we were amazed at all that had occurred, there was still an atmosphere of fear in the gathering. Perhaps, the teacher's enemies would now be looking for the teacher's disciples. Certainly, the empty tomb would now draw their attention and activity. If they would kill the teacher, what would they do when they heard of the newest event? The sound of racing feet filled our group with apprehension. Who was this that made such haste to our gathering room at this time of night?

The loud rapping on the door caused us all to hold our breath, but the voices that joined the rapping eased the fear in the room. Two more joined our group. These two had left earlier that same day, leaving the city for a small village from which they had come. They too had left dispirited by the events of the past few days but puzzled by the words of the women earlier in the morning. Now they stood before the group, out of breath, having run for much of the past few hours, returning from where they had stopped for the evening. Their story filled us all with wonder.

They finished telling us their story. Amazement filled the room. Multiple discussions began. Suddenly the two lamps that lit the room flared brightly, and a gentle breeze filled the shuttered room. All eyes turned, and silence filled the room. Another had joined us. He had appeared next to the table, in the middle of the room. Fear, wonder, and then his words, of which I heard many but remember these clearly, "See, it is I myself."

"The teacher is alive."

The old man put the stylus down again. There was no room left. He thought about all that would not be told.

The years that passed by. His marriage to Mary, the birth of his child. The breaking out of the great persecution after the death of Steven that claimed his twin brother's life, a sister and that of his parents. The truth had filled their life with purpose and direction. The fear that his parents had originally shown now replaced with a boldness that could only be explained from knowing the teacher. His parents had been with him and over five hundred others as the teacher had spoken and taught again before he had left. Wonder and joy had filled all the voids where fear had once resided.

His oldest brother Samuel had led the rabble to his father's house. Samuel succumbed to hatred and fear. Samuel had taken part in the stoning of Stephen. From there, it had been but a short step to confronting the rest of the family. He would inherit all that was left behind. The reward for betrayal would be short-lived.

Within another few years all that he had won would be lost in the rebellion that would destroy the great city. But it was of little consequence compared to what he had already lost. He never understood what he had lost.

He remembered his brother, Jason, who had offered himself up, delaying the search long enough to allow his own escape. His brother's final words, "Go, brother, I must stay. Your time is not yet, but I must bear witness to the truth here." His brother's wife, Ruth, had freely given herself up after her husband's arrest. They faced the end together, the joy at being together a mystery to those who took their lives. His parents, his brother, Jason and his brother's wife Ruth and his sister, Sarah, had all died within hours of one another. The old man's greatest joy was that of all his family, only one was truly lost.

His oldest sister Rachel left with Martha when the great persecution broke out. He had heard from Simon and Naomi that she had married a believer in Ephesus where they had finally settled. He had never seen her again but had prayed often that her life would be filled with joy and happiness. The last he had heard both she and Martha were providing much comfort for the saints there.

Simon and Naomi had visited him three times since his arrival among the Picts. Along with them had also come Jacob and his wife, Mariam. Together they had spent many hours remembering all that happened among them.

Simon and Naomi took up residence in Gaul. They had six children. Simon spent most of his wealth providing for the needs of so many in that province. He was noted as a generous and gracious man and was thought highly of by all in the province. Of him, a Roman governor writing the emperor pleading for wisdom related to the Christians, as we had become known, would say "He has taken care of the poor of his faith and our own poor as well." Despite the governor's observation and plea, Simon joined a host of others who gave up their lives the same year the edict on atheism was issued.

Naomi and their children escaped and still worked among the tribes that made up that province. Two of the children having escaped the Roman persecution found death at the hands of the tribes they worked among. Death and hate always followed love closely.

Jacob and his Mariam continued to live in the northern area around Galilee. Returning to the lake for his living, Jacob remained an ardent testifier for the teacher. Their children still lived in the area the last he had heard.

Restitutus, as he was now known, had visited their home once over twenty years ago. It had been a joyous occasion. He and Jacob had reminisced about the years of blindness and lameness and rejoiced in the great gift each had been given. Jacob's friends that had carried his stretcher for so many years still fished with him. The old man had not heard from them in over ten years, but in his spirit, he believed that they were still alive.

Lazarus had not fled the city when the great persecution broke out. His testimony was a burr that the leaders finally removed. Shortly after the breakout of the great persecution he was captured and tried. He shed no tears and spoke gloriously of the teacher's great works. The Roman's never had a chance to execute him. His own leaders and neighbors struck him down. It was said that as he died, he exclaimed aloud in a voice of great joy exclaiming "I have done this before! Lord, receive me again into your kingdom. "Few could comprehend the joy of this man who, freed once from death, no longer feared being bound by it again.

He remembered his own hot tears as he had escaped the city with Mary, his son, and Joseph of Arimathea and his family. Together they had made their way to the furthest reaches of the empire. Passing through Gaul, on their way to this distant island, they had almost decided to stay in Gaul. But with Simon and Naomi there, he felt the need to move further to an area where no witness yet resided. Along the way they had stopped, encouraging many and witnessing to even more of the truth they knew. The tradition would follow into history that the man with the sparkling eyes had resided in Gaul. It was only partially true.

They had chosen to live among the Picts. Here on the outskirts of the empire, there was both work and relative safety for many years. The Picts, viewed as barbarians by the Romans, had little of the sophisticated baggage of Greek philosophy and were a fertile field for the truth.

Yet, even here, the truth had finally come under attack as well. First to die was Joseph of Arimathea. Taken as he worked among the people of a small village, he had walked boldly into the Roman camp, refused to acknowledge the emperor as god, and then was killed in keeping with the recent laws related to "atheism."

He remembered the marriage of his own son and the birth of his three grandchildren. Two of the grandchildren had fled to Roman sanctuary as young teenagers where they had been raised with both the benefit of Roman wealth and culture and the curse of Roman beliefs.

His own grandson as a young man had turned against the teacher. His denial was richly rewarded, and in the end, had led to his betrayal of his own grandmother. Mary, like Joseph before her, refused to bow before the lie, and her final words were filled with joy as she saw the teacher even as the sword had fallen.

He remembered his own son, grieving over the loss of his mother, had briefly turned against the teacher and himself. His son could not understand why the teacher would not protect his followers from such experiences. Why would this teacher require that they yield themselves up to death? His son also could not believe that his father did not pull out a miracle to save his mother. After all, was not this Mary, the sister of the one returned to life by the teacher? Surely, if that story were true, then the teacher would rescue her? He had heard all the stories and had seen his father's unusual eyes. But in the end, despite his father's pleas and prayers, Mary had been killed.

Mary, the thought of her absence from his life, still brought pain that was only pushed back by the knowledge of whom she now resided. He longed for his journey to begin. He was tired of the struggle. He desired to look upon the teacher, to hear his voice and to once again know the tenderness of the woman that had been his companion for most of his life.

His own son had been the instrument to fulfill his longings. His son had turned him over to his grandson. His grandson was rapidly rising through the ranks of the Romans. One willing to betray his own family for rank was a man to be feared and honored among the Romans.

But his own son had repented of the evil he had done. Even now he knew, his son was grieving his betrayal. Shortly, he would turn over to this son, his own testimony and those of both his mother's brother and the others that had been written. They would be his son's burden and joy.

His green eyes sparkling, he had heard the voice clearly that had commanded him to write. He had obeyed the command, and his testimony lay now before him. So much was left to be said, but his smile crept across his face as he realized that all that was to be said had been. The rest would be remembered by some and remain unknown to most. He rolled the scroll closed.

Just as he did the door to his cell creaked. Turning, he saw his son being allowed into the cell. The cell door closed behind him. Once alone, his grieving son fell to the floor before him, grasping his legs and pleading for forgiveness. He allowed his hand to rest on his son's head and then drew him to his feet. In the short cell, it was awkward, but he wrapped his arms around his grown son and allowed his weeping to subside.

He stood his son up and then reached under his own tunic removing the small pouch. Reaching over his head, he freed the pouch and handed it to his son. He said, "The teacher told me to give this to you. It has been my emblem of hope for many years, and now it is to be yours." Turning to the table, he picked up the freshly closed scroll and handed it to his son. "This you must also take." He told his son where the other testimonies were kept and placed these into his trust as well. Finally, he gave his son the final puzzling command that he had received from the teacher.

With that, he hugged his dazed son again and told him, "Do not blame yourself, it is my time to testify, and I have longed for this day for many years. Do not weep for me, but for those who do not have eyes that see or ears that hear. Remember that where I go, you too will follow, although not today. You have still much to accomplish." Kissing his son, he sent him towards the door. Even as his son reached the door, it opened, and the soldiers entered in.

He smiled at the soldiers. The journey was beginning. He smiled again as his son slipped away and whispered a silent prayer for him. "Finally," was his last spoken word as he was led from the cell.

A short time later, the old man felt the embrace of the teacher's arms, heard his voice, saw his smile. Suddenly he was no longer old or tired. His embrace and touch removed all the former weariness and filled him with rapturous joy.

He turned and saw his own father and mother. His brother and sister and other family he had forgotten stood there as well. Then he heard her voice and turned to see once again his wife. Mary smiled. She was neither young nor old, but her form was now more glorious than what he remembered formerly. The teacher's glory burst from her smile. A warm and inviting light clothed her being, and her outstretched arms welcomed him home. The green lightning flashed from his eyes, completing the rainbow that swirled around him.

24

FINISHING THE RACE
IN ANOTHER TIME

Rubin looked down on the final sentence. "The teacher is alive." His pulse quickened again as he reread the last few paragraphs. There was so much more that he wanted to know. But as the thought flashed through his mind, another also filtered in. "What more did he need to know?"

The days at Carol's had passed quickly. He gauged the passage by the increasingly rumpled condition of his clothes. The weekend arrived after three days, and Carol had left early on Saturday morning returning shortly before lunchtime bearing gifts. Now Rubin owned two complete sets of new clothes as well as multiple sets of underwear and socks. Looking in the mirror that morning with a fresh set of clothes on, he smiled. The image that smiled back was an old man in new clothes. At least he felt cleaner.

The small group of students that had invaded Carol's home had grown every day. Molly and Arnold had many friends. It seemed that every day their excitement had spread like an infection. Sometimes a student would appear one day, and then seemingly disappear and return with another friend. By the weekend the group had swollen to fourteen students. Many had the same visage as Molly with both punctures and tattoos decorating their bodies. Some had heard Rubin at the university. All had heard of the strange discussion and the approaching debate.

The pastor and Cindy also came over every day, and the discussions and lessons filled Carol's home. Laura's classes kept her busy, but she hurried home, and the discussions lasted late into the evenings.

Rubin wondered when he would have time to prepare for his next visit to the university campus. He asked Carol for a large stack of index cards, and he started to outline his thoughts on them, as he had done for so many other lectures he had given in the past. But he was constantly interrupted. After three days he had completed only a few cards. At this rate, he would never be ready. He sat in the kitchen area, watching and listening as the pastor spoke to the students that were now a constant stream flowing in and out of the home. Often, the same questions were asked and answered many times over. He marveled at the pastor's patience and fortitude.

As he listened to the discussions and answered some of the questions that were being directed to him, he suddenly realized that he was being prepared, but not in the way he had expected. He finally put the index cards away and entered into the discussions fully. His concerns about the approaching challenge were forgotten, and the joy of seeing others suddenly understanding the truth-filled his mind with energy and excitement.

Finally, on Saturday, Rubin had escaped to the closed room and finished reading the first testimony while Carol was shopping. He had put the testimony back in its box and returned to his own room at the same time Carol had returned home. Now looking at the mirror and his new clothes he thought about the testimony. What was the purpose of the discovery? The voice had not returned, but he remembered what he had heard. How was it possible that the purpose of the testimonies was fulfilled in this generation? What had the voice meant when it said that they must be passed on? To whom and how was it to be passed on?

He thought about the other testimonies, and he wondered what he would learn from them. He suspected that each would fill in a little more of the experiences surrounding the teacher. The knock on the door broke his thought pattern, and he turned to see Laura's bright eyes looking approvingly at his new clothes.

"You look good!" she said. Rubin beamed in delight. Turning slowly looking in the mirror, he said, "Yep, clothes sure can make the man!" To which when he saw her frown, he added: "Just kidding!"

He followed Laura out to the kitchen and saw that Carol was on the phone while another pair of students entered the home with Molly and Arnold. Carol's waving suddenly gained his attention, and he walked over to where she was. Covering the mouthpiece, she said quickly, "It is Professor Dillington. He needs to talk with you."

Rubin took the phone from Carol and said, "Hello?" He listened intently as both Carol and Laura watched. Rubin's head was already nodding before his voice said, "That would be fine." A brief pause and then he said: " Yes, see you on Thursday, and I am looking forward to it as well." Putting the phone down, he turned to see both Carol's and Laura's questioning faces. Rubin said, "He was asking if it was okay to move the class from the lecture hall we were in to "Smith Hall." I told him it was fine. Both Laura's and Carol's eyes widened. Now it was his turn to look puzzled. Laura ended his confusion, "Smith Hall is the largest of all of the halls on the campus. It is where we hold our commencement exercises and where many of our public events are held.

It seats almost 5,000 people. Rubin slowly sat down. Five thousand people.

At nine o'clock, the pastor had finally left saying simply, "Tomorrow is Sunday, I need to finish preparing for the service." Rubin said to Carol after the pastor had left, "How is he going to do it? He has been here almost every waking moment for the last four days?"

The next morning Rubin arrived at the church and entered with Carol and Laura. A large contingent of students also followed them into the church. As with many Anglican Church buildings, this one was made of stone. The interior held three columns of wooden pews. Each pew row had red cloth colored kneelers that were in either vertical or horizontal positions depending on where the last user had left them. The center column was wider and sat 12 people easily on each pew. The two side pews were about half the size. Altogether the church was designed to hold 400 worshippers. Rubin had heard from Carol that on most Sundays under 50 attended and most were women, many grandmothers. Few young people normally attended and even fewer men. Looking at the large contingent of students, Rubin thought that this Sunday might be different.

By the time the service started the students outnumbered the normal contingent of parishioners. There were over 100 people there. The service was highly liturgical, following a pre-designed pattern, and outlined in a small missal of which each pew had numerous copies. Rubin chose to sit further back and watched with amusement as he realized that many of the students knew even less of the protocol than he did. But he also realized that the students were following the lead of the other parishioners and were intent on not causing a disturbance.

Laura sat with the students, and Carol sat next to him. Finally, the pastor made his way to the pulpit and looked out on the relative sea of faces compared to most of his Sundays. He looked up at the students and began simply with the reading. Rubin heard his words and felt their impact.

The passage was short and simple "The harvest is plentiful, but the workers are few. Therefore, beseech the Lord of the harvest to send out workers into His harvest." Rubin was transported. He looked about, and for a moment, he stood amid a great grain field. He had only seen such a field once, as a youth, when he had visited one of the great farms far from the city. The field was golden, and Rubin reached down and felt the head of one of the stalks of grain. The grain burst forth into his hand and had the sweet, nutty smell that filled his soul with pleasant memories. The wind blew, and the heads of grain seemed to form a great wave as the breath of the wind reached across the field, and the grain flowed with the wind racing towards him.

Just as suddenly Rubin was back, and the heads of the students and other parishioners suddenly replaced the vision of the grain. Their heads bobbed up and down and swayed as they listened to the pastor and took in his words. He heard the pastor's words and another's voice echoed in his ears. The voice said, "Who will go for me?" To this still, another voice answered, "Here I am Lord, send me!"

Suddenly he realized he knew the final voice. It had been his own. He looked around. Carol was still intent upon the pastor's words. He realized that those around him had not heard either voice. But then he saw Laura's face turn towards him, her green eyes flashed the lightning he had witnessed several times before, her smile warmed his soul again, and he realized, she had heard. Her smile said it all, and he was strangely relieved. Her smile said, "I will go with you as well."

The days flew by. More and more students poured into the home. Even two professors also made their way to Carol's home. Rubin marveled at the change that was occurring. The students continued to ask probing questions, and Rubin was finding his time spent more and more turning to the single book he owned that answered so many of the questions. He was still often forced to turn to the pastor for help, but every time the pastor pointed out where the answers might be found, Rubin learned. From time to time, even the pastor would say, "I do not know," but that was often followed by other observations that brought the discussion back on track. He began to realize that while he did not know everything, what he did know was enough to answer most questions. He heard the pastor quote a famous non-believer who had admitted, "It is not what I do not understand that bothers me, but that which I do understand that bothers me."

So, it was that Thursday approached.

In a blink of an eye, the morning arrived. Rubin spent a few minutes longer preparing his clothes that morning. He selected his favorite set of clothes from the two that Carol had purchased. He carefully got dressed and looked in the mirror. What he saw was not encouraging, an old man stared back at him. But as he looked closer, he realized that his eyes shone with a brightness he did not remember. He also saw that the lines of care and worry had faded from around his face. Yes, he was still old, and yet, he was different.

The trip to the university was uneventful. He sat beside Carol in the car, with Laura in the back seat. When they arrived at the University, Carol had parked where she had before. But unlike the former time, both Carol and Laura started walking towards the ultra-modern brick building that Laura had disappeared into the first time. Approaching the building, Rubin read the large brick placard in front of the building that bore the name of the building. It read "Smith Hall."

Upon entering the building, Rubin realized that it was much larger than the outside appearance led one to believe. To the left and right of the entry doors were both large stairwells that led both up and down to what must be numerous classrooms and other rooms on different levels. Students flowed in both directions through these disappearing in both directions. Straight ahead on the main floor, large offices appeared on either side of the huge hall. Walking down the hall, Rubin realized they were walking towards another wall, which was filled with large floor to ceiling glass doors. As Rubin approached the wall, he realized that he could see through the wall and looked down upon an enormous auditorium.

The seating in the auditorium was in stadium format with the chairs sweeping 270 degrees around a large central platform that was larger than many stages Rubin had seen before. Behind the platform, wall-sized glass looked out on a green field. The field sloped away, and the valley that the university overlooked stood revealed. In the center of the platform, a large screen could be lowered from above. The seats in the auditorium were already rapidly filling. Apprehension raised its head, but Laura slipped her hand in Rubin's, and they entered the auditorium together.

Rubin looked around again and realized that at key locations electronic equipment bristled. Several cameras were mounted on movable stands, and Rubin realized that events could be taped or broadcast from this location. Slowly, Rubin began the long trek down one of the isles, heading towards the platform.

Professor Dillington emerged from one of the rooms behind the stage and looked without humor as Rubin, Carol and Laura slowly made their way down the stairs. Laura released Rubin's hand about five rows from the front and then whispered in his ear, before turning to join a group of students who were already sitting close to the front and had obviously saved her a seat as well. He continued down the final stairs and then found that the pastor and Cindy were also there, and Carol squeezed Rubin's arm, planted a kiss on his cheek, and then turned to join them. Rubin continued the final few steps and then turned to follow around to the side to where steps led up to the platform.

Climbing the steps, he was suddenly aware of his age, and for a moment, fatigue weighed him down. Just as suddenly it passed.

Professor Dillington had made no movement to greet the arriving Rubin, but Rubin crossed the stage and stretched out his hand in greeting. The handshake was decidedly cold, reminding Rubin of the gravity of what he was about to undertake. On the stage stood two chairs beside two small square coffee-like tables, three podiums, and a larger central table. From both the larger table and the podiums different small microphones stood.

Rubin took the chair on the left and noticed the glass and water pitcher that resided on each smaller table. Sitting, he filled his water glass and sipped tentatively. The water was cold, and it loosened the frog that had already begun to form within his throat. Rubin turned and looked out on the auditorium that continued to fill. He found Carol, the pastor, and Cindy and smiled at them and then turned to look for Laura. He found Molly first and smiled again as he realized that the contingent of students from the last week was well represented in the section where Laura now sat.

He then began to glance around the rest of the auditorium, and then he froze. In disbelief, he looked again and realized that he recognized a number of the faces that were taking positions in the auditorium. He saw that many of his former colleagues and students were also present. He turned and looked at Professor Dillington, whose snide smile told Rubin volumes. Rubin closed his eyes briefly, spoke silently, and then continued to survey the auditorium. As soon as he opened his eyes, he had seen a tall, gangly figure, now aged and gray, slowly making his way down one of the paths as well. Rubin recognized Louis. Even his friend, the stork, was here. Carol had followed Rubin's gaze, seen Louis, and moved to greet him and draw him down to the row where she was. Rubin watched as Carol and Louis hugged and then both returned to the area where Carol had been.

He continued to look around and saw one other man enter. Also, gray and bent, he still wore a similar black suit and shoes that Rubin had remembered from so many years ago that had marked him as a ministry man. Back then, there had been two of them, but today, only one entered the room. The room continued to fill. Rubin had thought it would be unlikely that even 400 people would come, he had been very wrong. Already the large auditorium was more than half full. Where were all the people coming from?

Rubin also noticed the arrival of several people that were obviously from the press. Professor Dillington had made his way from the platform to greet these folks as they entered. He guided their way to the front of the auditorium where a row of seats had been reserved. He wanted to be sure that they had front row seats.

As he thought about that question, he noticed that Professor Dillington had also returned to the platform with a large box that he now sat on the large table. From this box, he now was removing a large number of books and was stacking those books onto the table. Rubin looked and recognized many of the books. Some were Rubin's own. Others were by authors that like Rubin had held the truth in great disdain for many years. Rubin noticed several of Professor Dillington's books as well.

By the time that Professor Dillington finally stood at the central podium and called the auditorium to order, it was almost three quarters filled. Four thousand faces looked down upon Rubin. Voices filled the room as most individuals were discussing something with the people surrounding them. Finally, Professor Dillington began, "Ladies and Gentlemen" the conversation began to die down, "Ladies and Gentlemen." Finally, a semblance of quiet returned, although a gentle murmur continued.

He continued, "First let me thank so many of you for coming. My name is Professor Dillington, and I am the chairman of the department of philosophy at this university. As some of you may know, I feel that it is important for the department chairman to continually interact with the students that are coming into our facilities. I am proud of what our department accomplishes, guiding, and helping free the bright minds of our future leaders. I often take out additional time to teach several different classes myself.

I could go into my extensive background but choose instead to provide for those of you that wish, a list of my degrees and publications, that you may pick up after the discussion today.

What many of you do not realize is that among the classes I teach is a class on the decline of Superstition and the increase of knowledge and reason. This class has had as its base the writings of a gentleman who was the foremost pioneer and leader in the field. A man who was my own guide for many of my university years and who I counted as being the champion of the new freedom and intellectual honesty that has been sweeping not only this campus but most respectable campuses across this country and the world as well."

"Last week the former champion of intellectual honesty paid a surprise visit to one of my classes. During the disruption that was caused by that visit, I discovered that this champion apparently has suffered a setback, and no longer apparently holds to his former honest appraisal of reality. It was at my invitation that he has returned today. It is my goal, through the use of my amply trained and wise students, to try and dissuade this gentleman of his current slippery views and hopefully draw him back to the reality that he has so adequately defined and defended in the past.

So many heard of this discussion that we have expanded the discussion to this wonderful hall. I am grateful to the administration for making it available to us." At this point, the Professor had clapped gently leading a small ripple of recognition for those of the administration that nodded their approval of the recognition.

He then continued, "I have chosen the style of discussion as it is one of which is fondly remembered by both myself and Professor James." Finally, Rubin had been identified.

Dillington continued: "We will use the tried and true thesis presentation method of discussion. Professor Rubin will have the opportunity to present his new thesis, and then we will all get the opportunity to question him on his thesis." "We will leave to you the decision as to whether the Professor's thesis bears merit. I suspect that before it is over, you will see that it does not, and hopefully, the professor will also." Gentle laughter flowed through the auditorium.

Dillington concluded: "And, yes, my students are being graded on their ability to both sway the professor as well as prove the true place of reason and knowledge in this discussion." He added to this statement another: "Of course, I will be the judge of that." Again, a ripple of laughter, although some was clearly a nervous laugh coming from an obvious set of students arrayed in the front row of seats in the auditorium.

Having said that, the Professor made no further introduction for Rubin but motioned to Rubin to take to the podium. Rubin slowly stood and shuffled more than walked over to the podium. He looked at Professor Dillington, whose impish smile communicated simply, "You asked for it." Rubin stared out at the sea of faces and then back at the Professor. He closed his eyes, listened intently, opened his eyes, and began.

"I wish to thank Professor Dillington for this opportunity to speak today. I am especially grateful that I have the opportunity to speak to so many colleagues, former students, and others today. I had not expected the privilege or the opportunity to correct the grievous harm I have done to so many of you all at the same time." A quiet hush fell across the great hall. Rubin continued, "Most of you probably are surprised that I am still alive? "

He asked it as a question and was greeted with a small murmur of laughter. He continued: "For those of you who do not know, I am still alive," more laughter, "and today I am celebrating another birthday."

It had dawned on him as he sat in the chair listening to Professor Dillington that today was his birthday. This was going to be a birthday to remember.

"Now many of you after listening to Professor Dillington and now knowing my age probably suspect that my current ideas are likely explained away by my age." A few heads bobbed, his age being a very acceptable explanation, even if they still had no idea as to what his current ideas were. He saw through the corner of his eye that even Professor Dillington smiled as the thought agreed with him as well, and Dillington stored it away for the future rebuttal.

Rubin continued " Let me assure you all, that although I may not walk as fast as I once did, and although I might drool more than I once did," a gentle wave of laughter filled the room, he continued, "my mind is still quite clear and in many ways, I see clearer today than ever before. So, let me tell you a story," and so it began.

Rubin started with his own history. He spoke freely of his family, his father and his mother, their own history and struggles, their fears and sorrows. He spoke of their deaths and the sorrows that rippled from those events. He then spoke of Anita, of his first Laura's birth, of Harry Brown and the impact of that man on his life. He spoke of Anita's death, Laura's gift, her rise in the academic world, his own rise as well.

He spoke of his belief in his own mind, his dependence on his own logic to form the reality he embraced. He skipped over the discovery, instead moving quickly to Laura's death, the anger and fear that filled his life. He spoke of his many works; through which he had tried to both remove his own responsibility and yet cement his own control over his life. He spoke of his relationship with Carol, without naming her. He spoke of the great damage he had done, the child he had not known, the driving away from himself of the woman who had loved him anyway and the family he did not realize he had.

He spoke of his daughter's beliefs, of Carol's beliefs, of his newest daughter's beliefs. He spoke of the tapes, his daughter's voice, and then he slowly withdrew a small worn book from his pocket and raised it up in his hand.

His voice broke for the first time as he said, "my daughter drew me to this book, as she herself had been drawn." He opened it to the passage she had marked years ago. Rubin looked out at the faces, all waiting to hear what he had mysteriously found. Rubin read, he introduced it simply, saying, "I am going to read you all a passage from a book in what we all know as the Bible. This is from the gospel of Saint John, starting in Chapter 9.

"And as He passed by, He saw a man blind from birth...."

Rubin read. Bright light filtered in through the windows. The valley below filled the scenery. Rubin looked, and saw all those faces, looking at him listening, and he saw his daughter's eyes, glowing a bright green, and saw her smile as he continued.

A small old man on a great stage spoke, some heard his voice, others heard another's. A gentle breeze swept unnoticed through the great room, and the lightning of the saints' eyes penetrated the souls of all who had been given ears to hear, and eyes to see.

25

All Things Made New

How does one measure a day? How does one measure a life? Rubin finally sat looking out on the auditorium, seeing it still more than a quarter full, numerous discussions still continuing. He measured the day and prayed softly again that the teacher might use it. He knew he had done his best.

He had watched as the core of students with Laura among them had fanned out among the others in the auditorium. Moving in pairs, they had engaged many who still lingered in the auditorium. He saw that most carried with them a copy of the same book he had read from. Even now as he looked, he saw many were listening intently as the students explained, read, and pointed out answers to the questions being asked.

He saw that Laura had paired herself with a rather stocky gentleman who appeared somewhat older than Laura and yet bore the trappings of a student. He watched as Laura had slipped her hand into his and moved together with him, seeking out another small group that still stood speaking together. Rubin smiled. Why was it he thought that our children so often seek out and find partners that remind them of their own parents? He had never thought about Laura in that way. Now as he saw her green eyes turn and listen to her partner's questions and answers, Rubin saw the flame of respect that spoke of a relationship that she had not bothered to discuss yet with him.

Professor Dillington had left almost immediately. Sweeping down upon the news contingent present, Rubin had heard his laugh shared by many of that contingent and listened as he invited them all for refreshments at the president's home. Some of his students, earning extra recognition from their teacher, handed out the professor's bio information, and leaped into action when asked for their opinions. That contingent had made its way out of the auditorium never even turning to acknowledge Rubin or to invite him as well.

Rubin stood and slowly moved over to the table where the many books remained piled. Many were open, lying with markers exposed, reminding Rubin of the grilling that the books had been used for. Gently he laid his own thin volume on the table, and in his mind, he saw the great scale tip decidedly towards his own small volume.

It was as he pondered this that he was aware that a small group of individuals had moved down the stairs and now waited for his awareness. The closest was the man, dressed in his black suit that looked around at the others. Rubin could see that the man was weighing whether to speak or to wait for the others to be done. Rubin stepped from the stage.

He looked at the man and smiled. He greeted the man, not remembering his name, saying simply "I thought you would have retired by now!" The man smiled and retorted, "And I thought you would be dead by now!" Both laughed and then the man said, "I have retired, many years ago as a matter of fact. But I still stay in touch with my office, and they have a problem. I learned that you were still alive and decided to come to see if perhaps you might aid them with their problem." He then described the situation, and Rubin suddenly knew the design of the events being related. After the man had described what was needed, Rubin shook his head and said, "I believe I can help, and I would be more than delighted, too if I can." To this, the man had smiled back, produced two cards, one worn with age that bore his own name and former office. On this card, the man had quickly scribbled another phone number on the back and said, "That is my home number." The other, much newer and fresher looking, still crisp from a recent package, bore the name of his replacement at the ministry. The name there was the one with the problem to solve.

Rubin invited the man, Peter Knowles II, the worn card said, to stay and to come over to Carol's house. Peter looked around, shook his head, and said, "You have so many others waiting for you, perhaps later?" To this, Rubin had slowly nodded but then added as he had already grasped and shaken the man's offered hand, "Are you sure you have later?" Their eyes locked, and suddenly Peter had crumpled in saying, "Yes, you are right, maybe I should come now." He stepped back from the crowd of others and said, "I'll just sit down over there while you finish." Rubin watched as Peter sat down, familiar fatigue and burden showing on Peter's face as it had shown on Rubin's own for many years.

The others who waited to greet Rubin were a mixture of students, professors, and others. He noted that two of Professor Dillington's own students were in the group, as well as several of his own former students. Rubin smiled warmly as he realized the many different ages, races, and nationalities represented even in this small group. The questions began. Rubin continued to answer as best he could. Through the corner of his eye, he saw Peter, listening in on all that was occurring, and Rubin relaxed as he was now sure that Peter was staying. Another face came into focus, one of the news people, a middle-aged woman, who had left with the other group, walked slowly down the steps and soon joined the group. Her eyes spoke of questions of her own that Rubin doubted would ever be read in her newspaper.

Later that evening, Rubin thought again, "How does one measure a day?" He smiled as he laid down on the bed, and thought, no matter how he measured this one; it had been one of the best days of his life. Carol's house was still packed to overflowing. Students, professors, seekers, one and all had flooded through and swirled around the small home until late in the evening. The Pastor and Cindy had taken some of the overflow to their own home as well. The discussions still ebbed and flowed even as Rubin had finally declared his need of rest.

Rubin had spent much of the evening speaking with Peter. For the first time, he had disappeared down the hall with someone else. He had unlocked the silent room, and together he and Peter had slipped inside. When they finally emerged, Peters' eyes were filled with mist. He shook Rubin's hand again and made his way towards the door. As Rubin watched Peter leave, he saw that Peter's fatigue had seemed to melt away. He was still an old man, yet something had occurred this day that had changed him as well. Both Carol and Laura had watched as Rubin had led the strange man dressed in black down the hall. They both had looked at one another with some apprehension, but also with the realization that Rubin understood the gravity of what he was doing. They saw Peter's departure and perceived the change within him. Carol looked over to Rubin, the question written on her face. Rubin's peaceful smile and nod spoke of answers yet to come but the knowledge that it was okay.

Rubin lay on his bed, still fully dressed and thought more of the day. He sensed his door opening and closing. He looked over and watched as Carol came and sat on the floor next to the bed, close to Rubin's head. Her eyes locked on his and before she could speak, Rubin said, "You know that you are a very beautiful woman." Carol's eyes filled with warmth. She said slowly, "I am so very proud of you, Rubin." Rubin slowly sat up, and Carol wrapped herself around Rubin's middle in an embrace, laying her head on one of his legs. Rubin slowly touched her hair and seeing the pencil-like stick that held her hair in its tight bun, removed it and allowed her hair to flow down around her face. Her once golden hair now was mostly silver, but it was still soft and wool-like. He sat there patting her head, smoothing her hair, with joy flowing through his being.

Finally, she looked up into his eyes and reached up, and their kiss joined them together again. After a little while, Rubin pushed them apart slowly standing her up and then he sank to his knees. Still looking up into Carol's eyes, he first said, "I need to ask your forgiveness, for not having loved you enough to do this many years ago. Carol's tears welled up again, but her eyes sparkled with hope, and then he said, "Carol, Would you marry me?"

It was a crisp December morning. The weather had turned decidedly colder, yet the blue sky and bright morning sun beckoned them out. November had been a blur of activity. Rubin had returned to his home, boxed up the tapes, still resting on his dining room table where he had left them. He had contacted the movers and made many trips disposing of much of the collection of junk that he no longer needed. The house had sold in less than three days, and he had moved. The former life was behind him. He took only the tapes, a few small books, and some pictures from the time past.

Carol and Rubin were married by the pastor on November 22. Rubin chose the date, coinciding with the death of a man whose works he had read years ago, but whose impact was only now registering in Rubin's life. There had been no honeymoon, as so much remained to be done. The greatest joy of his life occurred that first evening when for the first time in over twenty years, Carol had snuggled close to him in bed, and they had fallen together into a peaceful, dreamless sleep.

The pastor's church changed dramatically in November as well. The first Sunday after the presentation at the university, the church saw more than 200 people attend. The next Sunday the number had increased again. What was even more amazing, some of the women, who had been long-term parishioners, were accompanied by their men. The pastor's reaction at first was shock. Later he confided in Rubin and Carol his surprise, but also his realization that his response showed the depth of the lack of faith still evident in his own life. By the third week, the sudden growth and activity at his church had attracted the attention of the bishop who had attended the service the next Sunday. Rubin saw the bishop's body language radiate concern and disagreement with the pastor's message. Later as the congregation exited the church, Rubin saw the bishop did not know how to react to the "Molly" crowd, that the pastor had so embraced. Rubin was sure that there was trouble brewing for the pastor.

The next day was the wedding. So much needed to be done. Carol decided quickly many of the salient issues. It was to be a small, simple wedding. Laura would be her bridesmaid, and she would ask Cindy, the pastor's wife, also to stand as a witness. She decided quickly which dress she would wear. She had decided against a formal wedding gown, acknowledging that she did not feel comfortable with the purity of a white gown. She explained that she knew her earlier actions had been forgiven, but the facts remained. She would not pretend they had not happened.

Together they had looked for a ring for Carol without success. Finally, Laura had brought a small box out from her room. In it was a band that Rubin immediately recognized. It had belonged to his Anita and was the band that he had given her so many years ago. When Anita died, Rubin had taken the band and given it to his first Laura. Carol looked at the band, and then shared that Laura had given it to her just before she had died, asking that Carol give it to her yet unborn child.

"Somehow," Carol said, "She knew it was going to be a girl." Rubin looked at the ring and looked at Carol. Carol's sparkling eyes gave Rubin his answer.

Rubin had a more significant problem. He had so few friends, who could stand as best man and witness for him. The few friends he had made over the years were mostly gone. Part of the solution arrived at the dinner table two days after proposing to Carol. The expanding crowd of students and others continued to flow in and out of Carol's home. Many would stay for a least one meal, while others stayed for more. It seemed that both the message and their stomachs ruled the students' attention. The same young man that had accompanied Laura after the presentation arrived with Laura that evening. The normal discussions were already well underway having flowed and ebbed based on the number of people present at any given time. When Carol offered that "dinner" was served, the discussion had simply moved from various rooms to the dining area. Rubin had discovered that Laura's friend's name was Bertram Windsor. Laura introduced him simply as Bert. It was over dinner that Rubin had explained his dilemma and then turning to Laura asked her if she had any ideas. She did, and soon Bert was added to the wedding party both as Rubin's witness but also as

Laura's partner for the day. This left only one more problem…the best man.

Try as they may, neither Rubin nor Carol could come up with a suitable person. Both had thought about the pastor, but they realized that they preferred that he conduct the ceremony. With less than a week to go, no solution had arisen. It was the Wednesday before the wedding when the package had arrived for Rubin just as they had prepared to eat their evening meal. The small package contained his book that he had left behind on the stage after the presentation. The note was handwritten and Rubin recognized the scrawl. The note said simply, "You left this behind on the table, I thought about throwing it out, but thought better of it." It had no signature or other greeting.

Rubin got up and walked over to the telephone. Rubin had been praying about what contact he should have with the writer of the note. The idea came to him, and before he could chicken out, he picked up the phone and dialed the number.

The phone was answered after three rings, and the somewhat nasally "hello" identified for Rubin that he had reached the person he desired. He introduced himself and then said, "I am calling to thank you for sending my book back. I had plain forgotten what I had done with it!" Rubin listened briefly and then laughed a little saying, "well, I am sure I can do more damage with it now that I have it back!" Once again, Rubin listens to the response.

Rubin then said quickly, "Ah, before you go, I have a favor to ask." A pause followed by an "Ah ha, yes, I was wondering," for the first time Rubin stammered but then quickly recovered saying, to tell you the truth, I am getting married next Monday." Again, a little interruption from the other side and Rubin said, "to Carol, you remember, Carol Anders, who was my research assistant years ago."

After another brief pause, listening and another laugh, "Yes, it is quite amazing. I am so incredibly blessed." Rubin continued "Well, as you can imagine many of my friends are no longer here, and I thought that well since you know me as well as anyone and better than most that perhaps, well, perhaps you would do me the great honor of being my best man?" Silence ensued. Finally, Rubin said, "Hello, are you still there?" The voice on the other end of the line asked a question, and Rubin laughed and said, "Yes, I am very sure I would like you to do it!" Again silence, and then Rubin said, "That's great! I am so glad that you can.

Listen, we have a short practice on Saturday evening at 6 PM, you know just a run through to be sure that we do it right, could you join us? There is also a small dinner out at the Willard Pub afterward for the wedding party, you can bring someone along if you like." Another brief silence and then Rubin said, "That is tremendous, we are meeting at St Andrew's for the practice, I'll see you around six then?" Finally, Rubin said, "Thanks, see you, then."

Carol and Laura had both listened in on his conversation, their own curiosity growing by the syllable. Who in the world had he found to be his best man? Rubin turned from the phone, his smile reminding Carol of the cat who had swallowed the canary. Carol asked, "Who in the world was that?" Rubin's eyes twinkled, and his smile grew even bigger.

On the other side of town, a very bewildered man set the phone back on the phone cradle. His companion of many years said to him, "Whom were you talking to dear?" He turned to look at the woman who had been his student some twenty years ago and who had been his lover since. Lisa Martin was still a beauty. Her dark hair flowed around her slightly rounded face but her full mouth, shapely nose, and sparkling brown eyes more than made up for the roundness. The rest of her was also incredible. She had always remained active, with tennis and swimming keeping her in better shape than many of the newest potential conquests at the university.

She stood even with his height, and he had found that he enjoyed dancing with a partner that he could look straight in the eyes. The fact that she had adored the ground he walked on also had helped cement the attraction. He had played down her own intelligence but recently realized it too had been a lure for him. It helped that she agreed with most of his ideas. Those that she did not agree with, she very wisely kept silent about.

They had never married, and he marveled that she had stayed so long. She had been very aware of his roving eye and knew that faithfulness was not a word or a concept that he would ever grasp. Yet she had stayed.

He had taken a cue from his mentor, and having watched his life, felt sanctioned to play the field broadly. After all, his star was rising, and one thing that attracted attractive women was the thought of importance gained by being with someone important. Yet, as the time had worn on, he had begun to feel an emptiness that only grew with every new conquest. It seemed so odd that he could have so many and yet remain so lonely.

Only recently, had the strain begun to show on Lisa. Interestingly enough, it had been at the very time that he had found himself "too busy" to think about chasing all the other opportunities, that Lisa's own patience had begun to wear thin. After twenty years of waiting, he had sensed that time was finally running out.

He returned to the overstuffed armchair from which he had risen and looked at Lisa. He was still astonished, but he said, "It was

Professor James. He is getting married, and he wants me to be his best man!"

"You have got to be kidding!" she said. "No, it was him, alright. He said I knew him better than most." He was still looking lost by what had occurred. "What did you tell him?" she asked. Not for the first time, Professor Dillington wondered whether he should have declined the offer.

That Saturday evening Professor Dillington had arrived at Saint Andrew's at the appointed time, Lisa in tow as well. Rubin had greeted them at the door of the church enthusiastically. Rubin made very unneeded introductions, as everyone else in the wedding party knew who the professor was having seen him in action less than a month before. The professor saw Laura and Bert eyeing him with great suspicion, and once again, he wondered at the wisdom of having accepted such an invitation. It was Carol, Cindy, and the pastor that had made the difference. They had swept down on him, and Lisa and their energy and passion soon had both Lisa, and the professor won over. While Lisa had sat in one of the pews watching, the practice had begun. The pastor walked them through all the steps without faltering.

The problem began when the pastor introduced the passage that would be the charge to the bride and groom. Professor Dillington listened. The words thundered in his mind, and in the middle of the passage, tears had begun to flow down his face. Rubin had watched as the first tear made its way down his face. Rubin sensed a great tearing occurring within his former student. The curtain that had wrapped his soul for so many years was tearing, and soon, nothing would be able to seal up what had been opened. Rubin once again had the sensation of standing in the grain field, and smelling the ripe grain bursting forth as it waited to be harvested. Once again, the breeze moved, and so did

Rubin. Everyone had stood in muted silence as the tears had fallen from Professor Dillington's face. Everyone except Rubin, who had reached over and caught the professor as he had collapsed into a contorted, sobbing ball.

Rubin gently lifted his former student, and together, they had left the altar to a little room from which the pastor had emerged to start the practice. Carol looked, suspected what was happening and seeing Lisa sitting confused and worried left her spot to sit beside Lisa and talk with her.

After more than an hour had passed, the door that had swallowed Rubin and the professor reopened. Together the two men emerged. Both had tear tracks still obvious on their faces. The pastor went to greet them back and spoke in hushed tones with both.

Everyone saw that the professor kept looking up at Lisa. Lisa's own eyes had not left the professor since he had returned. Finally, the professor had broken loose from the pastor and Rubin and walked steadily towards her. Carol had stood and moved so that he might be closer, and everyone heard Lisa's question, "Are you alright?" To this, the professor had haltingly said, "yes and no." Then he surprised everyone as he knelt before her, taking her hand and burst into tears again saying. "Can you ever forgive me?" He had then laid his head down in her lap and wept. Everyone watched as an obviously surprised Lisa went from shock to acceptance, to forgiveness and then finally to joy.

Her own tears flowed freely as she brushed her hand across the professor's head and slowly bent her own down to his crown. Kissing the top of his head, through her tears, they all heard her say, "I have always loved you. I just could not believe that you could maybe love me as well." The professor's head had raised slightly, he had looked into her eyes and said, "I do now, I never knew how to before." Their kiss and tears mingled freely, and so did the tears and hugs of many others.

The rehearsal was done. Rubin announced that he was more than ready for Monday, and with a good deal of laughing and still some more tears, they all left for dinner and the pub.

Monday had arrived all too slowly in Rubin's own mind. Despite all that had happened, Rubin just could not wait for it to be over. He was amazed at the amount of activity in Carol's house on the morning of the wedding. He had been ready for over two hours, and yet Carol and Laura seemed to have just started. Finally, Bert had arrived, a full two hours before the wedding and Rubin had asked if it was okay that he and Bert go over to the church ahead of time. Carol had begun to protest, but Laura had seen the wisdom and simply quieted her mother and waved them both towards the door.

Rubin spent the time with Bert learning about how Bert and Laura had first met, and on discussing what he still did not understand about women, even after all his years of life. Rubin and Bert reached the church finding it empty of people but filled with the flowers and candles that Carol had wanted for the occasion. Rubin and Bert had retired to the little room set aside for them, which had also served as the site of Professor Dillington's waking as well as the pastor's study. About an hour before the wedding was to begin, the professor had also joined the small group, and together, they had sat reminiscing about the past and all that had occurred.

Finally, with less than ten minutes to go, the pastor had arrived in a rush. "Sorry, I've been delayed." He carried with him the late edition of the Sunday paper. He had turned the paper to a particular page and handed it to Rubin. Rubin looked and then began reading aloud, the article was titled "The Triumph of Faith and Reason" by Margaret

Fletcher. "Margaret Fletcher?" Rubin said, thinking back to the presentation at the university and the slightly overweight middle-aged female reporter who had returned to ask him some questions when all the rest of the press had followed the professor. Apparently, Rubin had misjudged again. The questions he had thought would never see the light of day in print were there staring up at him.

As he read, he discovered that Margaret Fletcher's mother had been a student with Anita and had been the cause of the late arrival of all of Anita's supporters to her thesis discussion so many years ago. That single act of spite and hate had been the catalyst that had led him here to this day. Her mother had never forgotten her act, and over the years had done everything possible to atone for the meanness she had discovered within herself. She had shared with her daughter the realization of her own evil nature and had found the teacher and his truth. Her daughter also knew the teacher but was curious about what had happened to the people involved in that act that had so molded her own mother.

The article spoke of Rubin's own history, the history of Professor Dillington, and had excerpts from the great debate, as she called it, at the university but a scant few weeks ago. Her language was filled with prose that painted the scenery of two giants welding incredibly brilliant swords striving mightily against one another. Neither giant was portrayed as a villain, although it was clear that she saw one giant as needing to be guided by the other. The only picture that accompanied the article was a picture of the table with the pile of books standing against the single volume that stood alone on its side of the table. Rubin knew the picture had to have been taken after he had left the room. He remembered that his book had been closed, in the picture it was obviously opened. If you looked closely enough, you could see that she had opened it to John 9.

She concluded her article with a surprisingly recent piece of information. The two giants were meeting again, except this time, together they were acting as best men for each other. Where conflict had been waged, now something better was emerging. Rubin and Professor Dillington looked at one another with surprise. How could she have learned of the change that occurred on Saturday in time for the newspaper on Sunday? It was a question that would have to wait. Even as they thought it, the pastor said, "Its time."

Together they exited from the room to face the arrival of their brides. As they exited the room, they looked up to see that the church was overflowing. Rubin and the Professor's surprise were evident. Rubin whispered almost too loud, "So much for the small and simple wedding!" As they looked out on the crowd, they together saw students, colleagues, and friends. Louis, the "stork" and Peter Knowles sat together with their wives on the second row. In the center of the fourth row back sat Margaret Fletcher, with a smile that could have split a smaller face in half. Both Rubin and Professor Dillington pointed to her as if to say, "shame on you," but their hands quickly fell back to their sides as Laura entered followed closely by Carol and Lisa.

That had been three weeks ago. In but a few more days, both Rubin and Professor Dillington would be joining for their first Christmas dinner as friends and as newlyweds.

Today, however, there was still another task to fulfill. Peter Knowles had arrived at the house early. He had called the evening before, and Rubin had assured him that everything would be ready. Rubin asked if he had completed his task as well and he also assured Rubin everything was ready.

CHARLES A. DE ANDRADE

Rubin and Laura walked in the brightness of the morning along the well-worn path. Rubin led the way, bearing the greater weight of the burden that swayed slightly between them. He knew the way having walked this path so many times over the past twenty years. Bert had argued that he should allow him to carry the burden, after all, Rubin was ninety-five, and Laura was a woman. Neither Rubin nor Laura would hear of it.

The wall appeared as they broke through the covering. Even in the day, it was an imposing sight. A tall line for as far as the eye could see. It stood a gray reminder of the past, its jagged rocks still imposing and grand. Man, though only an apprentice had learned much from the master builder. It was amazing what could be done when they put their minds to it.

They approached the area where the wall formed a corner. From here the wall made an abrupt right-angle turn. At the turn, the wall was more than double its normal thickness. The corner was their destination. It was here that the space for the burden had been prepared. A much younger man that was soon introduced to them as Peter's successor met them. It had been his problem that they had come to solve. And the problem was obvious. The stones had been removed from the spot, and the flimsy remains of an older mold were still lying on the ground where they had been tossed after being removed from the space. The blocks of stone had once again started to fall in as the molded box had lost its shape and form. "Strange," thought Peter's successor out loud, he had read the report of what that mold had been made of. It should have at least lasted a few hundred years.

After proper introductions were done, Rubin and Laura hefted the burden into the space that had been made for it. As before, it fit perfectly. Peter's successor had queried, somewhat worriedly, about the material used to make the replacement. He said, "It looks like wood! I would have expected some space-type synthetic." To that, Rubin said simply, "I can promise you that the material that this is made from will last two thousand years or longer if required." "Wow! The man said, "And I thought it was just wood, amazing what science is doing these days." To this, Rubin and Laura only looked at one another and grinned.

After the box was in place, Laura had almost lovingly rubbed her hand against it one last time. Her father stood back, understanding, and then finally said, we must hurry, we have much to do yet. Peter joined them, slowly handing back to Rubin the stones, in exactly the reverse pattern from which he had removed them. After two hours, the wall was almost complete, only the last two stones were required. Peter's successor jumped in picking up the stones and trying to force them into the opening. Finally, Rubin gently took the stones from him, formed them at the angle he remembered and slipped them back into place. A loud audible snap was heard, and the wall was intact once again. Peter's successor once again approached the wall and pulled on the stones to assure that they fitted together snuggly. Even as he touched the wall, a strange green light filtered through the cracks of the wall and before their eyes, all the cracks between the stones were instantly filled in and solid. Peter's successor jumped back, saying, "What in the world was that!" But only a few knew the answer to that question.

Once in the car going home, Rubin had chosen to sit in the back seat with Laura. Peter rode upfront with Carol, who was driving, and Bert sat in the trunk area of the station wagon. Rubin slid his arm around Laura, drawing her close, as he saw the sadness in her face.

Laura was lost thinking back over the years, and all that the testimonies had meant to her. Now, they were gone. Yet even as she thought about that, she realized that she had both the copies, the tapes, and even more so, the far greater testimony that was readily available to everyone.

She wondered what she was supposed to do with the copies. It was then that an idea began to take hold. She could still use them. And then she began to think, but not by themselves, no, she could use them if she embedded them in other works. She thought what she had been learning about advertising and communication. How thoughts could be embedded within seemingly innocent communications and how these thoughts could influence people.

She thought, and a title flashed before her. She would call the first book, "The Tears of the Saints."

Rubin remembered back to the evening before, as Laura had freely given up the two pouches she had worn for so long. The green stones had flowed back to their place, a clear indication that what they were doing was what was required. How the stones had come to leave their spaces was another story that Rubin knew Laura would reveal when she was ready.

The pouch with the gold coin she had begun to lay into the box as well, on top of the testimonies, but Rubin had stopped her. Instead, he had reached over his own head, and slowly removed another pouch that had resided there. He opened it slowly, took out a gold coin, and laid it in the palm of his hand. It was the twin. He said simply. "You are to keep your coin. It is your emblem of hope, and you should pass it on to your children and their children after them. Whispering in their minds all that it stands for and who it points to, until such time as it is needed in the light again." With that, he had returned the coin to the pouch and gently laid it on the testimonies. They then finished the assembly of the box.

Even now in the car, Rubin saw Laura's hand on her chest and realized she was clutching the small pouch through the fabric of her shirt. Her sadness though had seemed to ease. He placed his arm around her and drew her tight against his side. She entered his embrace easily, burying her head against his coat and side. She said in a quiet voice, "Thanks, Daddy." Rubin kissed the top of her head, even as his tears of joy splashed from his eyes.

A Peek at Book Two
in The Eyewitness Series:
The Risen Saints

I t was time.
Even across the unimaginable distance, his voice called me by name with a clarity seemingly impossible.

The past four days had been glorious. The journey to get here had been long and arduous. I had not wanted to make the trip and had labored for weeks to escape the need. The one who called me now had even been sent for, to see if he might be able to intervene, but he had not arrived in time. Yet, once I arrived, I was stunned by the beauty of this place and filled with joy inexpressible. The light in this place was unlike that produced by the sun that lite the land I had come from. Instead, this light flooded every crevice in my soul, filling me with peace and warming my thoughts. I realized that all that had troubled me before had disappeared, and a presence replaced the former emptiness I had often been aware of.

My mother and father greeted me first. They had left on their annual trip, collecting the species and harvesting the oils that were the basis of our business. They had not returned when expected, and now I had found them. They explained immediately the reasons behind their delayed return and then walked me around to other relatives and friends who were also sojourning with them in this place.

We spoke for hours, never getting tired, and the need for food or sleep seemingly missing. Yet there were two here, who appeared to still need to eat and who also still rested as we all had in the land I have traveled from. They were different from all the others here, their appearance remarkably solid compared to the ethereal nature of the rest of us.

I listened in awe as these two shared their own stories. Both were waiting to be summoned back, to the place I had left so unexpectedly. My parents had told me that I too would be returning, way before these two would arrive. The one man was one of the most famous personalities of our nation. His activities were still spoken of in awe, and his story was taught to every child as part of learning about our history. His mighty acts still inspired many to cling to the truths he had spoken openly about. He looked exactly like the image my teachers had embedded in my mind, as they told me his story.

The second man, I too had heard about, but his story was shrouded in mystery, and he shared little more insight into his arrival here, other than to say he was waiting the day when he would return, to serve as a witness to the amazing events leading up to an even more dramatic entrance of the one who had called me. He had been waiting here far longer than any of the others I met. He was a bear of a man, tall and stout, with a full beard, and blazing eyes. Both men's eyes were remarkably similar, as they seemed to burn with a fire that caused most to glance down when talking with them.

I waved at my mother and father, and cried out, "I'll be back," even as I started walking in the direction of the voice. I wondered whether the trip back would be as difficult as the trip here, but my fears were quickly put to rest.

AUTHORS NOTES

I was born into a Catholic family. My father and mother, but mostly my mother, read to us often from those written traditions regarding many of the saints of the past. These formerly oral traditions, now captured into writing, filled much of my youthful memories. I wish I could say that I had embraced the truth from an early age. The truth of the matter is that while I was gifted with a keen mind, I also was bound by earthly desires that controlled my thoughts and actions for many years.

Long after I became an adult, events occurred that slowly drew me to the truth of the Christ. Many people were instrumental in that process, including my grandparents, my parents, especially my mother, my wife, several godly pastors, and three dear friends who also bear the name "Charles," Charles Klein, Charles Lathe, and Charles Estes. All had profound impacts on my life. Many of those used by God to draw me to Himself, have gone to be with the One that was their center and foundation. I know the great privilege to be surrounded by a great host of saints of whom I long to be counted among.

The truth found me and drew me to where I am today. Today I am a Christian who attends a Presbyterian Church. As I close out my 66th year of life, I realize that much is to be gained from the testimonies of earlier saints and the traditions that have come from their lives. I also believe that the scripture must serve as the filter through which all traditions must pass. Only those in conformity with the scripture should be embraced as anything more than tradition. I am particularly mindful of the warnings of Christ to the Pharisees of his day who he scolded for having created traditions that allowed men to ignore the clear teaching of God.

This book is a novel. A novel, by definition, contains much that comes from the authors' own mind. I have struggled in writing this novel for fear that some might read too much into those parts that have come from my mind. It is my hope that the novel would instead drive the reader back to the text of scripture that is the true and reliable history of the events recorded. That is not to say that I do not also pray that those parts that come from my mind are also used. I hope that my thoughts have come from a sanctified mind that may in some places help explain more of the emotion of those events.

Some of the events that I have related are based on historical fact and passed on tradition.

The Hadrian Wall in Britain is real. The wall still exists, built by the Romans, in response to the threats of the various roaming tribes, including the Picts. The edicts related to the early persecution of the Christian church are well documented and known. The methods of execution have also been relayed through history. Christ's own words warned of the divisions that would occur in families, as the truth of Christ would split belief from unbelief, and in many cases shatter the family bond.

But what of the people the scripture talks about?

Unfortunately, often the individual people are swallowed by history with only brief glimpses surfacing of their existence. Some, normally, individuals of wealth and power, created artifacts that remain testifying to their former presence. We live in an age that has so come to trust artifacts that many demand this type of solid evidence that we can touch rather than believe what has been written and handed down through the generations to support the reality of an individual's former presence. Individuals who were written about in the scriptures but held by our generation as likely fictional suddenly surface through a new discovery confirming the reality of the existence of the person.

In the late 19th and early 20th-century photography added a here before unknown artifact into our culture. Pictures became the primary artifact of our time used to record and prove the history of recent ages. Until the advent of the computer, few would dispute the rise of many who were recorded visually for all of us to see and remember. The 20th century will be remembered as the most documented and recorded century in mans' existence.

The advent of computer enhancement now threatens the photographic artifact. New computer-generated "reality" has forced upon us a whole new realm. Experts now must examine photographic evidence for fraud, as the former tool of recording events becomes a tool for creating or manipulating events. The visual tool trusted to record reality now creates sensations as formerly impossible images are created and displayed. Our visual and auditory senses are now betrayed and often led astray by these new tools.

The next generation will be faced with even more difficult questions related to truth as our new tools continue to push our ability to recognize and respond to reality. Illusion is rapidly replacing reality as the new realm of experience for many. Recent movies show just how far our own ability has come in creating a reality where none actually exists. Illusion has become reality. Evidence of reality is being denied at increasing rates. Illusion instead provides an escape from the demands of reality. Objective truth, once the center of philosophical and historical debates has been replaced by the subjective perceptions of individuals and groups, permitting massive manipulations by those who are challenged or opposed by the truth.

Before the 20th century, visual representations of many individuals remain, captured in the many drawings and portraits that fill the museums of the world. Others are captured on the walls of caves and on the frescos hidden under the now submerged parts of the ancient towns of the world. Often walking through such museums or caves, one is prone to forget that these people were alive, and all had stories to tell. Their stories are often shadowed in the paintings or hidden surroundings that provide but a single snapshot into their stories. Some are remembered by their writings and the traditions surrounding those writings that were passed down through the generations. Much is learned as the ancient writings on walls, stones, and scrolls are discovered and slowly deciphered. Curiously again, if those writings only fill the pot of acquired knowledge, they raise little debate or concern.

It is when long-existing writings or newly discover artifacts point to the reality of the One who should be our center of focus, the very evidence is denied and questioned because the truth of His presence would demand a fundamental shift in our view of reality. It is no surprise then that many of the everyday, common people, touched by the Christ remain a mystery covered by the dust of time. Much of what we know about these people are found only in the oral traditions that are handed down over the spread of time until finally some were captured in written form.

These traditions often merge, grow, decline, and contradict one another. Yet, these traditions point to a common reality, and testify to the truth of many people who have lived and remember events that I now personally long to have seen and touched.

I understand the great gap that has caused many a Christian to disdain the "traditions of men" that have led so many astray into even greater errors. The debate between the position of tradition and the position of the scripture has led too much of the fragmentation in Christianity today. As "freedom of interpretation" has taken hold of the Christian church, more and more fragmentation has occurred. Many have forgotten the warning in the much-quoted passage from the epistle of Timothy regarding this issue or they have chosen a cavalier approach to the seriousness of the warnings found there.

It should be no small matter to so easily disturb the peace and tranquility that should reside within the church body. The debate between personal interpretation and the direct authority of the Church is not an easy debate to pick sides in. Both are filled with the potential of serious error. Both have led to fragmentation within the church and the surrendering of a clear understanding of God-given truth. Church split after church split has occurred often over issues that should have been resolved through Christian forbearance.

The strength of the church is in its many parts and not in the uniformity of those parts. The toe is not the same as the eye. Individually they do not make up the totality of the body. Together they are the body. Only when the toe claims to be an eye or even more severely claims to be the body in total and sheds its' identity as the toe should amputation even be considered. Before that time, much ointments and discussions must be applied, and every attempt be made to restore the toe to its toe-ness. After all, walking without all of ones' toes is a very painful matter for the rest of the body.

When one studies Church history, one discovers that most believers living in a body filled with unbelief had two principal conclusions. They either help lead the whole back to the truth or were eventually cast out by untruth. Few chose to leave. Like the blind man, whose testimony pointed out what was obvious (and not some secretly hidden minor event), did he find himself an outcast? But he did not leave of his own accord, he was "put out."

So, do not seek to be separated quickly. Instead, pray that your presence might lead to a great reformation within your body. Also, prayerfully consider and hold up to the Lord your position.

Remember, it is often easy for our corrupt nature to make us believe that we are in fact, something we are not. If it becomes obvious that what is at stake is the Lord's own truth, then we must be willing to run the race before us. We should never let our desire for comfort and tranquility override the true nature of God's peace that is often neither comfortable nor tranquil in this life.

At times, such foundational errors are present as to demand a reaction, especially when those errors lead to the denying of the very person and work that the scripture was given to reveal. There can be no forbearance if to do so would lead to the death of the very life the scripture is meant to reveal.

There exists in our generation a great falling away from the historic belief of the Church in the risen Lord. History records for us that the church has battled heresy during all its existence. A close examination of history since the time of Christ will show that almost every diversion from the truth already had its prototype within the first two centuries. Yet, in our age, the depth of unbelief and denial by those claiming to be Christians has reached a crescendo. The late nineteenth and twentieth centuries echoed with the unbelief that attempted to strip the scripture of the clearly divine intrusions into human history.

The fruits of these attempts produced entire congregations claiming the name of Christ yet unmoved or changed by the powerful presence of the Spirit. These fallen souls found the evidence of Christ stripped of power and therefore devoid of the very changing quality that provides evidence of His presence.

The church that has clung to the historic truths and presence of the divine intrusion into human history has reduced its significance to society as it has argued among its various parts and hurled anathemas at each other. Even more hideous is the fact that many have agreed with the truths of the scripture but have found it easy to slip into irrelevance desiring the "peace" peace of this world and sacrificing the peace that comes from following the one who gives the only true peace.

This is a lesson I have only recently begun to learn in my own life, and I now see the great error in knowing so much and doing so little.

This Lord that I claim to follow has demands that challenge my comfortable lifestyle. We are commanded to "contend for the faith once delivered." This requires that we cling closely to the Word of God and that we proclaim and live that word visibly in our society. Our actions and our life must be the visible display of the truth of the Savior's presence. Our repentance and our humble reliance upon Him must show the world that we stand not under our own power but by His power. It is His power to which they will be drawn and changed.

Do not forget that the unbelieving world uses our actions as an opportunity to blaspheme the very name we so desire to lift up. To the disbelieving world, squabbles within the family, merely bring smiles to their faces instead of tears to their eyes. Would that our eyes would also shed many tears and our minds think long and hard before choosing any path that brings the church ridicule.

Division, caused by different understandings of the scripture, was foreseen within the scripture itself. The warning, attached to this foresight, is often overlooked or downplayed. Splits bear with its great sorrow, the sure knowledge that the Lord of the Church will judge accurately the true intent of our hearts and the real facts of the matter.

There is no easy answer to how the filtering of the traditions occurs or how to make the final decision related to these traditions. This fact has led many rational people to claim to have discarded tradition in total only to discover that they have still embraced traditions that agree with their particular mindset. Tradition that "adds to the scripture" should be denied. Yet let us be sure that before we place any given tradition in that category that we have also asked the much more difficult questions. Does the tradition explain cultural realities pointed to by the scripture? Does the tradition support the scripture both in its testimony and its purpose? As we ask and answer these questions pray that the real role of tradition might be filled with the power of the Spirit who with the Father and the Son directs history and therefore all true tradition related to their presence. It is this same Spirit that guided and delivered the recording for us of the very Word of God.

There is a tradition surrounding the blind man cured by Christ. This tradition does not give the individual the name I have chosen in the book. Choosing his birth name is purely a result of my own freedom as the novel writer. The name Cain is a highly unlikely name given to any serious Jewish person, as his name bears with it the reminder of the first human murderer. But I choose it because it also bears within its history the title of "the marked one."

But the name Celidonius does come down to us through tradition as being a name that this man bore. The tradition of a relationship between this man and the family of Lazarus and Joseph of Arimathea also exist. My novels' display of a deeper relationship between this man and Lazarus's family again comes solely from my mind and not from any known tradition. Also, the earlier meetings of this man with the

Christ are totally of my own creation. His journey through France and finally to Britain are hinted at although the traditions contradict as to where he finally settled and what his final fate was.

The depth of the blind man's condition and the extreme nature of his cure is found principally in the Eastern Orthodox traditions related to this man. I feel that this tradition does not contradict the scripture, for even the scripture and the man's own words, hint to the profound nature of this miracle. Did it happen exactly the way I like to believe it did? I do not know. But I suspect that much more occurred that day than what most of us normally consider. The dust of time and forgetfulness covers the rest of what occurred to this man. He is remembered because he pointed to the One of who so much has been written. His testimony heard in his voice, and his words should echo through our minds and souls. Thanks, Be to God, they echo through mine!

God Says I Can

BETTY ZIKUSOOKA